A Demon Spirit

Arabic Hunting Poems

Letter from the General Editor

The Library of Arabic Literature makes available Arabic editions and English translations of significant works of Arabic literature, with an emphasis on the seventh to nineteenth centuries. The Library of Arabic Literature thus includes texts from the pre-Islamic era to the cusp of the modern period, and encompasses a wide range of genres, including poetry, poetics, fiction, religion, philosophy, law, science, travel writing, history, and historiography.

Books in the series are edited and translated by internationally recognized scholars. They are published as hardcovers in parallel-text format with Arabic and English on facing pages, as English-only paperbacks, and as downloadable Arabic editions. For some texts, the series also publishes separate scholarly editions with full critical apparatus.

The Library encourages scholars to produce authoritative Arabic editions, accompanied by modern, lucid English translations, with the ultimate goal of introducing Arabic's rich literary heritage to a general audience of readers as well as to scholars and students.

The publications of the Library of Arabic Literature are generously supported by Tamkeen under the NYU Abu Dhabi Research Institute Award G1003 and are published by NYU Press.

Philip F. Kennedy
General Editor, Library of Arabic Literature

الطرديّات من شعره

الحسن بن هانئ أبو نواس

Table of Contents

For Reggie and Ethel, who kept me company during the completion of this book.

To foe of His—I'm deadly foe—
None stir the second time—
On whom I lay a Yellow Eye—
Or an emphatic Thumb—

Though I than He—may longer live
He longer must—than I—
For I have but the power to kill,
Without—the power to die—

From Emily Dickinson, "My Life Had Stood a Loaded Gun"

The awareness we each have of being a living body, being "alive to the world," carries with it exposure to the bodily sense of vulnerability to death, sheer animal vulnerability, the vulnerability we share with them.

Cora Diamond, "The Difficulty of Reality and the Difficulty of Philosophy"

The duck landed, but the drake flew past. Suddenly realising he was alone, he turned to go back. As he turned, the peregrine dashed up at him from the marsh and raked him with outstretched talons. The teal was tossed up and over, as though flung up on the horns of a bull. He landed with a splash of blood, his heart torn open. I left the hawk to his kill; the duck flew back to the pond.

J. A. Baker, *The Peregrine*

Acknowledgments

I began this book eleven years ago, in the summer of 2012. The current versions of my translations bear little resemblance to my preliminary efforts. I owe their transformation to many people, especially the audiences who listened to me talk about the project and whose questions helped me plot its course. I must, however, say a special thank you to the following: my fellow laborers in the Library of Arabic Literature (LAL) field, Shawkat M. Toorawa and Philip F. Kennedy, for always supporting my harebrained schemes; the LAL editorial boards, past and present; the LAL editorial team, Chip Rossetti, Lucie Taylor, and Leah Baxter, for never visibly losing patience when the project was repeatedly delayed; the LAL production team, Stuart Brown, Keith Miller, and Wiam El-Tamami, for once again making my work look like a million dollars; our friends at the New York University Abu Dhabi Institute, Gila Waels, Manal Demaghlatrous, Antoine El Khayat, and Amani Al-Zoubi; Sir Mark Allen, CMG, for correcting all of my tyro's errors and misunderstandings about falcons and hawks; Michael Cooperson, Geert Jan van Gelder, Vahid Behmadi, and, above all, Lara Harb, for helping me make sense of the bizarreries of Poem 116; Bilal Orfali, for his help with the manuscripts; Charis Olszok, my colleague at Cambridge, for her ecocritical knowledge and for improving the Introduction; and Richard Sieburth, for sprinkling stardust over my work and turning it into a silk purse. Of course, it would all count for naught without my family's love—I can't believe we've actually managed to complete this book together, after all we've been through in the last decade!

Introduction

Heretic, Sufi, countercultural icon, Persian nationalist, brigand, court jester, alcoholic, catamite, sodomite, ritual clown, justified sinner, icon of transgressive sacrality, pleasure junkie—these are just a few of the identities that have been given to Abū ʿAlī l-Ḥasan ibn Hāniʾ al-Ḥakamī, better known as Abū Nuwās, "the man with the dangling curls," arguably the greatest poet of the Arabic language. Some of these identities are anachronistic and probably mistaken; others correspond to prominent strands of his collected poems. But beyond a few shards of biography, we know remarkably little about him. Of course, Abū Nuwās is not unique in this regard (there are plenty of authors, poets, and thinkers from the past about whom almost nothing is known for sure), but he is one of the few who may be responsible for our ignorance—he seems to have been a larger-than-life figure and was probably an architect of his own mythology.

Take the name we tend to use, Abū Nuwās. This name is known in Arabic as a *laqab*, a nickname. This particular nickname is somewhat unusual in that it is a riff on the *kunyah*, the teknonym used to identify an individual by paternity or filiality: in the case of our poet, his *kunyah* is Abū ʿAlī, "the father of ʿAlī." One account maintains that the *laqab* Abū Nuwās was given to the poet as a young man in Basra because his hair was habitually disheveled. A competing etiology positions it as a political act, a declaration of his fervent South Arabian partisanship, since it is patterned on the name Dhū Nuwās (d. AD 525), the celebrated Jewish king of ancient Ḥimyar. A third explanation follows this strain of thinking, but is somewhat more prosaic, identifying Nuwās with a mountain in South Arabia. It is unclear whether any or all of these identities originated with our poet. As improbable as it may seem, we should at least entertain the possibility. After all, should we be surprised that a poet who was so skilled at fashioning the world in his verse may have proved adept at self-fashioning?

Abbasid Self-Fashioning

Abū Nuwās was born in the province of Ahwāz in Khuzistan, on the eastern littoral of the Gulf, ca. 139–40/756–58.[1] His Persian mother, Jullanār, was a bamboo weaver and his Arab father was a soldier in the army of the last Umayyad caliph, Marwān II (r. 127–32/744–50). His father was the *mawlā*—a bondman, or protected member of the household—of a man of South Arabian descent, al-Jarrāḥ ibn ʿAbdallāh al-Ḥakamī: this is why Abū Nuwās's *nisbah*, tribal name, is al-Ḥakamī. His father's death when Abū Nuwās was very young prompted Jullanār to relocate the family to Basra.

Abū Nuwās attended a *kuttāb*, or elementary Qur'an school, and is said to have memorized the Qur'an at an early age. While working for an aloe cutter, Abū Nuwās made the acquaintance of Wālibah ibn al-Ḥubāb (d. 170/786–87), a poet who took him to Kufa as an apprentice of some sort. Wālibah was a member of a group, possibly a sodality, known as *mujjān al-Kūfah*, literally, "the transgressives of Kufa." Abū Nuwās's membership of such sodalities probably accounts for the descriptions of him dressed as a "brigand" (*shāṭir*), with his hair arranged in bangs, wearing a gown with voluminous sleeves, and clad in covered (that is, not open) leather sandals. Such an individual was known as a *fatā*, a "brave," a "fine young man." These sodalities also provide the context for many of Abū Nuwās's *Khamriyyāt* ("wine poems").[2]

Wālibah instructed Abū Nuwās in the art of poetry and is said to have taken him as his intimate. According to one anecdote, Wālibah beheld the naked Abū Nuwās on the first night they spent in each other's company and was so moved by his physical beauty that he kissed him on the backside, whereupon Abū Nuwās farted in his face, quipping that farts are meet rewards for those who kiss bums. Whatever the truth of the anecdote, it expresses one facet of the Abū Nuwās legend, his razor-sharp wit and ability to win a verbal contest. It is from Wālibah and his cronies that Abū Nuwās is said to have developed his love for boys and his penchant for the more risqué forms of poetry, the *khamriyyah* ("wine poem") and *mujūn* ("transgressive verse"), as well as the starring role Iblīs (Satan) plays in his verse.

Wālibah's death led to Abū Nuwās's return to Basra, where he studied with the notorious philologist and expert in ancient poetry and its tribal lore, Khalaf al-Aḥmar (d. 180/796). Khalaf, who had a capacious memory, was accused of forging as many poems from the ancient pre-Islamic tradition as he transmitted, especially one of the grandest of all pre-Islamic poems, the *lāmiyyat al-ʿArab* ("the poem of the Bedouin rhyming in *l*") by al-Shanfarā (d. 6th c.).[3] Khalaf instructed Abū Nuwās in the memorization of the pre-Islamic corpus and its battle lore: such instruction would have included a grounding in grammar. Abū Nuwās is said to have sought Khalaf's permission to compose and recite poetry, which he was granted on the condition that Abū Nuwās memorize and recite one thousand ancient poems. When Abū Nuwās returned and recited these poems over a period of several days, Khalaf ordered him to go away and forget them all. Abū Nuwās betook himself to a monastery for a period of seclusion and unremembered the poems. It was then that he was authorized by Khalaf. And so another facet of the legend was born: the paradoxical freshness and naturalness of Abū Nuwās's poetry, made possible by a large-scale intertextual embedding within, and allusiveness to, the ancient tradition.

Khalaf al-Aḥmar was not Abū Nuwās's only instructor in Basra. He acquired a basic grounding in *fiqh*, religious knowledge and legal jurisprudence, as well as in the Qur'anic disciplines, such as how one Qur'anic verse can be abrogated by a verse revealed later (*al-nāsikh wa-l-mansūkh*), recitation, and the science of variant readings (*qirā'āt*). His expertise in the battle lore of the Arabs was consolidated by studying with Abū ʿUbaydah Maʿmar ibn al-Muthannā (d. 209/824–25). He studied lexicography with Abū Zayd al-Anṣārī (d. 214 or 215/830–31), a specialist in recondite vocabulary, and Hadith with ʿAbd al-Wāḥid ibn Ziyād al-Thaqafī (d. 176–79/792–96). In his final examination with ʿAbd al-Wāḥid, Abū Nuwās is said to have delivered a stinging satire of the Hadith and its exponents. And thus, another facet of the legend is created: irreverence toward the religious sciences.

During these years in Basra, Abū Nuwās is said to have fallen in love with Janān, a slave girl and musician belonging to al-Wahhāb al-Thaqafī, the teacher of the legal experts Muḥammad ibn Idrīs al-Shāfiʿī (d. 204/820) and Aḥmad ibn Ḥanbal (d. 241/855). She rejected his advances. When she was given her master's permission to perform the pilgrimage, Abū Nuwās followed her to Mecca and attracted crowds eager to hear the pious verses he had composed for the occasion. He followed Janān as she circumambulated the Kaaba and engineered it such that he kissed the Black Stone at exactly the same time as she did, their cheeks touching in the process. When rebuked by an acquaintance, Abū Nuwās made it clear that this was his sole reason for performing the pilgrimage. Yet another facet of the legend emerges: disregard for the Islamic rites and proprieties.

At some point, perhaps during the accession to the caliphate of Hārūn al-Rashīd (r. 170–93/786–809), Abū Nuwās arrived in Baghdad. The leading patrons of poetry were the Barmakids, sponsors also of scientists and philosophers; the Āl Nawbakht, renowned astrologers from the province of Ahwāz; and the al-Rabīʿ family, who effectively controlled access to the caliphal court—al-Rabīʿ ibn Yūnus was the caliph's *ḥājib* (chamberlain).

Abū Nuwās found little success in securing the patronage of the Barmakids, a powerful clan from Balkh in Iran (*barmak* means a priest in a Buddhist temple) that had close ties with the caliph—Yaḥyā ibn Khālid was instrumental in Hārūn's accession to the throne—and that supported a large literary entourage. The principal figure of this entourage was a poet called Abān al-Lāḥiqī (d. ca. 200/815–16). He and Abū Nuwās developed a fierce mutual animosity. Abān denigrated Abū Nuwās's compositions and in return received stinging assaults on both his person and his mother. Abū Nuwās's prediction that Abān's verses would "be scattered in the wind" has come true: virtually none of his poetry has survived.

In 187/803, Hārūn destroyed the Barmakids in a palace coup that effectively annihilated the family and its power base. In the ensuing vacuum, al-Faḍl ibn al-Rabīʿ (d. 207/822–23 or 208/823–24) was appointed by Hārūn as his vizier, and he was more supportive of Abū Nuwās's endeavors to praise the caliph. Some fine panegyrics in the grand mode have survived (see Poem 122 for an example), but it is unclear whether Abū Nuwās ever actually delivered them in person at court in front of Hārūn al-Rashīd, despite the close and fun-loving companionship that exists between them in many tales in *The Thousand and One Nights*. Hārūn imprisoned Abū Nuwās twice, once for heresy and once for a satire composed against the northern Arabs, tantamount to an act of disloyalty to the caliph and the Abbasid elite. Abū Nuwās enjoyed more success in courting the caliph's son al-Amīn (r. 193–98/809–13), and we have a number of less formal eulogies of him in a somewhat intimate mode, presumably from before his accession to the caliphate.

The precariousness of Abū Nuwās's position in Baghdad was such that in 190/805–6 he left Baghdad and traveled to Egypt to secure the patronage of al-Khaṣīb ibn ʿAbd al-Ḥamīd, who was in charge of the country's land-tax registry. However, al-Khaṣīb's fall from grace in 191/806–7 brought an end to the poet's Egyptian sojourn.

On his return to Baghdad, Abū Nuwās was imprisoned. The death of Hārūn al-Rashīd in 193/809 and the oath of fealty to al-Amīn allowed the new caliph to free his erstwhile co-convivialist and favored poet. Abū Nuwās enjoyed his most successful, and arguably his most brilliant, years as court companion to al-Amīn, though even then he was never safe from imprisonment. A jeremiad by al-Ma'mūn from the pulpit in Khurasan denouncing the dissolute lifestyle of his brother and the debauched company he kept meant that Abū Nuwās was once again imprisoned. Jail notwithstanding, the three years of al-Amīn's caliphate were the culmination of Abū Nuwās's career as a successful poet. And tradition has it that their friendship was not purely platonic.

Shortly after the beheading of al-Amīn, Abū Nuwās died in the house of the Nawbakht family, sometime between 198/813 and 200/815. As befits the self-mythologizing poet, there are four accounts of the cause of his death: he was poisoned by the Nawbakhts; he died in a tavern, goblet in hand; he was beaten to death by the Nawbakhts for a vituperative poem he had composed about them; and he died in prison. None of these versions seems to be true: Abū Nuwās probably died from an illness. One powerful story persists, however: the tale of his deathbed repentance and pious return to the fold of Islam, the last installment of the myth.

The Royal Hunt

The royal hunt was an elite enterprise of symbolic, ceremonial, and political significance. It was frequently conducted on a lavish scale, and often in a paradise, a park constructed, managed, and cultivated for hunting. As Thomas T. Allsen notes, the royal hunt portrayed the ability of a ruler to govern through the marshaling of "labor, military manpower, and individuals (both humans and animals) with very special skills." It was central to "interstate relations, military preparations, domestic administration, communications networks, and [. . .] the search for political legitimacy" and it required the "preservation of natural resources."[4]

Many of the *Ṭardiyyāt* of Abū Nuwās describe hunting expeditions in the grounds of Iraqi Christian monasteries, expeditions that were modeled on and sought to replicate the lavish royal hunt. They often depict what Terence Clark has described as "the 'walked-up' hunt":

> The party would walk or ride in a line, with trained eagles or falcons flying overhead ready to stoop on any birds or small mammals that might break cover. If gazelle were spotted, the cheetah handlers would bring forward one of their charges, which would be slipped. The cheetah would run down and kill a buck that had already been pursued by huntsmen on horses until it was tired or stalk the prey by itself or trail a herd upwind until near enough to kill several at once. If a hare were "put up", a pair of saluqi hounds would be slipped. If a houbara bustard took off, a saker falcon would be flown at it. In

> wooded areas along the rivers, where water birds abounded, goshawks would be flown.[5]

Our corpus also contains instances of the hunting typical of the desert Arabs in which raptors are flown from the fist in a largely horizontal chase at quarry that is not flushed but spotted.[6]

Yet, despite the verisimilitude of the corpus, we should remember that Abū Nuwās, for all his familiarity with the hunt, was a poet, not a falconer, and that these poems are representations, rather than documentations, of events—they eloquently demonstrate that "fabulous beasts can only be slain by fabulous humans"[7] and remind us, in the words of Jonathan Bate, that "the language of art is a sign of our distance from nature: poets want to sing like nightingales or skylarks because they know they do not have the freedom of flight and the pure expressive capacity of real birds."[8]

Human Hunters

Do the poems tell us anything about the human animals who carried out the hunting? The answer is connected with which nonhuman hunters were used. In the majority of cases, the poets are the hunters, but this is not always the case. Some poems may describe a falconer or an austringer or a huntsman—say, a master of hounds or a cheetah handler—who accompanies the expedition. The hunter-poet, however, is always in command of the hunt team. In the case of the saluki sight hound, many poems in the *ṭardiyyah* genre concern fairly ordinary people who live off whatever their dogs can catch. But in this corpus we also meet, for example, cheetahs, and we must expect that only the elite could afford to hunt with such a creature.

Much of the language of the hunt and many of the adjectives used to describe raptors[9] and to convey falconry practices in particular reveal a Persian origin. And many of the practices, techniques, traditions, and iconography of the hunt were inflections of the royal hunt.[10]

Nonhuman Hunters

The poets of the *ṭardiyyāt* rarely name the nonhuman hunters. Rather than saying, for example, "I went on an expedition with a saluki," they prefer to use metonymy and say, "I went on an expedition with a lean, drop-eared," leaving the corresponding noun unsaid. That is, they take it for granted that the audience knows exactly which type of nonhuman they intend. My suspicion is that they also expect their audience to know exactly which individual bird or dog they intend. I suspect further that the nonhuman was present to hear and somehow to understand the poem. Yet, no matter how cherished or beloved the nonhuman, these nonhuman animals are rarely given names in the poems: they seem to resist humanizing, even when (or especially when?) they are circumscribed by terms deriving from human-made, domestic culture.[11] They are not enclosed in the anthropocentric orbit of the pet but retain a non-anthropocentric specificity and a particularity that, for all the interspecies blurring in depictions of the hunt, set them apart from the human hunter. At the same time, despite this particularity, they exist on a mythic plane of hyperbole and perfection almost as archetypes or universals and they often hunt in an idealized landscape, which could be any landscape. This mythologizing of the real is also the reason why the kill tallies are so excessive—these raptors are both real, particular birds and unreal, supreme death engines.

The Hunted

The quarry hunted depended on the terrain on which the hunting expedition took place and the kind of nonhuman hunter that formed part of the hunting team. In the *Ṭardiyyāt* of Abū Nuwās, we encounter highly generalized mentions of desert plains, rivers, and water holes, including wetlands, woodlands, shrublands, mountain ravines, wadis, lakes, and ponds. I presume that many of these hunting expeditions took place on the grounds of Iraq's Christian monasteries, where the hunting party could have easy access to wine and its associated pleasures.[12]

The quarry is not mentioned or described in every poem, so sometimes we don't know exactly what, for example, the saker falcon hunted and caught. And there are additional challenges in identifying the quarry even when it is named or referred to in the corpus. The first challenge—the metonymic riddle that sometimes besets our attempts to identify the nonhuman hunter—holds doubly true for the hunted nonhuman. In other words, the riddling metonyms are even more demanding and baffling when we seek to know exactly which hunted nonhumans are meant. The second challenge is that these nonhumans are rarely the primary focus of the poet's attention. So even when the poet mentions, say, a goose, we still do not know precisely which type of goose is meant.

This problem of identification looms large in the pellet-bow poems (poems in which a group of bowmen ambush birds in a wetland). In many instances, I have been reduced simply to transliterating the Arabic names.

The Inhuman Circuit of the *Ṭardiyyah*

As an enterprise, hunting is paradoxical. It is a costly, dangerous, and very unreliable method of providing sustenance. Despite the assertions of the poems, not all hunting expeditions would have been successful, and the expense of maintaining a hunting team, be it of raptors, dogs, horses, or cheetahs, would have been possible only for the wealthiest. There must also have been considerable danger involved. Given the cost and the peril, why was hunting so popular with the Abbasid elites? Hunting owed its elite popularity largely to its symbolism. It functioned as the theater in which culture heroes[13] could put themselves on display and embody the values that society and its regnal dynasty prized in its rulers: capability, prowess, decision-making, bravery, skill, and fortitude. It was the task of the culture hero to protect, disseminate, and at times enforce these values.

The feast of meat at the end of a hunting expedition also enjoyed significant symbolic capital. It was not only a testimony to the culture hero's investment and display of labor and skill but was also an occasion for a display of altruism and largesse of leadership. Hunting was thus a symbolic representation and enactment of fitness to rule, and its violence, inflicted on nonhuman animals, was thereby asserted over the enemies of the polity. Thus, the hunting poems of Ibn al-Muʿtazz (d. 296/908) celebrate and immortalize his royal status and prestige and communicate his status as embodiment of heroic masculinity.[14] The poems in this volume are a further attestation to the dominance of these values among the Abbasid elite.

Hunting scenes occur in a liminal zone: they take place at dawn and are set in a paradise—a secluded enclosure or garden, often inviolate, such as the grounds of a monastery or a game reserve. The hunt, however, does not function as a rite of initiation, for the skilled hunter takes center stage and he is already an initiate. The hunt is an arena in which the hunter's heroic masculinity is put to the test. In this liminal space, the heroic hunter must not only exercise all his skills of decision-making, coordinating the hunt team and controlling the nonhuman hunters, but in order to vanquish the quarry must penetrate the phenomenology of the nonhuman world, of both nonhuman hunter and prey. To do this, the hero must merge his consciousness with that of the nonhumans involved in the chase—in a sense, he must efface himself but also be able at the end of the hunt to recover his self. Short of combat and warfare, this was the ultimate crucible for heroic masculinity.

In his article "Medieval Blood Sport," William Marvin discusses with great insight the "depths of experience with animal consciousness among medieval hunters," noting the delicate balance that is required for a successful hunt in which "the ferocity of the hunting instinct" must be spurred in "the animal team" until it reaches a critical point and results in a kill, at which point the discipline of training is required in order to halt the "destruction of the prey."[15] In order to achieve and maintain this balance, and in order to catch the quarry, the hunter must enter into a deep and instinctual familiarity with the prey as well as with the hunting team. All three—human hunter, nonhuman hunter, and nonhuman prey—enter, in Marvin's words,

> the same phenomenology by having to (a) register sudden stimuli, (b) assess the level of threat, (c) process the immediate time-distance-ground problems, and (d) execute the run with maximum potential for speed and stratagem.[16]

Marvin refers to the attendant "powers of hyper-focus" and notes that the hunt endows "lesser-seeming creatures" with superpowers.[17]

The hunting poems in this volume provide numerous examples of a microscale conceptualization of relationality and a blurring, at the phenomenological level, of human and nonhuman animal, mediated by the poet, who is simultaneously participant, observer, and creator. In the meticulous attention paid by the poets to the stages of the hunt, the chase, and the kill, these poems blur distinctions between the perceptions of the poet as hunter and the perceptions of the nonhuman hunters.

As a genre, the *ṭardiyyah* eschews generalization and thrives in the particular, in the moment, in the detail, in the "little flickers of consciousness coaxed by memory."[18] The microscale conceptualization of relationality, which is typical of Abbasid poetics, becomes, in the context of the *ṭardiyyah*, another index of Marvin's "hyper-focus." And the attendant power of hyper-focus, a feature that might have seemed unique to the pointillism of the Arabic poetic aesthetic, turns out, in essence, also to belong to a widespread phenomenology of the hunt.

The phenomenological blurring so typical of the *ṭardiyyah* is an indication that what is at play in these poems is the phenomenon designated by the theorists Gilles Deleuze and Félix Guattari as "agencement"—that is, an "assemblage" or a "circuit."[19] The human hunter, the nonhuman hunter, the paraphernalia of hunting (be it the raptor's jesses and bell, or the dog's collar and leash), and the quarry form ephemeral nodes of being in which

> no single object or body has meaning [. . .] without reference to other forces, intensities, affects, and directions to which it is conjoined and within which it is always in the process of becoming something other, something new.[20]

In the resultant (evanescent) circuit, or assemblage, it becomes difficult to isolate an individual falcon or saluki as distinct from the falconer or saluki handler or even as distinct from the hunting gear or the quarry. The species line is dissolved into "a dispersive network of identity that admixes the inanimate and the inhuman," which disregards bodily boundaries and creates "an amalgam of force, materiality, and motion." [21] Furthermore, the art of hunting requires a rigorous regimen of training on the part of both human and nonhuman hunter—it depends on "an intersubjective discipline"; that is, one that seeks to transcend or erase or dematerialize interspecies boundaries in a reconfigured embodiment.[22]

Jeffrey J. Cohen, in his discussion of what he labels "the chivalric circuit," notes that steed and warrior and accoutrements become simultaneously active and receptive points within a transformative assemblage. Agency, potentiality, and identity are mobile, the product of relations of movement rather than a static residuum contained in discrete bodies (horse, man) and inanimate objects (saddle, stirrups, spurs, armor, sword).[23] In its translation into verse of this phenomenological blurring, of this inhuman circuit or assemblage, the *ṭardiyyah* expresses the dismantling and transformation of material form into a blended species whose coherence and movements are no longer exclusively human, no matter how hegemonic the role occupied in the circuit by the poet-as-hunter.[24] The *ṭardiyyah* becomes, in Deleuze's terms, a site of "combat-between," "a center of metamorphosis."[25]

Interspecies Encounter

In two of the most striking English poems of the twentieth century, D. H. Lawrence's "Snake" (1921) and Elizabeth Bishop's "Moose" (1972), the nonhuman animals emerge in all their unhuman mystery and majesty, and "the loss of creatureliness [. . .] that comes from living apart from the natural, both within and outside our bodies,"[26] is lamented. The poets confront two distinct zones of being: that of human animals, on the one hand, and nonhuman animals, on the other—what Jacques Derrida identifies as the "abyssal limit," "an existence that refuses to be conceptualized."[27] In "His Heart Whispered Caution" (Poem 30), Abū Nuwās describes a situation in which a concealed hunter watches a sparrow standing just out of reach of his trap net. The bird's world is miniaturized, and it is a world that demands of its audience the keenest attentiveness in order to adequately respond to it.[28] The hunter's tense yet powerless attentiveness to the bird exudes an air of mystery, and the poet anthropomorphizes the bird's indecision, with its heart whispering caution and its exemplary trust in God's protection. The poet turns the failure of the trap into a lesson on the inscrutability of God's decree, the mutability of Fate, and the need to accept life's uncertainties.

For all its humanizing strategies and its apparent inability to avoid being interested in the nonhuman only insofar as it is a reflection of what is significant to the human, the poem suggests a different way of conceiving relationality. It recognizes that humans are not the only selves in the world and attends to "living thoughts in the world," highlighting not only the centrality of God's decree in all living creatures, but also how confusion and uncertainty can become a mechanism for appreciating that relationality might operate across the species divide, that nonhumans might interpret the world every bit as much as humans do.[29] The poem suggests that we do not need certain knowledge in order to know how the sparrow is interpreting its reality, that the poet's provisional explanation of the sparrow's interpretation of what it was thinking might suggest a different form of interspecies attentiveness, one less grim that Derrida's "abyssal limit." In this poem, Abū Nuwās, like William Wordsworth, sees "into the life of things."[30]

Abū Nuwās's Oeuvre

Abū Nuwās's poetry is sheer joy: it never fails to delight, surprise, and excite. His diwan, his collected poems, encompasses the principal early Abbasid poetic genres: panegyrics (*madīḥ*), renunciant poems (*zuhdiyyāt*), lampoons (*hijā'*), hunting poems (*ṭardiyyāt*), wine poems (*khamriyyāt*), love poems (*ghazaliyyāt*) to males (*mudhakkarāt*) and females (*mu'annathāt*), and transgressive verse (*mujūn*). What is most striking in his poetry is its apparent effortlessness and the naturalness of its Arabic, despite the deployment of the full panoply of the new rhetorical style known as the *badīʿ*. Abū Nuwās represented the poetic trend the critics termed *muḥdath*, which means both "modern" and "modernist." The ease with which he celebrates the accepted features of the pre-Islamic and Umayyad corpus, often inverting and subverting them, and innovates at both the level of the individual verse and of the macro structure of the poem is virtually unparalleled. Such simplicity is deceptive, for it is usually the result of deep artifice.

Ṭardiyyāt

This edition and translation of the *Ṭardiyyāt* of Abū Nuwās are based principally upon the recension of the poet's diwan by Ḥamzah al-Iṣfahānī (d. 360/971). Ḥamzah devoted considerable attention to his presentation of this hunting corpus. He divided the corpus into poems that his authorities averred were authentic (Poems 1–30) and poems attributed to Abū Nuwās without sufficient testimony to corroborate their authenticity (Poems 36–106). He also added an in-between category of two kinds of poems: those that were genuine compositions by Abū Nuwās but were not, in the strictest sense, on the subject of the hunt (Poems 31 and 32), and poems that were of indeterminate authenticity and also were not, in the strictest sense, on the subject of the hunt (Poems 33–35). He further subdivided the authentic poems into *urjūzah*s, which are pieces composed in *rajaz* meter (Poems 1–26), and qasidas (Poems 27–30).

Much uncertainty has surrounded the number of genuine poems by Abū Nuwās. This is how al-Iṣfahānī describes the situation:

> Ibn Abī Ṭāhir quotes Ibn Ḥarb, citing ʻAlī ibn Abī Khalṣah who had it from Abū Diʻāmah, as stating that Abū Nuwās composed twenty-nine *urjūzah*s on hunting, while the remainder were attributions. Abū l-ʻAbbās al-ʻUmmārī, however, quotes Ibn Mahrawayh as citing al-Ḥasan ibn al-Ḥusayn al-Sukkarī's comment that Ibrāhīm ibn Maḥbūb showed him a jotter that Ibrāhīm said contained more than seventy *rajaz* poems on hunting dictated and signed by Abū Nuwās himself. Abū Nuwās's transmitters Muḥammad ibn Ḥarb ibn Khalaf, Sulaymān ibn Sakhṭah, al-Yu'yu', al-Jammāz from Basra, Ibn al-Dāyah the Baghdadi Slave Trader, and ʻAlī ibn Abī Khalṣah told Abū Hiffān that Abū Nuwās composed no more than twenty-nine *rajaz* pieces and four qasidas on the subject, while the remainder are attributions.[31]

It is immediately apparent that there is some discrepancy between the numbers of this statement (twenty-nine *urjūzah*s and four qasidas) and the version of al-Iṣfahānī's recension in the extant manuscripts, which preserve thirty poems (*urjūzah*s and qasidas) in total. Somewhere along the chain of transmission, three *urjūzah*s have fallen by the wayside. The discrepancy is further evident in the list of twenty-six opening lines given by al-Iṣfahānī, one of which has no corresponding poem in the collection and another of which is in fact one of the attributions (Poem 60). No matter the fluctuations in the tradition, we must thank al-Iṣfahānī for his scrupulosity in preserving so maximally the *Ṭardiyyāt*, because we have many examples of the genre that would otherwise have been lost.

Al-Iṣfahānī's attention to detail did not stop at the level of determining authenticity and attribution; it extended also to the arrangement of compositions within his chosen categories. He elected to organize them not alphabetically, as was often the case, but by animal.

What I find most striking about Abū Nuwās's *Ṭardiyyāt* is their fertile inventiveness; the smoothness of the diction, in which the demands of the meter (admittedly, *rajaz* is one of the most accommodating of the Arabic meters) and the naturalness of the Arabic are in harmony; and the poet's powers of observation.[32] The narrative economy of the corpus is also notable. Some of the poet's images are unforgettable, as, for example, in Poem 22, where Abū Nuwās describes a lark, killed by a merlin: "Its beak flopped / on top of a cairn."[33] Few poets can match the skill of Poem 14, remarkable for the way in which the poet's description follows the bird's anatomy from head to foot.

There are few extant *ṭardiyyāt* that predate Abū Nuwās's *Ṭardiyyāt*.[34] As a genre, it seems to emerge fully formed, like Athena from Zeus's head. Like almost all classical Arabic poetry, the *ṭardiyyah* was occasional—that is, it was composed for a specific occasion or purpose. It was, in fact, doubly occasional, in that its structure and contents were largely determined by the occasion it was composed for—the format and structure of the hunting expedition. Invariably, the hunting expedition began in the dead of night, proceeded to an early-morning hunt before the sun was high in the sky, and ended with a feast in which the game was cooked and shared, accompanied by a drinking session. Many of the poems included here would have been composed or declaimed during these festivities at the conclusion of the hunt. The structure of the hunting expedition, then, by and large determined the structure of the poem.

The standard opening of the *ṭardiyyah* was inspired by what is probably the earliest extant hunting scene in Arabic, the one in the *Muʿallaqah*, or "Suspended Ode," of Imruʾ al-Qays (d. AD 544), which begins with the formula *wa-qad aghtadī*, literally, "often I depart early in the morning."[35] Three of the earliest extant *ṭardiyyāt* begin with this formula.[36] Abū Nuwās's inventiveness is conspicuous in the opening lines of his authentic corpus: eleven of his poems begin with the *qad aghtadī* formula (or a variant thereof).[37] The "dawn motif," but without the *qad aghtadī* formula, familiar from an early *ṭardiyyah* by Ghaylān ibn Ḥurayth,[38] is also used (Poem 13), but Abū Nuwās is equally ready to dispense with both the *qad aghtadī* formula and the "dawn motif" in four poems (Poems 4, 6, 8, and 9). He begins four further poems with the pre-Islamic device of introducing a new sequence in a qasida with the particle *wa-* with or without *rubba*, meaning "many's the . . ." or "there was a . . . ," employed for a *ṭardiyyah* by Abū l-Najm al-ʿIjlī.[39] To the best of my knowledge, Abū Nuwās is the first poet to deploy the *lā ṣayda illā* (literally, "there can be no hunting unless . . .") introduction and, in terms of the *ṭardiyyah* genre, the *anʿatu* ("I describe") opening.[40]

The poet's subversive wit is in evidence in the phallus description (Poem 31), which begins with the *qad aghtadī* formula, and in the dirham description (Poem 32), which begins with the poet's hallmark rejection of the pre-Islamic topos in which the poet describes how he chances upon a now-abandoned encampment where once he lived in the company of his beloved and is moved to tears by the memories.[41] Ibn al-Muʿtazz, the tradition's second great *ṭardiyyah* poet, may have crafted the genre into a miniaturist's art, with his startling and vivid portraits and his keen, bold images,[42] but who can match Abū Nuwās's brilliance, bravura, and panache?

Panache, wit, and inventiveness are most acute in a hunting poem that is not classified as a *ṭardiyyah* but is categorized among the *khamriyyāt* (wine poems), though a strong case could also be made for classifying it among the *ghazal* (love poems): the line between *khamriyyah* and *ghazal* was very porous, as was the line between *ṭardiyyah* and *ghazal*.[43]

> No heart can keep its secrets safe
> from the spell of your gazelle eyes.
> They ask what I'm hiding and whisper
> all my feelings in your ear. One look
> and all is revealed—you seem to control
> my thoughts. How have you been able
> to break me yet stay free of how Time
> has ravaged me? I watch you kill me
> with no fear of reprisal, as if my murder
> were a sacrifice offered up to God.

So hand me my morning cup of wine—
yes, it's forbidden, but God forgives our sins—
a pale wine that builds bubbles in the mix,
like pearls chased by gold, Noah's prize
on board the ark when the earth was flooded,
as light as a soul incarnated in the body
of an amphora sealed with pitch
then wrapped with linen and palm leaves.
A Persian lord chose to conceal it
from its life in the world, hidden in a cavern
for eons in a land where neither Kalb,
ʿAbs, nor Dhubyān pitched their tents,
where neither Dhuhl nor Shaybān dwelled,
in the home of the elect where Khusro built
his palaces, never sullied by a Basran, free
of that smell of *ʿarfaj* and taste of acacia
the Bedouin love so much, where pomegranate
grows surrounded by myrtle in a garland
of roses and lilies. One sniff, and your nose
is filled with the aroma of sweet basil.
What a night of auspicious stars,
as drunkard ambushed drunkard
and we worshipped Iblīs, in his thrall
until the monks tolled the death of night.
You got up, dragging your sumptuous clothes
soiled by my wicked hand, wailing, in tears,
"Oh no! You have robbed me of my virtue!"
"A lion spotted a gazelle and jumped on it,"
I replied. "Sic transit gloria mundi!"

Abū Nuwās's poem is an elaboration of the topos of the deadly gaze of the love object who is figured as a gazelle—the vulnerable doe, hunted by the leonine poet, turns her eyes on him and is metamorphosed from hunted to hunter.[44] The poet is transformed into the quarry and, unable to resist, dies the death of love. With his customary wit and ebullience, Abū Nuwās begins with his sanctioned death under the bewitching gaze of his love-object-cum-gazelle. In the next move of the poem, the bacchanal, he calls for wine, and thus subverts another topos of the pre-Islamic tradition, the motif in which the poet consoles himself for the loss of the love object, either in a desert journey, a feat of arms, or inebriation. The wine description leads to the third move in the poem, the drunken, carnal orgy at the end of the debauch. But once again the hunted becomes the hunter as Abū Nuwās, no longer the victim, becomes the victimizer and exacts his revenge by violating the love object.

Of the Arabic poetic genres, the *ṭardiyyah* is semiotically closest in spirit to the love lyric (*ghazal*), and in particular those compositions in which the poet-lover is hunted and ensnared by the love object, male or female. The epic hunter, vanquisher of the nonhuman world, abjectly and voluntarily surrenders himself to the snares and charms of a young boy or girl. The love object hunts down and destroys the hunter, who is then wounded by the very object of his heart's desire. Unlike the *ṭardiyyah,* which culminates in a successful kill, the *ghazal* usually terminates in failure: the love object is always out of reach and unattainable, and should that object be attained, it is quickly replaced by another unattainable object. The epic hunter of the *ṭardiyyah* is always a victim in the *ghazal,* his masculinity ever undone. However, the true hunter in the *ghazal* is not the pursued love object; rather, it is the poet's own desire, which desire is powerless and without choice, invariably indulging in the chase and thus becoming a victim, enthusiastically embracing perpetual failure.[45]

In Abū Nuwās's wine poem, the customary power dynamic is restored: the once vanquished lion kills the erstwhile victorious gazelle. Only Abū Nuwās could have turned this whole dynamic on its head.

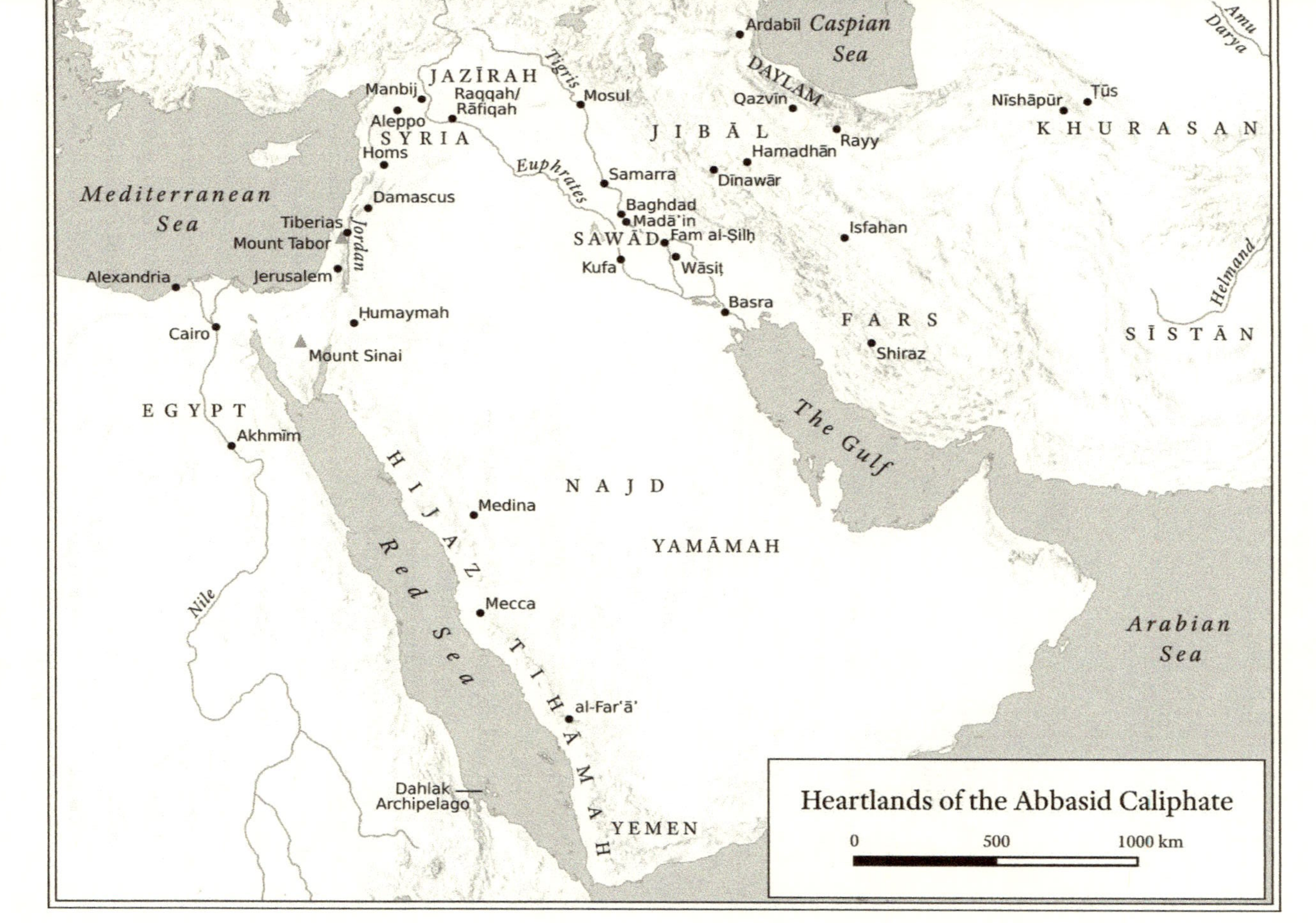
Heartlands of the Abbasid Caliphate
0
500
1000 km
Caspian Sea
Ardabīl
DAYLAM
Amu Darya
Nīshāpūr
Ṭūs
KHURASAN
Qazvīn
Rayy
JIBĀL
Hamadhān
Dīnawār
Isfahan
Helmand
SĪSTĀN
FARS
Shiraz
JAZĪRAH
Tigris
Mosul
Manbij
Raqqah/
Rāfiqah
Aleppo
SYRIA
Homs
Euphrates
Samarra
Baghdad
Madā'in
SAWĀD
Fam al-Ṣilḥ
Kufa
Wāsiṭ
Basra
Mediterranean Sea
Damascus
Tiberias
Mount Tabor
Jordan
Alexandria
Jerusalem
Ḥumaymah
Cairo
Mount Sinai
EGYPT
Akhmīm
The Gulf
NAJD
HIJAZ
Medina
YAMĀMAH
Red Sea
Nile
Mecca
TIHĀMAH
al-Far'ā'
Arabian Sea
Dahlak
Archipelago
YEMEN

Note on the Text

The Edition

Editorial Principles

My decision to edit and translate the *Ṭardiyyāt* of Abū Nuwās for the Library of Arabic Literature presented me with a conundrum. Unlike the work of many poets from the tradition, Abū Nuwās's poetry is available in an excellent edition, established on sound scientific principles and meticulously documented. The first volume of Ewald Wagner's edition appeared in 1958 (a second revised and enlarged edition was published in 2001), with the fifth and final volume published in 2003.[46] Two volumes of indexes appeared in 2006. Prior to embarking on his edition of the diwan, in 1957 Wagner produced an extensive study of the manuscript tradition ("Die Überlieferung des Abū Nuwās-Dīwān und seine Handschriften"). Why burden scholarship with yet another edition? What contribution, I wondered, could I possibly make?

Initially, I contemplated using Wagner's excellent edition of Abū Nuwās's *Ṭardiyyāt* and approached him with a view to securing his permission, which I'm honored to say I received. Philip Kennedy suggested that I consider editing Abū Bakr al-Ṣūlī's recension (Wagner's edition is based on the recension of Ḥamzah al-Iṣfahānī [d. 360/971]). Al-Ṣūlī's recension is available in a fine edition by Bahjat ʿAbd al-Ghafūr al-Ḥadīthī from 2001, and I seriously considered this alternative. In fact, in the initial stages of the project I entertained both options and refrained from making a decision.

As my work on the *ṭardiyyah* tradition progressed and I became more familiar with its varieties, I was led to the important insight that as a genre, the *ṭardiyyah* was especially prone to internal variations, often to the point of entire poems. This is especially evident in the case of the *Ṭardiyyāt* of Ibn al-Muʿtazz (see Ibn al-Muʿtazz, *In Deadly Embrace*). My work on Abū Bakr al-Ṣūlī's (d. 355/947) recension of Ibn al-Muʿtazz led me to a second insight, that al-Ṣūlī's recension of this mode of Ibn al-Muʿtazz's poetry (and, by inference, of his recension of the whole diwan) did not exist in a stable form. Despite our understanding of al-Ṣūlī as a scholar who published his work in book form, his recension of Ibn al-Muʿtazz seems to have circulated in several versions (see my forthcoming scholarly edition of the *Ṭardiyyāt*). This stage of my work was dominated by a third consideration: I wanted my study to be as comprehensive as possible, to try to make available as many poems from the heyday of the tradition as I possibly could.

Armed with these insights, I revisited the question of which recension of Abū Nuwās's *Ṭardiyyāt* to use. My desire for comprehensiveness ruled out al-Ṣūlī's recension: al-Ṣūlī was only interested in what he considered to be the genuine Abū Nuwās and often refers to poems he considered spurious by their first lines without offering full versions.[47] Al-Iṣfahānī too was driven to establish what he considered to be the genuine Abū Nuwās, but in the case of the *Ṭardiyyāt*, and to our great good fortune, he decided to offer versions of Abū Nuwās's apocrypha. Thus, his recension includes thirty genuine pieces, five pieces of indeterminate authenticity on subjects contiguous to those of the *ṭardiyyah* as a genre, but not necessarily *ṭardiyyāt* proper, and sixty-nine apocrypha, in addition to a list of the first lines of a further sixteen *ṭardiyyāt* that he found in various sources accredited to Abū Nuwās, but in his view demonstrably incorrectly.[48] In order to be comprehensive, therefore, the project required that I base my edition on al-Iṣfahānī's recension.

In terms of editorial method, Ewald Wagner's edition is synthetic—that is, his edition does not rely on one manuscript to the exclusion of other testimonies in the corpus but produces its own version of the poems based on an integrative approach to as many manuscripts as he had at his disposal. In other words, it is a work of restoration: the resultant versions are effectively restored and are often not actually attested to by the tradition. They represent a new, combinatorial, reading that seeks to produce as complete a text as possible. Wagner's detailed critical apparatus meticulously charts his restorations and thereby mitigates most of the confusion that can arise from such synthetic editions. However, this editorial method does not accord with the editorial approach promoted by the LAL, which requires scholars to base their edition on a single manuscript as principal witness, to avoid the creation of versions of texts that are not attested in the tradition, and to keep editorial intrusion or interference to a minimum.[49] In light of this, and of my realization that the *ṭardiyyah* as a genre was more likely than most to attest to the genuineness of divergent versions of any given poem, I decided that I could not use Wagner's edition for my project. I hasten to emphasize my admiration for, and dependence on, Wagner—I could not have produced my edition without his work. What is at stake is a question of editorial approach that seeks to represent as far as possible the perceived nature of the tradition under study.

My edition of Abū Nuwās's *Ṭardiyyāt* is therefore based on a single witness: MS Fātiḥ 3773 preserved in the Sülemaniye Library in Istanbul, an undated copy made for private use by a certain Aḥmad ibn Muḥammad ibn ʿAbdallāh ibn al-ʿAsqalānī.[50] This manuscript contains approximately half of al-Iṣfahānī's recension of the diwan: the *Ṭardiyyāt* are on folios 197b–260b. It is in a clear hand, regularly and correctly vocalized, and with a minimum of marginalia.

Editorial Decisions

The opening lines of Poem 5 required some editorial interference. Al-Iṣfahānī notes that this poem has an alternative two-verse opening.[51] I have restored these as the first two lines of the poem, with al-Iṣfahānī's preferred opening beginning with line 3. The sequence of lines in the version of Poem 11 in al-Ṣūlī's recension and Wagner's edition makes slightly better sense than the version contained in our manuscript. Al-Ṣūlī's version is four lines shorter than the version in Fātiḥ 3773, and its line sequence is 1–3, 7–11, 13–14, 4–6, 16–26; the sequence in Wagner is 1–3, 7–12, 4–6, 13–28.[52] Al-Ṣūlī's recension reads the events of the last four lines of Poem 47 in a different sequence: see *Dīwān Abī Nuwās* (ed. al-Ḥadīthī), 226. In Poem 94, lines 11–17 are problematic. I have transposed lines 12 and 13 of the version contained in the manuscript to provide a referent for the description of line 12. In the case of Poem 99, al-Iṣfahānī includes a shortened version at the end of the section of his diwan devoted to the reproach (*ʿitāb*): see Fātiḥ 3773, 132a–132b.[53] Al-Iṣfahānī notes there: "The following verses will be found in a long *rajaz* poem I have included at the end of a section of the chapter on hunting." The "reproach" version contains the following verses of my edition: 1–6, 51–70, 73–76. I have incorporated the variant readings of this version into the apparatus.[54]

Oddly, al-Iṣfahānī includes nine pellet-bow poems in the apocryphal chapter (Poems 91–99), though the manuscripts specify "eight." I have not emended the text and retained the inconsistency.

For some reason, the Fātiḥ 3773 manuscript omits one *ṭardiyyah* included in other manuscripts of al-Iṣfahānī's recension: Poem 106, a saluki description.[55] I have decided not to position it in the place it occupies in the other manuscripts but have included it as the first of the poems supplementary to al-Iṣfahānī's recension as preserved in Fātiḥ 3773. Furthermore, al-Ṣūlī preserves a poem not recorded by al-Iṣfahānī, either as genuine or apocryphal, and edited by Wagner.[56] I include it as Poem 107.

The edition concludes with poems attributed to Abū Nuwās but not preserved by either al-Iṣfahānī or al-Ṣūlī. Wagner's revised and enlarged edition of volume one of the diwan (2001) includes nine poems preserved only by Ibrāhīm ibn Aḥmad al-Ṭabarī Tüzün.[57] In addition, I have added five poems attributed to Abū Nuwās by Abū l-Ḥasan ʿAlī ibn Muḥammad al-Shimshāṭī (fl. second half of fourth/tenth century)[58] and also two qasidas by Abū Nuwās (Poems 122 and 123), which feature respectively a goshawk and a saker description: see Fātiḥ 3773, folios 50a–53a, and Fātiḥ 3773, folios 144a–46b.[59]

Divergent Attributions

Several of the poems in the collection are attributed to other poets. A version of Poem 10 is attributed by Abū ʿUthmān al-Jāḥiẓ (*Kitāb al-Ḥayawān*, 6.472–73) to al-Faḍl ibn ʿAbd al-Ṣamad al-Raqāshī. According to al-Ṣūlī, Poems 12 and 17 are not genuine, but are classed by him in the category of "attributed" to Abū Nuwās.[60] An alternative version of Poem 107 (preserved only in al-Ṣūlī's recension[61]) is attributed to al-Shamardal ibn Sharīk.[62] Poem 109, preserved in Tüzün's recension, is ascribed by al-Iṣfahānī, on the authority of Abū Ḥāṭim al-Sijistānī (d. 255/869), to Ghaylān ibn Ḥurayth. The poem's first line is quoted by al-Iṣfahānī in his inventory of the first lines of poems he has excluded from his section of attributions:[63] see the version ascribed to Ghaylān in Montgomery, *Fate the Hunter*, Poem 12, 74–75. The first line of Poem 110 is included by al-Iṣfahānī in his inventory of the first lines of poems he has excluded from his section of attributions.[64] He attributes it to "a poet of Balʿanbar." Lines 1–3 and 5–8 of Poem 111 are attributed to al-Shamardal ibn Sharīk.[65] Tüzün prefaces Poem 113 as follows: "A description of a horse. According to Abū Ḥātim (that is, al-Sijistānī), this poem is by Ḥumayd al-Arqaṭ: Ḥumayd compares his horses with a saker." The version in Montgomery, *Fate the Hunter*, Poem 11, has three extra lines: two between lines 5 and 6 and one between lines 10 and 11. The seventeen-line version of Poem 118 in this collection is a version of the forty-nine-line poem by Abū l-Najm reconstructed from a variety of sources in Montgomery, *Fate the Hunter*, Poem 24, 124–29. The sequence of lines in this version, compared to that of Abū l-Najm's poem, is: 7, 13, 16, 17, 18, 8, 21, 30, 9, 10, 11, 33, 39, 12, 40, 46, 47.

Finally, for some reason al-Shimshāṭī includes a version of Poem 104, identified as an equine description in our collection, in his section on dogs (*Kitāb al-Anwār wa-maḥāsin al-ashʿār*, 2.125–26).

The Translation

The *ṭardiyyah* in Arabic conveys an at times breathless intensity and rapidity, perfectly facilitated by the flexibility of its metrical form. I have striven to recreate this intensity in English, insofar as I am able. To achieve this, I have prioritized clarity above all, be it of expression, image, or poetic structure, in an English I have endeavored to keep uncluttered and economical. I aimed for English renderings that could stand on their own.

The art of falconry and hawking boasts a developed and sophisticated vocabulary in English. I have dipped into its lexical riches to capture features and behaviors of the raptors as described by Abū Nuwās. I have included these terms in the Glossary. I have also opted quite frequently to transform into proper nouns common epithets for both nonhuman hunter and hunted.

However, despite my best efforts, there remain many poems and lines that are obscure, be it because the vocabulary has been forgotten, the practice or behavior described unclear, or the syntax condensed to the point of puzzlement. Consequently, much of my translation remains conjectural, and in such instances I have dispensed with endnotes that signpost my failings.

Notes to the Introduction

1 This potted biography is heavily indebted to Wagner, *Abū Nuwās: Eine Studie zur arabischen Literatur der frühen ʿAbbāsidenzeit*; Wagner, "Abū Nuwās"; Kennedy, "Abu Nuwas (circa 757–814 or 815)"; and Kennedy, *Abu Nuwas: A Genius of Poetry*.

2 For Abū Nuwās as a *shāṭir*, see Kennedy, *Abu Nuwas: A Genius of Poetry*, 17. On the sodalities, see van Ess, *Theology and Society in the Second and Third Centuries of the Hijra: A History of Religious Thought in Early Islam*, vol. 3, 113–15; Tor, *Violent Disorder: Religious Warfare, Chivalry, and the ʿAyyār Phenomenon in the Medieval Islamic World*; Robinson, *Empire and Elites after the Muslim Conquest: The Transformation of Northern Mesopotamia*, 113 ("these figures were not parochial bandits, dressed by the late and urban literary tradition in the garb of religious revolutionaries. These were warrior saints who did have a programme; and they were bandits only in the sense that they were drawn from the same surplus of rural leadership that produces banditry, many of whose techniques they employed with considerable success"); and Cooperson, "Bandits."

3 For a translation and discussion, see Montgomery, *Fate the Hunter*, 27–33.

4 Allsen, *The Royal Hunt in Eurasian History*, 8, 12.

5 Clark, "The Noble Art of the Chase in the Arab World," 49.

6 Allen, *Falconry in Arabia*.

7 Allsen, *The Royal Hunt*, 12. See also Vidal-Naquet, *The Black Hunter: Forms of Thought and Forms of Society in the Greek World*, 5: "the 'culture heroes' of the Greek legends are all hunters and destroyers of wild beasts."

8 Bate, *The Song of the Earth*, 62. See Armitage, *A Vertical Art*, 152: "the speaker's underlying envy of the bird's attributes [. . .] disguising a deep-lying admiration bordering on covetousness [. . .] a covetousness subliminally intimated through the hypnotised speaker's obsession with the hawk's eye."

9 The exact meaning of some of the epithets is unclear, and many of my renderings are either conjectural or approximate.

10 Allsen, *The Royal Hunt*.

11 See Bate, *The Song of the Earth*, 65: "Typically [Elizabeth] Bishop will compare something in nature with something man-made [. . . .] Bishop's imagery always respects nature as it is and for itself, while at the same time recognizing that we can only understand nature by way of those distinctively human categories, history [. . .] and language."

12 See for examples al-Shabushtī, *The Book of Monasteries*.

13 By "culture heroes," I mean, for example, senior males in the Abbasid family as well as the superelites who wielded power (such as the Barmakids in Abū Nuwās's day and other prominent families), in tandem with the poets in their entourages who sang their praises and intoned the qualities that qualified them to be culture heroes. I think the notion can also be applied, for example, to the eponymous founders of the law schools and other emergent disciplines whose disciples cast them in such a mold: see Michael Cooperson, *Classical Arabic Biography*.

14 See further Ibn al-Muʿtazz, *In Deadly Embrace*, xx–xxi.

15 Marvin, "Medieval Blood Sport," 57.

16 Marvin, "Medieval Blood Sport," 66.

17 Marvin, "Medieval Blood Sport," 68, 69.

18 Foster, *Being a Beast*, 85.

19 The concept of the assemblage is explored in Deleuze and Guattari, *A Thousand Plateaus: Capitalism and Schizophrenia*.

20 Cohen, *Medieval Identity Machines*, 76.

21 Cohen, *Medieval Identity Machines*, xxiv and 38.

22 Cohen, *Medieval Identity Machines*, 50. See also *Medieval Identity Machines*, 46: "this medieval technology of the self relies upon a complex assemblage capable of catching up human, animal, objects, and intensities into what also might be called a nonhuman body."

23 Cohen, *Medieval Identity Machines*, 50.

24 As Steel notes in *How to Make a Human: Animals and Violence in the Middle Ages*, 15: "the knight owns the horse and may separate himself from a chivalric circuit by killing and eating his possession."

25 Deleuze, *Essays Critical and Clinical*, 132, 134.

26 Burnside, *The Music of Time: Poetry in the Twentieth Century*, 217.

27 Derrida, "The Animal That Therefore I Am (More to Follow)," 381 and 379, respectively.

28 Compare this poem with Poem 121, "God's Unseen Realm."

29 Kohn, *How Forests Think: Toward an Anthropology beyond the Human*, 72.

30 Bate, *The Song of the Earth*, 149.

31 Abū Nuwās, *Dīwān al-Ḥasan ibn Hāniʾ*, ed. Wagner, 2.176.10–177.5.

32 See Wagner, *Abū Nuwās*, 265–89, for a survey of Abū Nuwās's *Ṭardiyyāt*.

33 The merlin tends to break the neck of its quarry in flight.

34 Some of them are collected in my book *Fate the Hunter*. The remainder will feature in a subsequent publication.

35 See Montgomery, *Fate the Hunter*, 2–11.

36 See Montgomery, *Fate the Hunter*, Poems 11, 12, 14, and 21 (a fragment).

37 Poems 7, 10, 11, 12, 16, 17, 18, 21, 22, 23, 28, and 29 (*rubbamā aghdū*). See also Poem 33, *qad asbiqu* (lit., "I anticipate"), which mirrors the *qad aghtadī* formula and the "dawn motif"; and Poem 33, *qad ashhadu l-lahwa* (lit., "I witness the sport").

38 See Montgomery, *Fate the Hunter*, Poem 13 and the fragmentary Poem 19, by al-Shamardal ibn Sharīk.

39 Abū Nuwās, Poems 24 and 25 (*wa-*); 20 and 26 (*yā rubba*); Montgomery, *Fate the Hunter*, Poem 22 (Abū l-Najm). See further Abū Nuwās, Poems 34 and 35.

40 The verb occurs in a hunting context prior to Abū Nuwās's use by al-Muzarrid ibn Ḍirār: see Montgomery, *Fate the Hunter*, Poem 8, line 64; Stetkevych, *The Hunt in Arabic Poetry: From Heroic to Lyric to Metapoetic*, 95–104 and 296–97, gives other examples of *naʿt*.

41 For examples, see Montgomery, *Fate the Hunter*, Poems 1, 3, and 7.

42 See Ibn al-Muʿtazz, *In Deadly Embrace*.

43 Abū Nuwās, *Dīwān al-Ḥasan ibn Hāniʾ*, ed. Wagner, 3.323.8–325.12. See the studies by Meisami, "Abū Nuwās and the Rhetoric of Parody," and Kennedy, "Perspectives of a Ḫamriyya: Abū Nuwās' *Yā Saḥir al-Ṭarf*."

44 See Bürgel, "The Lady Gazelle and Her Murderous Glances."

45 See the discussion of this in Ibn al-Muʿtazz, *In Deadly Embrace*, xxi–xxii.

46 Volume 4 was edited by Gregor Schoeler (1982).

47 My scholarly edition of the *Ṭardiyyāt* for the Library of Arabic Literature will include an edition of al-Ṣūlī's recension.

48 Abū Nuwās, *Dīwān al-Ḥasan ibn Hāniʾ*, ed. Wagner, 2.324–25.

49 See the arguments to this effect in my *Dīwān ʿAntarah ibn Shaddād: A Literary-Historical Edition.*

50 For details, see Wagner, "Die Überlieferung des Abū Niwās-Dīwān," 328–29.

51 Abū Nuwās, *Dīwān al-Ḥasan ibn Hāniʾ*, ed. Wagner, 2.187.3–17.

52 Abū Nuwās, *Dīwān Abī Nuwās*, ed. al-Ḥadīthī, 189–91; *Dīwān al-Ḥasan ibn Hāniʾ*, ed. Wagner, 2.202.13–204.16

53 Abū Nuwās, *Dīwān al-Ḥasan ibn Hāniʾ*, ed. Wagner, 1.402.6–403.8.

54 For a further version, see also al-Azdī, *The Portrait of Abū l-Qāsim al-Baghdādī al-Tamīmī* (*Ḥikāyat Abī l-Qāsim al-Baghdādī al-Tamīmī*), 303–4.

55 Abū Nuwās, *Dīwān al-Ḥasan ibn Hāniʾ*, ed. Wagner, 2.269.4–10.

56 Abū Nuwās, *Dīwān al-Ḥasan ibn Hāniʾ*, ed. Wagner, 2.325.16–327.5; *Dīwān Abī Nuwās*, ed. al-Ḥadīthī, 217–18.

57 Abū Nuwās, *Dīwān al-Ḥasan ibn Hāniʾ*, ed. Wagner, 1.417–22. On the manuscripts, see Wagner, "Die Überlieferung des Abū Nuwās-Dīwān," 356–58.

58 Al-Shimshāṭī, *Kitāb al-Anwār wa-maḥāsin al-ash'ār*, 2.160–61; 219–20; 283–84; 288.

59 Abū Nuwās, *Dīwān al-Ḥasan ibn Hāni'*, ed. Wagner at 1.111.15–22.4 and 2.35.18–40.18, respectively.

60 See Abū Nuwās, *Dīwān Abī Nuwās*, ed. al-Ḥadīthī, 184 and 188, respectively.

61 Abū Nuwās, *Dīwān Abī Nuwās*, ed. al-Ḥadīthī, 217–18.

62 Montgomery, *Fate the Hunter*, Poem 16, 86–88.

63 Abū Nuwās, *Dīwān al-Ḥasan ibn Hāni'*, ed. Wagner, 2.325.1.

64 Abū Nuwās, *Dīwān al-Ḥasan ibn Hāni'*, ed. Wagner, 2.325.8.

65 See Montgomery, *Fate the Hunter*, Poem 19, 94–95.

ما رواه الرواة عنه من الرجز والقصيـد

*Urjūzah*s and Qasidas Recorded by the Experts

نعت الكلب تسع أرجوزات

~ ١ ~

قال ينعته [الرجز]

أَنْعَتُ كَلْبًا أَهْلُهُ فِي كَدِّهِ
قَدْ سَعِدَتْ جُدُودُهُمْ بِجَدِّهِ
فَكُلُّ خَيْرٍ عِنْدَهُمْ مِنْ عِنْدِهِ
وَكُلُّ رِفْدٍ عِنْدَهُمْ مِنْ رِفْدِهِ
يَظَلُّ مَوْلَاهُ لَهُ كَعَبْدِهِ
يَبِيتُ أَدْنَى صَاحِبٍ مِنْ مَهْدِهِ
وَإِنْ غَدَا جَلَّلَهُ بِبُرْدِهِ
ذَا غُرَّةٍ مُحَجَّلًا بِزَنْدِهِ
تَلَذُّ مِنْهُ ٱلْعَيْنُ حُسْنَ قَدِّهِ
تَأْخِيرَ شِدْقَيْهِ وَطُولَ خَدِّهِ
تَلْقَى ٱلظِّبَاءُ عَنَتًا مِنْ طَرْدِهِ
تَشْرَبُ كَأْسَ شَدِّهَا بِشَدِّهِ
يَصِيدُنَا عِشْرِينَ فِي مُرْقَدِّهِ
يَا لَكَ مِنْ كَلْبٍ نَسِيجِ وَحْدِهِ

Dog Descriptions: Nine *Urjūzah*s

~ 1 ~

In His Gift

I sing of a dog who feeds his folk—
good fortune and well-being are in his gift.
His master sleeps by his bed, wraps him in his cloak
on dawn hunts, and waits on him like a slave.
The eye exults in his beauty: the bright blaze
on his head, his white forelegs, fire-stick
thin, his long cheek, his scissor bite.
He brings death to the *ẓaby*s,
drinking their speed to the dregs,
felling twenty in a single run.
What a dog you are—the best of dogs!

~ ٢ ~

وقال ينعته [الرجز]

أَنْعَتُ كَلْبًا لَيْسَ بِٱلْمَسْبُوقِ
مُطَهَّمًا يَجْرِي عَلَى ٱلْعُرُوقِ
جَاءَتْ بِهِ ٱلْأَمْلَاكُ مِنْ سَلُوقِ
كَأَنَّهُ فِي ٱلْمِقْوَدِ ٱلْمَمْشُوقِ
إِذَا عَدَا عَدْوَةَ لَا مَعُوقِ
يَلْعَبُ بَيْنَ ٱلسَّهْلِ وَٱلْخُرُوقِ
بِأَرْنَبٍ وَثَّابَةٍ عَقُوقِ
لِعْبَ وَلِيدِ ٱلْحَيِّ بِٱلدَّبُّوقِ
يَشْفِي مِنَ ٱلطَّرْدِ جَوَى ٱلْمَشُوقِ
فَٱلْوَحْشُ لَوْ مَرَّتْ عَلَى ٱلْعَيُّوقِ
أَنْزَلَهَا دَامِيَةَ ٱلْحُلُوقِ
ذَاكَ عَلَيْهِ أَوْجَبُ ٱلْحُقُوقِ
لِكُلِّ صَيَّادٍ بِهِ مَرْزُوقِ

~ 2 ~

Bred by Salūq's Kings

I sing of a dog, unbettered in any race,
lean to perfection, bred by Salūq's kings,
clad in collar and leash, running on legs
thin as veins. Through plains flat and wide,
he's unstoppable, playing with a pregnant hare
jinking like a boy with a *dabbūq*. He slakes
your thirst for the hunt! If the oryx
were to fly to ʿAyyūq, he'd bring them down to earth
by the bloody throat. Lucky the hunter
who owns a dog who fulfills this sacred duty.

~ ٣ ~

وقال ينعته [الرجز]

أَنْعَتُ كَلْبًا جَالَ فِي رِبَاطِهِ
خَوْفَ مُصَابٍ خَافَ مِنْ إِسْعَاطِهِ
عِنْدَ طَبِيبٍ خَافَ مِنْ سِيَاطِهِ
هِجْنَا بِهِ وَهَاجَ مِنْ نَشَاطِهِ
كَٱلْكَوْكَبِ ٱلدُّرِّيِّ فِي ٱنْخِرَاطِهِ
عِنْدَ تَهَاوِي ٱلشَّدِّ وَٱنْبِسَاطِهِ
يُقَحِّمُ ٱلْقَائِدَ فِي حِطَاطِهِ
وَقَدِّهِ ٱلْبَيْدَاءَ فِي ٱعْتِبَاطِهِ
لَمَّا رَأَى ٱلْعَلْهَبَ فِي أَقْوَاطِهِ
سَابَحَهُ وَمَرَّ فِي ٱلْتِبَاطِهِ
كَٱلْبَرْقِ يَذْرِي ٱلْمَرْوَ بِٱلْتِقَاطِهِ
مِثْلَ قَلِيٍّ طَارَ فِي إِنْفَاطِهِ
وَٱنْصَاعَ يَتْلُوهُ عَلَى قِطَاطِهِ
أَغْضَفَ لَا يَيْأَسُ مِنْ خِلَاطِهِ
يَصِيدُ بَعْدَ ٱلْبُعْدِ وَٱنْبِسَاطِهِ
إِنْ لَمْ يَبُتَّ ٱلْقَلْبَ مِنْ نِيَاطِهِ
فَلَمْ يَزَلْ يَأْخُذُ فِي لِطَاطِهِ
كَٱلصَّقْرِ يَنْقَضُّ عَلَى غِطَاطِهِ
يَقْشِرُ وَجْهَ ٱلْأَرْضِ مِنْ بَلَاطِهِ
بِأَرْبَعِ تَقُولُ مِنْ إِفْرَاطِهِ
لِشِدَّةِ ٱلْجَرْيِ وَلِٱسْتِحْطَاطِهِ
مَا إِنْ تَمَسُّ ٱلْأَرْضَ فِي أَشْوَاطِهِ

~ 3 ~

Greek Fire

I sing of a dog pulling on the leash
like a lunatic terrified of needles
bolting from a doctor. We provoked him
but we needn't have—he crackled
with pure energy, set to run like a star
shot from the sky.
He strained at the leash, 6
his handler stumbled, then in a whirlwind
he sped across the desert. Old Bull stood
amid his herds. The chase was on—
a scream of lightning, he sliced the *marw*
popping like seeds in a frying pan.
Old Bull cut across, swerving at his heels,
but Drop Ear didn't tire of his company.
He'll get him soon, but it won't be easy,
if his heart doesn't burst first!
He lunged at Old Bull's neck, like a saker
on a grouse, peeling back the earth's
crust with legs so dizzying in their speed
you'd swear they hardly touched the ground.

قَدْ خَدَشَتْ رِجْلَاهُ فِي آبَاطِهِ
وَخَرَّمَ ٱلْأُذْنَيْنِ بِٱنْتِشَاطِهِ
خَلْجُ ذِرَاعَيْهِ إِلَى مِلَاطِهِ
يَنْقَدُّ عَنْهُ ٱلصِّيقُ بِٱنْغِطَاطِهِ
فِي هَبَوَاتِ ٱلصِّيقِ أَوْ رِيَاطِهِ
فَأَدْرَكَ ٱلظَّبْيَ وَلَمْ يُبَاطِهِ
وَلَفَّ عِشْرِينَ إِلَى أَشْرَاطِهِ
فَلَمْ يَزَلْ يَقْرُنُ فِي رِبَاطِهِ
وَيَخْمِطُ ٱلشَّاوُونَ مِنْ خِمَاطِهِ
وَيَطْبَخُ ٱلطَّابِخُ مِنْ أَسْقَاطِهِ
حَتَّى عَلَا فِي ٱلْجَوِّ مِنْ شِيَاطِهِ
كَدَاخِنِ ٱلنَّفْطِ إِلَى نَفَّاطِهِ

His armpits were scraped by his paws, his ears
were pummeled by his strong legs raised
shoulder high. The dust cloud billowed,
the mirage shimmered—into the waves
he dove, giving the *ẓaby*s no quarter.
Twenty were added to the tally.

Back on the leash, he tugged as the meat
was roasted on a spit and the giblets
were boiled by the cooks. The sky filled
with clouds of thick, greasy smoke—
like Greek fire ignited for war.

~ ٤ ~

وقال ينعته [الرجز]

أَعْدَدْتُ كَلْبًا لِلطِّرَادِ سَلْطَا
مُقَلَّدًا قَلَائِدًا وَمُقْطَا
كَأَنَّهُ ٱلصَّقْرُ إِذَا مَا ٱنْحَطَّا
أَوْ لَهَبُ ٱلنَّارِ أُذِيقَتْ نَفْطَا
فَهْوَ ٱلْجَمِيلُ وَٱلْحَسِيبُ رَهْطَا
تَرَى لَهُ شِدْقَيْنِ خُطَّا خَطَّا
وَمَلْطَمًا سَهْلًا وَلَحْيًا سَبْطَا
ذَاكَ وَمَتْنَيْنِ إِذَا تَمَطَّى
قُلْتَ شِرَاكَانِ أُجِيدَا قَطَّا
مِنْ أَدَمِ ٱلطَّائِفِ عُطَّا عَطَّا
يَفْرِي إِذَا كَانَ ٱلْجِرَاءُ عَبْطَا
بَرَاثِنًا سُحْمَ ٱلْأَشَافِي مُلْطَا
يَنْشِطُ أُذْنَيْهِ بِهِنَّ نَشْطَا
تَخَالُ مَا دَمَّيْنَ مِنْهُ شَرْطَا
مَا إِنْ يَقَعْنَ ٱلْأَرْضَ إِلَّا فَرْطَا
كَأَنَّمَا يُعْجِلْنَ شَيْئًا لَقْطَا
أَسْرَعَ مِنْ قَوْلِ قَطَاةٍ قَطَّا
يَكْتَالُ خِزَّانَ ٱلصَّحَارَى ٱلرُّقْطَا
يَلْقَيْنَ مِنْهُ حَاكِمًا مُشْتَطَّا

~ 4 ~

A Pitiless Judge

I readied[1] a long-tongued dog
with collar and leash, who stoops
like a saker or explodes like naphtha in battle.
He's a rare pedigree—look at his pincer jaws
like thin lines, cheeks smooth,
dewlaps tight, and, in the stretch,
a well-balanced back that you'd swear
was a pair of fine Ṭā'if thongs.

The chase kicked up a dust storm. 11
He primed his nails, like black awls
or unfletched arrows,
pulling and tearing at his ears—
you'd think the blood ran
from scars left by cupping—
his legs barely touched the ground,
for just a second, as if scooping seeds
at speed, faster than a pin-tail's call.[2]
He was lenient to all the mottled hares
dragged into court before a pitiless judge.
Black blood lustered in the dust.

لِلْعَظْمِ حَطْمًا وَٱلْأَدِيمِ عَطَّا
فَرْيَ ٱلصَّنَاعِ سَابِرًا وَقُبْطَا
إِذَا ٱلنَّجِيعُ بِٱلْغُبَارِ شَمْطَا
فَٱلْحَمْدُ لِلّٰهِ عَلَى مَا أَعْطَى

A Pitiless Judge

He's a bone crusher, a skin ripper,
a skilled tailor of Sābir and Coptic cloth.
Praise God for His gifts!

~ ٥ ~

وقال ينعته [الرجز]

قَدْ أَغْتَدِي وَٱلصُّبْحُ فِي إِيَابِهِ
بِفِتْيَةٍ كُلُّهُمُ يُعْنَى بِهِ
لَمَّا تَبَدَّى ٱلصُّبْحُ مِنْ حِجَابِهِ
كَطَلْعَةِ ٱلْأَشْمَطِ مِن جِلْبَابِهِ
وَٱنْعَدَلَ ٱللَّيْلُ إِلَى مَآبِهِ
كَٱلْحَبَشِيِّ ٱفْتَرَّ عَنْ أَنْيَابِهِ
هِجْنَا بِكَلْبٍ طَالَمَا هِجْنَا بِهِ
يَنْتَسِفُ ٱلْمِقْوَدَ مِنْ كَلَّابِهِ
مِنْ مَرَحٍ يَغْلُو إِذَا ٱغْلَوْلَى بِهِ
وَمَيْعَةٍ تَغْلِبُ مِنْ شَبَابِهِ
كَأَنَّ مَتْنَيْهِ لَدَى ٱنْسِلَابِهِ
مَتْنَا شُجَاعٍ لَجَّ فِي ٱنْسِيَابِهِ
كَأَنَّمَا ٱلْأُظْفُورَ فِي قِنَابِهِ
مُوسَى صَنَاعٍ رُدَّ فِي قِرَابِهِ
تَرَاهُ فِي ٱلْحُضْرِ إِذَا هَاهَا بِهِ
يَكَادُ أَنْ يَخْرُجَ مِنْ إِهَابِهِ
شَدًّا يَطِنُّ ٱلْقَاعُ مِنْ إِلْهَابِهِ
يَتْرُكُ وَجْهَ ٱلْأَرْضِ فِي ذَهَابِهِ
كَأَنَّ نَشْوَانًا تَوَكَّلْنَا بِهِ
يَعْفُو عَلَى مَا جَرَّ مِنْ ثِيَابِهِ
إِلَّا ٱلَّذِي أَثَّرَ مِنْ هُدَّابِهِ

~ 5 ~

Coiled Like a Viper

Night went back home. On her return,
dawn dropped her veil, a flash
of an Ethiopian's smile. I crossed the dark
with a fine troop. We enraged the dog;
how we maddened him! So much pent-up
energy, so much fury that he tore the leash
from his handler. Sicced, focused,
his back coiled like a viper,
his nails set in his toes like a razor
in its handle. "Go on! Go on!"
we urged. Look—he's so fast
he almost jumped out of his skin.
The light touch of his pace
made the valley sing—it was as if
we'd put our trust in a man so drunk
he trails the hem of his cloak
and wipes away his footprints.[3]

تَرَى سَوَامَ ٱلْوَحْشِ تُجْتَلَى بِهِ
فَهُنَّ أَسْرَى ظُفْرِهِ وَنَابِهِ

Look at the herd of war slaves—
oryx brides rounded up
by swift legs and fierce jaws!

~ ٦ ~

وقال ينعته [الرجز]

لَمَّا غَدَا ٱلثَّعْلَبُ مِنْ وِجَارِهِ
يَلْتَمِسُ ٱلْكَسْبَ عَلَى صِغَارِهِ
جَذْلَانَ قَدْ هُيِّجَ مِنْ دُوَّارِهِ
عَارَضْتُهُ مِنْ سَنَنِ ٱمْتِيَارِهِ
بِضَرِمٍ يَمُوجُ فِي شَوَارِهِ
فِي ٱلْحَلَقِ ٱلصُّفْرِ وَفِي أَسْيَارِهِ
مُضْطَمِرِ ٱلْقُصْرَى مِنَ ٱضْطِمَارِهِ
قَدْ نَحَتَ ٱلتَّنْهِيمُ مِنْ أَقْطَارِهِ
مِنْ بَعْدِ مَا كَانَ إِلَى أَصْبَارِهِ
نَحْضًا كَسَتْهُ ٱلْخُورُ مِنْ عِشَارِهِ
أَيَّامَ لَا يُحْبَسُ عَنْ أَظْآرِهِ
وَهْوَ طَلًا لَمْ يَدْنُ مِنْ شِغَارِهِ
فِي مَنْزِلٍ يُحْجَبُ عَنْ زُوَّارِهِ
يُسَاسُ فِيهِ طَرَفَيْ نَهَارِهِ
حَتَّى إِذَا أُحْمِدَ فِي ٱبْتِيَارِهِ
وَآضَ مِثْلَ ٱلْقُلْبِ مِنْ نُضَارِهِ
كَأَنَّمَا قُرِّبَ مِنْ هِجَارِهِ
يَجْمَعُ قُطْرَيْهِ مِنَ ٱنْضِمَارِهِ
وَإِنْ تَمَطَّى تَمَّ فِي أَشْبَارِهِ
عَشْرًا إِذَا قُدِّرَ فِي ٱقْتِدَارِهِ

~ 6 ~

A Star Scream

Fox left his lair early to look for food,
merrily out and about—I attacked him
with a hungry sight hound, surging forward
in his gear—yellow collar and leather leash.
After a hard fast, his well-sprung ribs
were now chiseled out of flesh
once plump to the touch, nurtured
on camel's milk when a puppy too young
to lift his leg, his wet nurses' darling.
Morning and evening, he'd be trained
in seclusion till he passed every test
and his golden coat turned white as heart
of palm, his slinky flanks as lean as his leash,[4]
measuring ten spans at full stretch.

كَأَنَّ لَحْيَيْهِ لَدَى ٱفْتِرَارِهِ
شَكُّ مَسَامِيرَ عَلَى طَوَارِهِ
كَأَنَّ بَيْنَ مُلْتَقَى أَشْفَارِهِ
جَمْرُ غَضًا يُدْمِنُ فِي ٱسْتِعَارِهِ
سِمْعٌ إِذَا ٱسْتَرْوَحَ لَمْ تُمَارِهِ
إِلَّا بِأَنْ تُطْلِقَ مِنْ عِذَارِهِ
فَٱنْصَاعَ كَٱلْكَوْكَبِ فِي ٱنْكِدَارِهِ
لَفْتَ ٱلْمُشِيرِ مَوْهِنًا بِنَارِهِ
حَتَّى إِذَا أَحْصَفَ فِي إِحْضَارِهِ
خَرَّقَ أُذْنَيْهِ شَبَا أَظْفَارِهِ
حَتَّى إِذَا مَا ٱنْشَامَ فِي غُبَارِهِ
عَافَرَهُ أَخْرَقَ فِي عِفَارِهِ
فَتَلْتَلَ ٱلْمَفْصِلَ مِنْ فَقَارِهِ
وَفَرَّ عَنْهُ جَانِبَيْ صِدَارِهِ
قَدَّ ٱلْأَدِيمَ عُطَّ فِي ٱقْتِوَارِهِ
لَا خَيرَ لِلثَّعْلَبِ فِي ٱبْتِكَارِهِ

A smile from his tight scissor bite
is like a crack made by a nail at the tip
of a stick; flaming coals burn
between the slits of his eyelids.[5]
He's a ferocious *sim‘*—when he gets the scent,
don't try to control him, just let slip!

He shot loose, a star scream, a torch 27
carried at night by a guide. At full speed
he kicked up stones and dirt,
ripping his ears with his nail tips.
He plunged into Fox's dust cloud,
wrestled him brutally to the ground,
snapping his spine like an expert furrier.
Fox had run out of luck!

~ ٧ ~

وقال ينعته [الرجز]

قَدْ أَغْتَدِي وَٱلطَّيْرُ فِي مَثْوَاتِهَا
لَمْ تُعْرِبِ ٱلْأَفْوَاهُ عَنْ لُغَاتِهَا
بِأَكْلُبٍ تَمْرَحُ فِي قِدَّاتِهَا
تَعُدُّ عِينَ ٱلْوَحْشِ مِنْ أَقْوَاتِهَا
قَدْ لَوَّحَ ٱلتَّقْدِيحُ وَارِيَاتِهَا
وَأَشْفَقَ ٱلْقَانِصُ مِنْ خُفَاتِهَا
مِنْ شِدَّةِ ٱلتَّلْوِيحِ وَٱقْتِيَاتِهَا
وَقُلْتُ قَدْ أَحْكَمْتَهَا فَهَاتِهَا
وَأَدْنِ لِلصَّيْدِ مُعَلَّمَاتِهَا
وَٱرْفَعْ لَنَا نِسْبَةَ أُمَّهَاتِهَا
فَجَاءَ يُزْجِيهَا عَلَى شِيَاتِهَا
شُمَّ ٱلْعَرَاقِيبِ مُؤَنَّفَاتِهَا
مُشْرِفَةَ ٱلْأَكْتَافِ مُوفِدَاتِهَا
سُودًا وَصُفْرًا وَخَلَنْجِيَّاتِهَا
غُرَّ ٱلْوُجُوهِ وَمُحَجَّلَاتِهَا
كَأَنَّ أَقْمَارًا عَلَى لَبَّاتِهَا
مُفَدَّيَاتٍ وَمُحَمَّيَاتِهَا
زُلَّ ٱلْمَآخِيرِ عَمَلَّسَاتِهَا
مَفْرُوشَةَ ٱلْأَيْدِي شَرَنْبَثَاتِهَا

~ 7 ~

A Lion's Brutal Paws

As the dawn chorus slept silently in their nests,
I crossed the dark with lively hounds on the leash—
black-eyed oryx are their specialty.
After a harsh regime, their flesh, once fat,
was now hard as wood—the hunter fearing they'd die
from overtraining with so little to eat.
"What a great job," I said. "Fetch your best pupils,
tell me who their mothers are!" He brought the pack,
in their coats of different colors—black, fawn, striped,
with tendon-taut hocks well let down,
round withers on sloping shoulders, light patches
of fur on forehead and leg, moon-bright chests,[6]
a lion's brutal paws when outstretched, and a wolf's
lean, sleek croup. Magnificent creatures!

تَسْمَعُ فِي ٱلْآثَارِ مِنْ وَحَاتِهَا
لِتَفْثَأَ ٱلْأَرْنَبَ عَنْ خَبَاتِهَا
إِنَّ حَيَاةَ ٱلْكَلْبِ فِي وَفَاتِهَا
حَتَّى تَرَى ٱلْقِدْرَ عَلَى مِثْفَاتِهَا
كَثِيرَةَ ٱلضِّيفَانِ مِنْ عُفَاتِهَا
يَقْذِفُ جَالَاهَا بِجَوْزَيْ شَاتِهَا

Listen to the sound of their feet hitting the ground!
Their task—to flush the hare from his flatlands,[7]
for the death of a hare is the life of a dog.[8]
See how the cauldron rocks on its stand,
how the guests and petitioners gather around,
how the two oryx boil away.[9]

~ ٨ ~

وقال ينعته [الرجز]

إِذَا ٱلشَّيَاطِينُ رَأَتْ زُنْبُورَ
قَدْ قُلِّدَ ٱلْحَلْقَةَ وَٱلسُّيُورَ
دَعَتْ لِخِزَّانِ ٱلْفَلَا ثُبُورَ
أَدْفَى تَرَى فِي شِدْقِهِ تَأْخِيرَ
تَرَى إِذَا عَارَضْتَهُ مَفْرُورَ
خَنَاجِرًا قَدْ نَبَتَتْ سُطُورَ
مُشْتَبِكَاتٍ تَنْظِمُ ٱلسُّحُورَ
أُحْسِنَ فِي تَأْدِيبِهِ صَغِيرَ
حَتَّى تَوَفَّى ٱلسِّتَّةَ ٱلشُّهُورَ
مِنْ سِنِّهِ وَبَلَغَ ٱلشُّغُورَ
وَعَرَفَ ٱلْإِيحَاءَ وَٱلصَّفِيرَ
وَٱلْكَفَّ أَنْ تُومِئَ أَوْ تُشِيرَ
يُعْطِيكَ أَقْصَى حُضْرِهِ ٱلْمَذْخُورَ
شَدًّا تَرَى مِنْ هَمْزِهِ ٱلْأُظْفُورَ
مُنْتَشِطًا مِنْ أُذْنِهِ سُيُورَ
فَمَا يَزَالُ وَالِغًا تَأْمُورَ
مِنْ ثَعْلَبٍ غَادَرَهُ عَقِيرَ
أَوْ أَرْنَبٍ جَوَّرَهَا تَجْوِيرَ
فَأَمْتَعَ ٱللَّهُ بِهِ ٱلْأَمِيرَ
رَبِّي وَلَا زَالَ بِهِ مَسْرُورَ

~ 8 ~

Hornet

At the sight of Hornet in collar and lead,
the demons cried, "Death to the desert hares!"[10]
His neck is long, his back arched,
and just look at the scissor bite of his teeth,
like a range of daggers tightly packed in a row,
which can bore holes in a hare's lungs
as if piercing pearls. Trained well as a pup,
at six months he began to lift his leg
and know the calls—the hand signs,
the whistles, the pointings, the nods.[11]
In the dash, he gives you his full store of speed.
Look at how, in full flight, his nails scrape
the skin from his ears. He laps the thick black blood
of a fox, hocked and slain, or a hare, quartered.

God grant my emir every joy and delight in him![12]

~ ٩ ~

وقال ينعته [الرجز]

يَا رُبَّ بَيْتٍ بِفَضَاءِ سَبْسَبِ
بَعِيدِ بَيْنَ ٱلسَّمْكِ وَٱلْمُطَنَّبِ
لِفِتْيَةٍ قَدْ بَكَّرُوا بِأَكْلُبِ
قَدْ أَدَّبُوهَا أَحْسَنَ ٱلتَّأَدُّبِ
مِنْ كُلِّ أَدْفَى مَيَسَانِ ٱلْمَنْكِبِ
يَشُبُّ فِي ٱلْقَوْدِ شُبُوبَ ٱلْمُقْرَبِ
يُلْحِقُ أُذْنَيْهِ بِحَدِّ ٱلْمِخْلَبِ
فَمَا تَنِي وَشِيقَةٌ مِنْ أَرْنَبِ
عِنْدَهُمُ أَوْ تَيْسِ رَبْلٍ عَلْهَبِ
وَفَرْوَةٌ مَسْلُوخَةٌ مِنْ ثَعْلَبِ
مَقْلُوبَةُ ٱلْجِلْدَةِ أَوْ لَمْ تُقْلَبِ
وَعَيْرُ عَانَاتٍ وَأُمُّ تَوْلَبِ
وَمِرْجَلٍ يَهْدِرُ هَدْرَ ٱلْمُصْعَبِ
يَقْذِفُ جَالَاهُ بِجَوْزِ ٱلْقَرْهَبِ

~ 9 ~

In the Open Desert

Tents stood in the open desert, tall pavilions
pitched by nobles who hunt in the early hours
with hounds trained to perfection, their backs
arched, their shoulders proud, pure breeds
curvetting in their collars, their ears ripped
by the tips of their nails in the dash.
Cornucopia of cured hare and oryx meat—
it's Old Bull, the buck—a trove of wild onager jacks
and mothers of foals, of unskinned foxes
and of stripped fox skins, turned inside out.[13]

The cauldron roars like an untamed male camel 13
as Old Bull's carcass boils briskly in the pot.

نعت الفهد وهو أرجوزة واحدة

~ ١٠ ~

قال ينعته [الرجز]

قَدْ أَغْتَدِي وَٱللَّيْلُ أَحْوَى ٱلسُّدِّ
وَٱلصُّبْحُ فِي ٱلظَّلْمَاءِ ذُو تَعَدِّي
مِثْلَ ٱهْتِزَازِ ٱلْعَضْبِ ذِي ٱلْفِرِنْدِ
بِأَهْرَتِ ٱلشِّدْقَيْنِ مُرْمَئِدِّ
أَزْبَرَ مَضْبُورِ ٱلْقَرَا عِلَّكْدِ
طَاوِي ٱلْحَشَا فِي طَيِّ جِسْمٍ مَعْدِ
كَرْهِ ٱلرُّوَا جَمِّ غُضُونِ ٱلْخَدِّ
دُلَامِزٍ ذِي نَكَفٍ مُسْوَدِّ
وَسَحْرِ بُخْتِيٍّ بِنَحْرٍ وَرْدِ
شَرَنْبَثٍ أَغْلَبَ مُصْمَعِدِّ
كَٱللَّيْثِ إِلَّا نُمْرَةً بِٱلْجِلْدِ
لِلشَّبَحِ ٱلْحَائِلِ مُسْتَعِدِّ
عَايَنَ بَعْدَ ٱلنَّظَرِ ٱلْمُمْتَدِّ
عَلَى قَطَاةِ ٱلزَّرْدِ رِدْفَ ٱلْعَبْدِ
سِرْبَيْنِ عَنَّا بِجَبِينٍ صَلْدِ

Cheetah Description: One *Urjūzah*

~ 10 ~

An Ambush

Dawn quivered like a fine, glistering blade
waging war on darkness. I crossed
the black-cloud night with a spry, wide-
jawed cheetah, thick necked, with bulky
scapulae welded fast to his spine
and a lean-bellied body tightly twisted
like a well rope. When he scowls, his cheek
folds are plump and sheeny; he has black
teardrops on the muscles of his face,[14]
a Bactrian's lungs in a saffron ribcage,
heavy paws, a bull neck, and a sudden dart,
alert to any shapes that shift—his spotted
coat the only sign he's not a lion—
mounted behind the rider.[15]
A long search 13
revealed two herds on a plain flat as a man's brow.

فَٱنْقَضَّ يَأْدُو غَيْرَ مُجْرَهِدِّ
فِي لَهَبٍ مِنْهُ وَخَتْلٍ إِدِّ
مِثْلَ لِسَانِ ٱلْحَيَّةِ ٱلْعِرْبَدِّ
بِكُلِّ نَشْزٍ وَبِكُلِّ وَهْدِ
حَتَّى إِذَا كَانَ تُجَاهَ ٱلْقَصْدِ
صَعْصَعَهَا بِٱلصَّحْصَحَانِ ٱلْجَرْدِ
وَعَاثَ فِيهَا بِفَرِيغِ ٱلشَّدِّ
بَيْنَ شَرِيجَيْ طَمَعٍ وَحَرْدِ
لَا خَيْرَ فِي ٱلصَّيْدِ بِغَيْرِ فَهْدِ

An Ambush

He was off, in a stealthy stalk, an ambush, a trap
ready to explode,[16] like a viper's tongue[17]
moving over ground high and low. Then,
creeping over the ground, face to face
with his prey, he scattered them across the desert
plain, wreaking havoc at full stretch,
full tilt, torn between anger and greed.
When hunting, a cheetah is the only way to go!

نعت البازي وهو خمس أرجوزات

~ ١١ ~

قال ينعته [الرجز]

قَدْ أَغْتَدِي وَٱللَّيْلُ فِي مُسْوَدِّهِ
وَرْدٌ يُرَقِّي ٱلطَّيْرَ فِي مُنْقَدِّهِ
غُدُوَّ بَاغِي قَنَصٍ مُعِدِّهِ
فِي قُرْطُقٍ خُيِّطَ بِٱزْبَكَنْدِهِ
مِنْ خَالِصِ ٱلدِّيبَاجِ أَوْ فِرِنْدِهِ
مُشَمَّرَ ٱلتَّخْصِيرِ دَامَنْ فَرْدِهِ
بِدَسْتَبَانٍ فَاضِلٍ عَنْ زَنْدِهِ
وَسُهْرَدَازِ ٱللَّوْنِ أَوْ سَمَنْدِهِ
سَائِلَةً غُرَّتُهُ بِخَدِّهِ
قَدْ قَدَّهُ ٱلصَّانِعُ أَحْلَى قَدِّهِ
فَهْوَ شَبِيهٌ قَبْلُهُ بِبَعْدِهِ
ذُو غُرَّةٍ مَنْ يَرَهُ يُفَدِّهِ
يَرْنُو إِذَا ٱلصَّيْدُ ٱرْتَأَى مِنْ بُعْدِهِ
بِمُقْلَةٍ تَلْحَقُ قَبْلَ شَدِّهِ
سَجْرَاءَ لَيْسَ جِلْدُهُ كَجِلْدِهِ
مَا كَانَ إِلَّا حَلُّنَا مِنْ عَقْدِهِ
وَخَرْطُنَاهُ مِنْ شِكَارِبَنْدِهِ

Goshawk Descriptions: Five *Urjūzah*s

~ 11 ~

At the Falconer's Tally

Night, in stygian mood,[18] was torn
and turned red, rousing the birds.
I crossed the dark in search of game
with a hawk in a needle-sewn tunic
of pure silk or fine cloth, her arms bare
to the waist, train feathers stretching
past her feet, sitting on a glove
that covered my elbow. A *suhradāz* gos;
no, a *samand*, her cheek a blaze of white,
given the sweetest form by our Maker,
unchanged by the hunt. If you saw her white face,
you'd pledge her your life! Before flight, she stares
at the prey she sights from afar, tracking it down
with eyes inflamed red against the white
of her coat. Releasing the jess, we cast her

فَمَرَّ يَفْرِي ٱلْأَرْضَ فِي مُرْقَدِّهِ
فَجَالَ وَٱرْتَدَّتْ عَلَى مُرْتَدِّهِ
كَأَنَّهَا إِذْ وَأَلَتْ مِنْ حَدِّهِ
وَٱعْصَوْصَبَتْ لَمَّا رَأَتْ مِنْ جِدِّهِ
أُسْرَةَ كِسْرَى يَوْمَ دَسْتَبَنْدِهِ
فَصَادَنَا قَبْلَ ٱنْتِصَافِ جَهْدِهِ
خَمْسِينَ أَحْصَتْهَا يَدَا مُعْتَدِّهِ
فَنَحْنُ فِي نَائِلِهِ وَرِفْدِهِ
أَبُو عِيَالٍ قَاتَهُمْ بِكَدِّهِ
فَكُلُّ خَيْرٍ عِنْدَهُمْ مِنْ عِنْدِهِ
يَا لَكَ مِنْ بَازٍ نَسِيجِ وَحْدِهِ

from the glove. In a circuit, at great speed,
she cut up the terrain and brought the quarry
round, trying to outrun her. When they saw
how determined she was, they flocked together
like Khusro's kin on the day of the *dastaband*.
She hunted fifty, at the falconer's tally,
and had more than half her energy to spare.
We depend on her grace and favor as a family
depends on the father who feeds them—
whatever good they have derives from his labors.
What a fine gos! One of a kind!

~ ١٢ ~

وقال ينعته [الرجز]

قَدْ أَغْتَدِي وَٱللَّيْلُ ذُو دَيَاجِي
قَبْلَ طُلُوعِ ٱلْفَجْرِ بِٱنْبِلَاجِ
فِي فِتْيَةٍ سَرَّهُمُ ٱدِّلَاجِي
بِبَازِيٍ صِيدَ عَلَى ٱبْتِهَاجِ
كُرِّزَ عَامٍ جَاءَ مِنْ مِنْهَاجِ
أَلْبَسَهُ وَشْيًا بِلَا نَسَّاجِ
مَوْشِيَّةِ ٱلرِّيَاشِ كَٱلدِّيبَاجِ
مُنَقَّطٍ ظَاهِرُهُ بِزَاجِ
كَأَنَّمَا يَنْظُرُ مِنْ سِرَاجِ
عَنْ مُقْلَةٍ وَاسِعَةِ ٱلْحَجَاجِ
وَمِنْسَرٍ أَكْلَفَ ذِي ٱعْوِجَاجِ
تَخَالُهُ صُدْغًا عَلَى مِغْنَاجِ
زَرْفَنَهُ إِذْ قَامَ لِلْيَرَاجِ
فِي وَجْنَةٍ تَبْرُقُ مِثْلَ ٱلْعَاجِ
حَتَّى إِذَا صِرْنَا لَدَى ٱلْفِجَاجِ
مِنْ مَوْضِعِ ٱلصَّيْدِ عَلَى ٱرْتِهَاجِ
لَمَّا تَبَدَّى ٱلصُّبْحُ بِٱلْإِبْلَاجِ
مِنْ ظُلَمٍ كُمْتٍ عَلَى رِتَاجِ
حَلَلْتُ سَيْرَيْهِ فِعَالَ ٱلرَّاجِي
ثُمَّ دَعَوْتُ دَعْوَةَ ٱلْمُنَاجِي
فَمَرَّ كَٱلْبَرْقِ بِلَا ٱنْعِرَاجِ

~ 12 ~

Dots of Dark Vitriol

I crossed the pitch-black night before dawn smiled
upon the company of a noble troop happy
to be out early with me, hunting with a gos,
intermewed, trapped when carefree in her home,
her pattern coat embroidered with brocade feathers
not woven by human hand, her mail covered
in surface dots of dark vitriol, eyes lamp-bright
beneath high ridges, and a tawny curved beak—
imagine a coquette's curl twirled upon an ivory-
sheen cheek as she fiddles with her jewels.

Despite the dust storm, we reached the Ravines
to hunt. The color of a bay horse,
dawn smiled at night's door. I loosened
the ties on her halsband, cocky at the prospect
of a kill. I gave the call and she exploded—
a lightning bolt, fatal to her quarry.

لَيْسَ ٱلَّذِي يَطْلُبُـهُ بِنَـاجِي
فَصَـادَ قَبْـلَ بَـارِحِ ٱلْعَجَاجِ
خَمْسِـينَ مِنْ وَزٍّ وَمِنْ دُرَّاجِ
أَحْصَيْتُهَـا عَـدًّا بِلَا تَـلَاجِ
نِعْـمَ ٱلرَّفِيقُ لِلْفَتَى ٱلْمُحْتَـاجِ

Before the wind kicked up the dust,
she hunted fifty geese and coursers—
I counted them myself, without cheating.
What a fine friend to the needy!

~ ١٣ ~

قال ينعته [الرجز]

لَمَّا رَأَيْتُ ٱللَّيْلَ قَدْ تَسَرَّرَ
عَنِّي وَعَنْ مَعْرُوفِ صُبْحٍ أَسْفَرَ
أَلْبَسْتُ كَفِّي دَسْتَبَانًا مُشْعَرَ
فَرْوَةَ سِنْجَابٍ لُؤَامًا أَوْبَرَ
تَقِي بَنَانَ ٱلْكَفِّ أَنْ لَا تُخْصَرَ
وَغَمْرَةَ ٱلْبَازِي إِذَا مَا ظَفَّرَ
فَشِمْتُ فِيهِ ٱلْكَفَّ إِلَّا ٱلْخِنْصِرَ
أَعْدَدْتُ لِلْبِغْثَانِ حَتْفًا مُمْقِرَ
أَبْرَشَ بُطْنَانِ ٱلْجَنَاحِ أَقْمَرَ
أَرْقَطَ ضَاحِي ٱلدَّفَّتَيْنِ أَنْمَرَ
كَأَنَّ شِدْقَيْهِ إِذَا تَضَوَّرَ
صَدْعَانِ مِنْ عَرْعَرَةٍ تَفَطَّرَ
كَأَنَّ عَيْنَيْهِ إِذَا مَا أَتْأَرَ
فَصَّانِ قِيضَا مِنْ عَقِيقٍ أَحْمَرَ
فِي هَامَةٍ غَلْبَاءَ تَهْدِي مِنْسَرَ
كَعَطْفَةِ ٱلْجِيمِ بِكَفٍّ أَعْسَرَ
يَقُولُ مَنْ فِيهَا بِعَقْلٍ فَكَّرَ
لَوْ زَادَهَا عَيْنًا وَفَاءً ثُمَّ رَ
فَٱتَّصَلَتْ بِٱلْجِيمِ كَانَتْ جَعْفَرَ
فَٱلطَّيْرُ يَلْقَيْنَ مِدَقًّا مِدْسَرَ
مَشْقًا هَذَاذَيْهِ وَنَهْسًا نَهْسَرَ

~ 13 ~

Piledriver Force

Night had bedded down with his woman.
I saw dawn's kind gift of light and put
on a pad lined with a squirrel's pelt,
tightly matted, fleecy, to protect my hand
from the gos's savage grip, covering
all but my little finger. I readied
a bitter death for the ibis—with freckled
underwing coverts, dusty-white spangled
sails, leopard spots. When she shrieks,
her mandibles are thin cleft juniper sticks,
with eyes that stare like red gems chipped
from a Yemeni stone. A bulky crown
directs a beak like the loop of a *jīm*
drawn by a left hand—astute men
would look at it and say, "Add *ʿayn*,
fāʾ and *rāʾ*, and it spells Jaʿfar."[19]

Piledriver force, a whirlwind of spear
thrusts more ravenous than wolves,
beaked the birds to shreds.

~ ١٤ ~

قال ينعته [الرجز]

أُطْـرِيكَ يَا بَازِيَّنَا وَأُطْـرِي
مُـرْتَجِزًا وَفِي قَصِـيدِ ٱلشِّعْـرِ
أَقْمَـرُ مِنْ ضَـرْبِ بُـزَاةٍ قُمْـرِ
يَصْقُلُ حِمْلَاقًا شَدِيدَ ٱلطَّحْرِ
كَأَنَّـهُ مُكْتَحِـلٌ بِتِـبْرِ
فِي هَـامَـةٍ لُمَّتْ كَلَمِّ ٱلْفِهْـرِ
وَجُؤْجُؤٍ كَٱلْحَجَـرِ ٱلْقَهْقَـرِّ
يُـرِيـحُ إِنْ أَرَاحَ لَا مِنْ بُهْـرِ
مِنْ مِنْخَرٍ رَحْبٍ كَعَقْدِ ٱلْعَشْرِ
فِي مِنْسَرٍ أَقْنَى رُحَابِ ٱلشَّجْرِ
شَثْنُ سُلَامَى ٱلْكَفِّ وَافِي ٱلشِّبْرِ
أَخْـرَقُ طَبٌّ بِٱنْتِـزَاعِ ٱلسَّحْـرِ
فَـلِلْكَرَاكِيِّ بِكُلِّ دَبْـــرِ
وَقَـائِعٌ مِنْ عَنَـتٍ وَأَسْـــرِ

~ 14 ~

Her Brutal War

I salute you, my gos! In odes
formal and songs informal,
I sing your praises!

A dusty-white bird, her eyes 3
burnished by a strong blink
as if kohled with gold, a bulky crown
like a pestle, a mail like a boulder,
swelling when she breathes,
but not from fatigue, crines
as round as fingers making
the sign of the number ten,[20]
a hooked beak, a wide throat,
coarse beam feathers, broad-
span talons—a doctor skilled
at performing throat surgery.

The cranes in the canals and the fields 13
are helpless against her brutal war.

~ ١٥ ~

قال ينعته ويمدح الصقر بن الصفّاق بن حجر الأزديّ من ولد الجلندى وكان ينزل خلف سيراف والناس يظنّون أنّ الأرجوزة في وصف الصقر [الرجز]

يَا صَقْرَ غَيْثٍ يَجْبُرُ ٱللَّهِيفَا
مِنْ فَرْعِ عِزٍّ لَمْ يَكُنْ خَلِيفَا
وَشَرَفٍ قَدْ زِدْتَهُ تَشْرِيفَا
أَتْبَعْتَ مِنْهُ ٱلتَّالِدَ ٱلطَّرِيفَا
مَا زِلْتُ أَرْجُو مُذْ قَدِمْتَ ٱلسِّيفَا
أَقْمَرَ مِنْ بُزَاتِهَا غِطْرِيفَا
لَا قَاتِمَ ٱللَّوْنِ وَلَا خَصِيفَا
وَلَا إِلَى سَائِسِهِ مَأْفُوفَا
رَبَا بِهِ مُنْذُ رَبَا مَشْعُوفَا
لَوْ لَمْ يَجِدْ يَوْمًا لَهُ عَدُوفَا
حَزَّ لَهُ مِنْ أُذْنِهِ ٱلْغُضْرُوفَا
كَانَ ٱفْتِلَاهُ ضَرَعًا نَحِيفَا
تَرَى لَهُ مِنْ زَغَبٍ شُفُوفَا
صُفْرًا تَرَى لِلَوْنِهَا رَفِيفَا
كَأَنَّ وَرْسًا عَلَّهُ مَدُوفَا
فَٱرْتَبَّهُ رَبًّا بِهِ رَؤُوفَا
وَلَقِنًا فِي فَهْمِهِ عَسُوفَا

~ 15 ~

Yellow Gossamer Down

A description of a gos and a panegyric for al-Ṣaqr ibn al-Ṣaffāq ibn Ḥujr al-Azdī, one of the sons of al-Julandā, when he had taken up residence in the hinterland of Sīrāf. Nonexperts generally suppose that this *urjūzah* is a description of al-Ṣaqr. [21]

Ever faithful to the mighty tree of honor
and glory you inherited and helped raise high,
Ṣaqr, your bounty rains down on us poor wretches.

Since your move to Sīf, I have been hoping
for one of its dusty-white eyas hawks,
not a gray or a dappled gos, black on white,
or one who causes the austringer to say, "Ugh!"
but rather the apple of his eye, smothered
in love: if one day he had nothing to feed her,
he'd slice the helix from his ear as a tidbit!
As a tiny chick, he'd cosset her—look,
you can see her yellow gossamer down
as if dyed deep in powdered Yemeni spice—
and rear her, a lord and master loving
and yet harsh (what skill, what expertise!),

حَتَّى إِذَا مَا جَرَّمَ ٱلْمَصِيفَا
وَشْيًا وَقَدْ ثَقَّفَهُ تَثْقِيفَا
وَٱجْتَابَ مِنْ طِرَازِهِ تَفْوِيفَا
وَشْيًا تَرَى بَسِيطَهُ مَكْفُوفَا
مِثْلَ ٱسْتِرَاقِ ٱلْكَاتِبِ ٱلْحُرُوفَا
يَصْقُلُ حِمْلَاقًا لَهُ مَشُوفَا
فِي هَامَةٍ تَرَى لَهَا حُرُوفَا
يَعْتَامُ بَطَّ ٱللُّجَّةِ ٱلْعُكُوفَا
مِنْهُ بِكَفٍّ تَرْحَبُ ٱلْكُفُوفَا
تَخَالُ فِي جِلْدَتِهَا تَوْسِيفَا
بِحَيْثُ ضَمَّ ٱلْكَمَعُ ٱلْوَظِيفَا
وَلَا تَكُونَنْ عِدَتِي تَسْوِيفَا
فَقَدْ أَرَاكَ ذَا حِجًى خَصِيفَا
يَدْرَأُ عَنْكَ رَبُّكَ ٱلْمَخُوفَا

until, trained and taught well, after a summer
in the mews, she was clad in a white-striped cloak
of patterned stitches, the furled feathers
on her mail like a scribe's half-formed calligraphy,
her eyes, burnished and bright, set in a crown
where the brows are clear and distinct.[22]
Of the ducks captive[23] on the lake, she takes
her pick with a welcoming hand opened wide—
you'd think her skin was chapped where the jesses
clasp her arm.[24]
Don't put off your promise— 29
you're a man of excellent sense, God keep you!

نعت الزرّق وهو أرجوزتان

~ ١٦ ~

قال ينعته [الرجز]

قَـدْ أَغْـتَـدِي بِزُرَّقٍ جُـرَازِ
مَحْضٍ رَقِيقِ ٱلزِّفِّ وَٱلطِّرَازِ
دُبِّقَ مِنْ نَعْـمَانَ سُهْـرَدَازِ
يَصِيدُنَا زَرْقًا وَدَسْتَخَازِ
زَيْنُ يَدِ ٱلْحَامِلِ وَٱلْقُفَّـازِ
فَكَمْ وَكَمْ مِنْ طُوَّلٍ جَمَّـازِ
مُغَـامِـرٍ يُكْنَى أَبَا كُرَّازِ
جَمِّ ٱلْوِقَاعِ مُوجِزِ ٱلْإِيجَازِ
قَدْ طَالَ مَا أَوْطَنَ بِٱلْأَهْوَازِ
بِحَجِنَاتٍ صَدْقَةِ ٱلتَّوْخَازِ
مِثْلَ أَشَافِي ٱلصَّنَعِ ٱلْخَرَّازِ
يَعْـتَامُهَا فَـرْدًا بِلَا جِلْوَازِ
وَلَا مُـرَاآةٍ عَـلَى فَـرْوَازِ
مَشْقًا يَقُـدُّ ثَبَجَ ٱلْأَجْوَازِ
قَدَّ ٱبْنِ بَازٍ وَصَنِـيعَ بَـازِ
نِعْمَ ٱلْخَلِيلُ سَاعَةَ ٱلْإِعْوَازِ

Tiercel Goshawk Descriptions: Two *Urjūzah*s

~ 16 ~

A Farrier's Hard Needles

I crossed the dark with a pure tiercel on the glove,
keen as a blade, *suhradāz,* with soft,
downy patterned coverts, lime-trapped
in Na'mān then intermewed—this hunter's
a fine sight mounted on his carrier's hand
and perched on the block. From the wrist
he flies straight into combat, a berserker,
the essence of speed—he slaughters
many high-stepping waders, long-term
residents of Ahwāz,[25] seizing them and rapidly
lancing them with a farrier's hard needles,
like a deft tanner's awls. He selects them
when they're alone and unguarded,
then isolates them, without guile,
slashing through their backs to get at the heart,
with typical goshawk skill, just like his sire.
What a fine friend in time of need!

~ ١٧ ~

وقال ينعته [الرجز]

قَدْ أَغْتَدِي بِزُرَّقٍ صَبِيحِ
مَحْضٍ لِمَنْ يَنْسُبُهُ صَرِيحِ
صَلْتِ ٱلْجَبِينِ وَاضِحٍ مَلِيحِ
وَلَيْسَ مَا يُغْمَزُ كَٱلصَّحِيحِ
بِكَفِّ ضَنَّانٍ بِهِ شَحِيحِ
مِمَّا ٱشْتَرَى بِٱلثَّمَنِ ٱلرَّبِيحِ
فَلَمْ يَزَلْ بِٱلنَّهْمِ وَٱلتَّقْدِيحِ
وَرَشِّهِ بِٱلْمَاءِ وَٱلتَّلْوِيحِ
حَتَّى ٱنْطَوَى إِلَّا جَنَانَ ٱلرُّوحِ
وَعَرَفَ ٱلصَّوْتَ وَوَحْيَ ٱلْمُوحِي
فَكَمْ وَكَمْ مِنْ طُوَّلٍ طَمُوحِ
لَمْ يُنْجِهِ طُمُورُهُ فِي ٱللُّوحِ
مِنْ فَلَتَاتِ صَلَتَانٍ شِيحِ
تُرْجِلُهُ ٱلرِّيحُ بِكَفِّ ٱلرِّيحِ
وَضَرْبَةٍ بِنَيْزَكٍ مَذْرُوحِ
فَٱصْطَادَ قَبْلَ ٱلْأَيْنِ وَٱلتَّبْرِيحِ
خَمْسِينَ مُسْتَحْيًى إِلَى مَذْبُوحِ

~ 17 ~

The Coded Signs

I crossed the dark with a fine tiercel on the glove,
a purebred according to the genealogists.
His brow is clear and bright and noble—
you can tell true witness from false—
sitting on the hand of a man devoted to him,
bought at a good price, disciplined by fasting
and inanition, calmed with water, and trained
with the lure. Then, fit and lean but with a demon
spirit,[26] he could recognize the falconer's
voice and interpret the coded signs.

So many farsighted waders vaulted 11
into the air but couldn't escape his sudden
precise, steely blows, forced back to the ground
by a flight as fast as the wind, and a thwack
of spearheads smeared with poison.
Before giving in to fatigue, he caught
a full fifty—some left at death's door,
others slaughtered outright.

نعت الصقر وهو ثلاث أرجوزات

~ ١٨ ~

قال ينعته [الرجز]

قَدْ أَغْتَدِي وَٱللَّيْلُ ذُو غَيَاطِلِ
هَابِي ٱلدُّجَى مُنْضَرِجُ ٱلْخَصَائِلِ
بِتَوَّجِيٍّ مُرْهَفِ ٱلْمَعَاوِلِ
حَامِي ٱلْحُمَيَّا مِخْلَطٍ مُزَايِلِ
يُوفِي ٱنْتِصَابَ ٱلْمَلِكِ ٱلْحُلَاحِلِ
فَوْقَ شِمَالِ ٱلْقَانِصِ ٱلْمُخَاتِلِ
أَفْحَجَ مَخْشِيِّ ٱلشَّدَا قُصَامِلِ
حَتَّى إِذَا أُطْلِقَ غَيْرُ وَائِلِ
إِلَّا بِمَا ٱعْتَامَ مِنَ ٱلْعَقَائِلِ
صَكَّ ٱلْمُغَالِي هَدَفَ ٱلْمُخَاصِلِ
وَٱلسِّرْبُ بَيْنَ خَرِقٍ وَوَائِلِ
كَأَنَّهُ حِينَ سَمَا كَٱلْخَاتِلِ
مُنْقَلِبَ ٱلْحِمْلَاقِ غَيْرَ غَافِلِ
مُنْكَفِتًا لِسِرْبِهِنَّ ٱلْحَافِلِ
جَنْدَلَةً تَهْوِي إِلَى جَنَادِلِ
يَدْوَيْنَ بَيْنَ دَنِفٍ مُنَاقِلِ
وَبَيْنَ مَفْرِيِّ ٱلْقَرَا خَرَادِلِ

Saker Descriptions: Three *Urjūzah*s

~ 18 ~

In Denial of Death

I crossed the tamarisk-thick night,
dawn still but a bud in the smoky dark,
with a Tawwajī saker on the glove,
armed with sharp pickaxe talons.
She's fierce, spirited, daunting in attack,
carried on a canny hunter's left hand
like a king on a throne, with a solid frame,
a fearsome beak, and a killer bite.
When cast off, she thwacks into her prey
like an arrow rocking its target
and brings home the finest spoils.

A startled flock took flight; others 11
froze in fear. She climbed and feinted,
blinked her eye, then wheeled—
she hadn't missed her chance—
into a stoop, then down fast, an avalanche
from the sky. The birds lay like stones
on the ground, some in denial of death,
others with mustard-seed holes in their backs.

كَأَنَّهُ فِي جِلْدِهِ ٱلرَّعَابِلِ
لَابِسُ فَرْوٍ نَائِسٍ ٱلذَّلَاذِلِ

She stood tall, her coat matted
with the tattered feathers of her dead.

~ ١٩ ~

وقال ينعته [الرجز]

لَا صَيْدَ إِلَّا بِٱلصُّقُورِ ٱللُّمَّحِ
كُلِّ قَطَامِيٍّ بَعِيدِ ٱلْمِطْرَحِ
يَجْلُو حَجَاجَيْ مُقْلَةٍ لَمْ تُجْرَحِ
لَمْ تَغْذُهُ بِٱللَّبَنِ ٱلْمُضَيَّحِ
أُمٌّ وَلَمْ يُولَدْ بِسَهْلِ ٱلْأَبْطَحِ
إِلَّا بِأَشْرَافِ ٱلْجِبَالِ ٱلطُّمَّحِ
يُلْوِي بِخِزَّانِ ٱلصَّحَارَى ٱلْجُمَّحِ
يَنْحَى لَهَا بَعْدَ ٱلطِّمَاحِ ٱلْأَطْمَحِ
بِسَلِبٍ كَٱلنَّيْزَكِ ٱلْمُذَرَّحِ
وَمِنْسَرٍ أَقْنَى كَأَنْفِ ٱلْمِجْدَحِ
وَهْوَ رُدَافَى بِٱلْبَسَاطِ ٱلْأَفْيَحِ
مُتَيَّحَاتٌ بِخُفَافٍ مِتْيَحِ
فَٱصْطَادَ قَبْلَ ٱلتَّعَبِ ٱلْمُبَرِّحِ
وَقَبْلَ أَوْبِ ٱلْعَازِبِ ٱلْمُرَوِّحِ
خَمْسِينَ مِثْلَ ٱلْعِتْرِ ٱلْمُسَدَّحِ
مَا بَيْنَ مَذْبُوحٍ وَمَا لَمْ يُذْبَحِ
أَحَصَّ أَطْرَافِ ٱلْقُدَامَى وَحْوَحِ
أَبْرَشَ مَا بَيْنَ ٱلْقَرَا وَٱلْمَذْبَحِ

~ 19 ~

The Altar of a Hungry Idol

A lightning-bolt saker—that's how to hunt!
Mad for the kill,[27] never missing a season,
her bright eyes a stranger to the needle's
seel, never milk-fed in the dull plain
but born wild on the craggy peaks.

She towers high and long, then she's off. 7
Jinking desert hares twirled and tossed
in the grip of poison-tipped spears
and a curve-beaked scoop. She rides
shotgun on the flat plain beside hares
fated to meet a sidewinder, fully fueled.[28]

Before fatigue's bite, before the cattle 13
return from the fields, she hunts fifty,
victims on the altar of a hungry idol—
some slaughtered, others not yet dead.

Enseamed, she stands dappled from mail 17
to throat, her beams hard-penned.

~ ٢٠ ~

وقال ينعته ويقال إنّها في البازي وقيل في اليؤيؤ [الرجز]

يَا رُبَّ غَيْثٍ آمِنِ ٱلسُّرُوبِ
مُلَازِمَاتٍ جَلْهَتَيْ مَلْحُوبِ
إِلَى ٱلْقُطَيْبِيَّاتِ فَٱلذَّنُوبِ
رَوَافِلٍ دَأْبَ ٱلنَّصَارَى ٱلشِّيبِ
تَخْطِرُ فِي بَرَانِسٍ قُشُوبِ
مِنْ حِبَرٍ حُودِثْنَ بِٱلتَّذْهِيبِ
فِي يَوْمِ عِيدٍ مُبْرِزِ ٱلصَّلِيبِ
ذَعَرْتُهَا بِمُلْهَبِ ٱلشُّؤْبُوبِ
مُفَهَّمٍ إِهَابَةَ ٱلْمُهِيبِ
وَكَلِمَاتِ كُلِّ مُسْتَجِيبِ
أَقْنَى إِلَى سَائِسِهِ حَبِيبِ
وَقَدْ جَرَى مِنْهُ عَلَى تَأْدِيبِ
يُوفِي عَلَى قُفَّازِهِ ٱلْمَجُوبِ
مِنْهُ بِكَفٍّ سَبْطَةِ ٱلتَّرْحِيبِ
كَأَنَّهَا بَرَاثِنٌ مِنْ ذِيبِ
يَضْبِثُهُنَّ فِي ثَرًى مَصْبُوبِ
إِلَى وَظِيفٍ فَاتِقِ ٱلظُّنْبُوبِ
وَجُؤْجُؤٍ مِثْلَ مَدَاكِ ٱلطِّيبِ
فِي قَصَبٍ مُسْتَأْزِرِ ٱلْكُعُوبِ

~ 20 ~

A Pleuritic Cough

Some scholars say this is a description not of a saker but of a goshawk, while others maintain it is a merlin.

Rain-grass—there's always game
to be had clinging to the parched slopes
as far as Quṭaybiyyāt and Dhanūb,
sauntering about in their bright hoods
burnished with gold, like gray-haired
Christians parading the Cross on a holy day.

I terrified them with Curve Beak, 8
an exploding supernova trained
to heed the call and listen for the shout,
cherished by her expert handler.
She sits astride the glove, her claws
with long talons eager to extend
their welcome, like the toes of a wolf
furiously digging at wet soil, arms
with bulky shins, a piledriver mail

تَحْتَ جَنَاحٍ مُوجَدِ ٱلتَّنْكِيبِ
وَحْفِ ٱلظُّهَارِ عَصِلِ ٱلْأُنْبُوبِ
آنَسَ بَيْنَ صَــــرْدَحٍ وَلُوبِ
بِمُقْلَةٍ قَلِيلَةِ ٱلتَّكْذِيبِ
طَرَّاحَةٍ خَلْفَ لَقَى ٱلْغُيُوبِ
فَٱنْقَضَّ مِثْلَ ٱلْحَجَرِ ٱلْمَنْدُوبِ
مُنْكَفِتًا تَكَفُّتَ ٱلْجَنِيبِ
بِٱلشَّطْرِ مِنْ حِمْلَاقِهِ ٱلْمَقْلُوبِ
عَلَى رِفَلٍّ بِٱلضُّحَى ضَغُوبِ
بِذِي مَوَاسٍ مُرْهَفِ ٱلْكُلُّوبِ
غَادٍ فِي جُؤْشُوشِهِ ٱلْمَنْقُوبِ
جَيَّاشَةً تَذْهَبُ فِي أُسْلُوبِ
بِصَائِكٍ مِنْ عَلَقٍ صَبِيبِ
فَٱصْطَادَ قَبْلَ سَاعَةِ ٱلتَّأْوِيبِ
خَمْسِينَ فِي حِسَابِهِ ٱلْمَحْسُوبِ
فَٱلْقَوْمُ مِنْ مُقْتَدِرٍ مُطِيبِ
وَمُعْجِلِ ٱلنَّشْلِ عَنِ ٱلتَّضْهِيبِ
يَفْثَأُ حَرَّ ٱلْوَجْهِ مِنْ لَهِيبِ

under a wing fitted to a hard wrist,
quills with chunky knobs, beams
thick, on bent short-sided shafts,
and keen of sight—in the flats
and lava strips, her eye rarely fails
to spy the nests in the tangled underbrush.

Midmorning she wheeled on her side
like an invalid with a pleuritic cough,
and, after a blink of a rolled eye,
she stooped like a rockfall straight
down upon grumbly Bush Tail the hare.
A fistful of razors, treacherous meat hooks,
sliced the hare's punctured chest, ripped
his neck in hot-blood gashes, her beak gooey
with gushing clots. Before it was time
to return, she'd hunted fifty, her tally told.

Some of us boiled the meat in a stew,
sweet-smelling; others scoffed it down half-
cooked, wiping the sweat from their brows.

نعت الشاهين أرجوزة واحدة

~ ٢١ ~

قال ينعته [الرجز]

قَدْ أَغْتَدِي قَبْلَ ٱلصَّبَاحِ ٱلْأَبْلَجِ
وَقَبْلَ نَقْنَاقِ ٱلدَّجَاجِ ٱلدُّجَّجِ
بِسُهْرَدَازِ ٱللَّوْنِ أَوْ سَبَهْرَجِ
يُوفِي عَلَى ٱلْكَفِّ ٱنْتِصَابِ ٱلزُّجِّ
مُشَمِّرٍ ثِيَابَهُ عَنْ مَوْزَجِ
كَأَنَّمَا غُلَّ بِصِبْغِ ٱلنِّيلَجِ
كَأَنَّ وَشْيَ رِيشِهِ ٱلْمُدَرَّجِ
مِنْ قَائِمٍ مِنْهُ وَمِنْ مُعَوَّجِ
بَاقِي حُرُوفِ ٱلسَّطَرِ ٱلْمُخَرْفَجِ
أَبْرَشِ أَوْتَادِ ٱلْجَنَاحِ ٱلْخُرَّجِ
بَيْنَ خَوَافِيهِ إِلَى ٱلدَّهْفَرَّجِ
يَنْهَسُ سَيْرَ ٱلْمِقْوَدِ ٱلْمُحَمْلَجِ
مِنْ نَهَمِ ٱلْحِرْصِ وَإِنْ لَمْ يَلْمُجِ
يَنْحَازُ جَوْلَانُ ٱلْقَذَى ٱلْمُنَجْنَجِ
عِنْدَ ٱمْتِدَادِ ٱلنَّظَرِ ٱلْمُحَمَّجِ
مِنْ مُقْلَةٍ وَاسِعَةِ ٱلْمُحَجَّجِ

Peregrine Description: One *Urjūzah*

~ 21 ~

No Singsong

I crossed the dark before the early light,
before the raspy hens began to cluck,
with a peregrine, *suhradāz*
or *sabahraj* like a goshawk,
full on the fist, eagle-tall, with a booted arm
beneath her gown dyed deep indigo.
Her folded sails, straight and curved,
are embroidered with plush penned
letter shapes. She's freckled at the jutting
wrists between her flags and beams.
Before she tastes flesh, she snaps
at the twisted jess in kill-lust,
flushes away the dust with a wink
of her keen, wide-browed eye

كَأَنَّمَا يَطْـرِفُ عَنْ فَيْرُوزَجِ
مِنَ ٱلشَّوَاهِينِ كُلَافٍ كُنْفُجِ
فِي هَامَةٍ مِثْلِ ٱلصَّفَا ٱلْمُدَمَّجِ
وَمِنْسَرٍ أَقْنَى رُحَابِ ٱلْمِضْـرَجِ
حَتَّى قَضَيْنَا كُلَّ حَاجٍ مُحْوَجِ
مِـنْ دَارِجِ ٱللَّوْنِ وَغَـيْرِ ٱلدُّرَّجِ
مُبَـرْنَسِ ٱلْهَامَـةِ أَوْ مُـتَوَّجِ
مُكَحَّـلِ ٱلْآمَاقِ أَوْ مُـزَجَّجِ
يَصْفِـرُ أَحْـيَانـًا إِذَا لَمْ يَهْـزَجِ
مِنْ مِثْلِ حَرْفِ ٱلْمِجْدَحِ ٱلْمُعَيَّجِ
فَظَلَّ أَصْحَابِي بِعَيْشٍ سَجْسَجِ
مِنْ زَهَمِ ٱلصَّيْدِ وَشُرْبِ ٱلْبُخْتَجِ
تَـرَاهُـمُ مِنْ مُعْجِلٍ أَوْ مُنْضِـجِ
وَقَـــادِحٍ أَوْرَى وَلَمْ يُؤَجِّـجِ

whose glance is turquoise bright—
a rusty-black, lush-feathered
falcon with a wide hooked beak
and a crown like a stone worn smooth.

We got all the dappled quarry we wanted, 21
birds with heads crowned with hoods,
eyes kohl-dark or with plucked brows.
Our peregrine screamed, no singsong,
from a spindly beak. My comrades
lived large on fat flesh and mulled
grape juice. Look—some ate the meat
rare, others waited for it to cook,
others couldn't get their fires going.

نعت اليؤيؤ وهما أرجوزتان

~ ٢٢ ~

قال ينعته [الرجز]

قَدْ أَغْتَدِي وَٱلصُّبْحُ فِي مُكْتَمِّهِ
وَرْدٌ تَرَقَّى ٱلطَّيْرُ فِي مُقْتَمِّهِ
بِيُؤْيُؤٍ أَسْفَعَ يُدْعَى بِٱسْمِهِ
مُقَابَلٍ مِنْ خَالِهِ وَعَمِّهِ
فَأَيُّ عِرْقٍ صَالِحٍ لَمْ يُنْمِهِ
وَقَانِصٍ أَحْفَى بِهِ مِنْ أُمِّهِ
يُوحِي إِلَيْهِ كَلِمَاتِ عِلْمِهِ
لَوْ يَسْتَطِيعُ قَاتَهُ بِلَحْمِهِ
يَقِيهِ مِنْ بَرْدِ ٱلنَّدَى بِكُمِّهِ
تَفْدِيَةَ ٱلْأُمِّ ٱبْنَهَا فِي ضَمِّهِ
لِمَا يُلِذُّ أَنْفَهَا مِنْ شَمِّهِ
يُنَازِلُ ٱلْمُكَّاءَ عِنْدَ نَجْمِهِ
بِٱلْغَتِّ أَوْ يَنْزِلُ عِنْدَ حُكْمِهِ
يَرْكَبُ أَطْرَافَ ٱلصُّوَى بِخَطْمِهِ
وَكَمْ جُمَيْلٍ حَطَّهُ بِرَغْمِهِ

Merlin Descriptions: Two *Urjūzah*s

~ 22 ~

Against Their Will

Dawn was a rose in bud above birds enfolded in night.
I crossed the dark with a dappled black merlin on the glove,
who responds to the call of his name—the product
of excellent breeding, his maternal and paternal lines
equally matched—and a falconer who loves him
more than his mother,[29] instructing him in the secrets
of his science. He'd feed him his own flesh if he could,
his sleeve protecting him from the cold dew, like a mother
tenderly cuddling her infant, elated by his scent.

The lark appeared. Combat mode. The merlin throttled it 12
until it tumbled, his verdict delivered. Its beak flopped
on top of a cairn. So many *jumayl*s killed against their will.[30]

~ ٢٣ ~

وقال ينعته [الرجز]

قَدْ أَغْتَدِي وَٱلصُّبْحُ فِي دُجَاهُ
كَطُـرَّةِ ٱلْبُـرْدِ عَلَى مَثْنَـاهُ
بِيُؤْيُؤٍ يُعْجِـبُ مَنْ يَــرَاهُ
قَـانِصُـهُ مِنْ وَكْرِهِ ٱفْتَـلَاهُ
مَـا فِي ٱلْيَـآيِي يُؤْيُؤٌ شَـرْوَاهُ
مِنْ سُفْعَـةٍ طَـرَّ بِهَا خَـدَّاهُ
أَزْرَقُ لَا تَـكْذِبُـهُ عَـيْنَـاهُ
فَلَوْ يَـرَى ٱلْقَـانِصُ مَا يَـرَاهُ
فَـدَّاهُ بِٱلْأُمِّ وَقَـدْ فَـدَّاهُ
مِنْ بُعْدِ مَا تَذْهَبُ جِمْلَاقَاهُ
لَا يُوئِـلُ ٱلْمُـكَّاءَ مَـنْكِبَـاهُ
وَلَا جَـنَـاحَـانِ تَـكَـنَّفَـاهُ
مِنْـهُ إِذَا طَـارَ وَقَـدْ تَـلَاهُ
دُونَ ٱنْتِزَاعِ ٱلسَّحْرِ مِنْ حَشَاهُ
لَوْ أَكْثَـرَ ٱلتَّسْبِيـحُ مَا نَجَّاهُ
هُوَ ٱلَّذِي خَوَّلَنَـــاهُ ٱللَّهُ
تَبَـارَكَ ٱللَّهُ ٱلَّذِي هَـدَّاهُ

~ 23 ~

His Airborne Chase

Morning was like the hem fold of a patterned gown.
I crossed the dark with a merlin on the glove, reared
from the nest by the hunter. A marvel to see!
No merlin's like him—blue-gray,[31] cheeks dappled black,
eyes that see so far that if the hunter could see
what he sees, he'd sacrifice his mother to save him.

The lark beat its wings hard, but found no refuge 11
from his airborne chase until the jack ripped his lungs
clean from his guts. The lark could pray to the Almighty
over and again but still not escape evade God's gift!

نعت قوس البندق وهو ثلاث أرجوزات

~ ٢٤ ~

قال ينعته [الرجز]

وَأُوقَةٍ لِلطَّيْرِ فِي أَرْجَائِهَا
كَلَغَطِ ٱلْكُتَّابِ فِي ٱسْتِمْلَائِهَا
أَشْرَفْتُهَا وَٱلشَّمْسُ فِي خِرْشَائِهَا
لَمْ يَبْرُزِ ٱلْمَقْرُورُ لِٱصْطِلَائِهَا
بِشِقَّةٍ طَوْلُكَ فِي إِيفَائِهَا
إِذَا ٱنْتَحَى ٱلنَّازِعُ فِي ٱنْتِحَائِهَا
لَمْ يَرْهَبِ ٱلْفُطُورَ فِي سِيسَائِهَا
يُعْزَى ٱبْنُ عُصْفُورٍ إِلَى بَرَّائِهَا
حَتَّى تَأَيَّاهَا إِلَى ٱنْتِهَائِهَا
وَٱسْتَوْسَقَ ٱلْقِشْرُ إِلَى لِحَائِهَا
وَأَشْمَسَتْ فَيَبِسَتْ مِنْ مَائِهَا
فَٱلْحُسْنُ وَٱلْجُودَةُ مِنْ أَسْمَائِهَا
ثُمَّ ٱبْتَدَرْنَا ٱلطَّيْرَ فِي ٱعْتِلَائِهَا
بَنَادِقًا تُعْجِبُ لِٱسْتِوَائِهَا
مِنْ طِينَةٍ لَمْ تَدْنُ مِنْ غَضْرَائِهَا
وَلَمْ يُخَالِطْهَا نَقَا مَيْثَائِهَا

Pellet Bow Descriptions: Three *Urjūzah*s

~ 24 ~

They Soared with the Birds

The birds choked the pond, muttering like clerks
dictating their texts. The sun had yet to slough its skin;
chilled invalids had yet to venture out into the warmth.
I took my position behind a knoll with a bow;
when you aim it, leaning hard into the draw
with no fear of its back snapping, it always gives
more than it promises—crafted by Ibn 'Usfūr,
who, stripping the bark and drying the sap
in the sun, waited for the wood to be right.
We had wondrous pellets ready, spheres
selected to match the birds' flight, made of dark,
sticky clay, with no mixture of soft soil or sand—

لَا يَحُوجُ ٱلرَّامِي إِلَى ٱنْتِقَائِهَا
فَهْيَ تُرَاقِي ٱلطَّيْرَ فِي ٱرْتِقَائِهَا
مِثْلَ تَلَظِّي ٱلنَّارِ فِي ٱلْتِظَائِهَا
مِنْ سُودِ أَعْجَازٍ وَمِنْ خَضْرَائِهَا
وَمِنْ شَرَوْقَاهَا وَمِنْ صَبْغَائِهَا
كُلِّ حَبَنْطَاةٍ عَلَى ٱحْبِنْطَائِهَا
طَرَّاحَةٍ لِلْحُوتِ مِنْ جَرْبَائِهَا
تَحُطُّهَا لِلْأَرْضِ مِنْ سَمَائِهَا
تَرْفُلُ فِي نَعْلَيْنِ مِنْ أَمْعَائِهَا
مَرْثُومَةَ ٱلْخَطْمِ بِطِينِ مَائِهَا

each perfect for a shot. In the air
they soared with the birds, like a bonfire
exploding into flames. Black-tails, dark-tails,
meaty mallards and white-tails, potbellied
and pudgy birds, spearing fish with their mottled beaks,
fell from the sky, riddled with pellet shot—
on the ground, they swayed from side to side,
their guts at their feet, their beaks smeared with mud.

~ ٢٥ ~

وقال ينعتها [الرجز]

وَمَنْهَلٍ يَعْتَمُّ بِٱلْغَلَافِقِ
حَرًى مِنَ ٱلْإِوَزِّ وَٱلشَّرَاوِقِ
وَٱلْغُرِّ مِنْ مُسِنَّةٍ وَعَاتِقِ
سُودِ ٱلْمَآقِي صُفُرِ ٱلْحَمَالِقِ
وَأُخَرٍ فِي خُضُرِ ٱلْيَلَامِقِ
كَأَنَّمَا يَصْفِرْنَ مِنْ مَلَاعِقِ
صَرْصَرَةَ ٱلْأَقْلَامِ فِي ٱلْمَهَارِقِ
يَخْرُجْنَ مِنْ مُقَارِبٍ وَمَاشِقِ
صَبَّحْتُهَا قَبْلَ ٱلصَّبَاحِ ٱلْفَاتِقِ
وَقَبْلَ وَعْوَاعِ ٱلْغُرَابِ ٱلنَّاعِقِ
مُسْتَحْقِبِي خَرَائِطِ ٱلْبَنَادِقِ
وَشِقَقٍ مِنَ ٱلْقَنَا رَشَائِقِ
مَحْزُومَةِ ٱلْأَوْسَاطِ بِٱلْمَنَاطِقِ
مِنْ بَرْيِ بَرَّاءٍ بِهِنَّ حَاذِقِ
أَنْشَبَ فِي أَحِشَّةِ ٱلْأَفَاوِقِ
مَرْبُوعَةً شَزْرًا بِكَفِّ ٱلطَّائِقِ
تَقْذِي مَآقِيهِنَّ بِٱلْفَلَائِقِ
حَتَّى إِذَا قَامُوا مَقَامَ ٱلرَّامِقِ
وَحَسَرُوا ٱلْأَيْدِي إِلَى ٱلْمَرَافِقِ
وَلَقَّحَ ٱلرَّمْيُ بِنَزْعٍ صَادِقِ
وَجَادَهَا عَارِضُ مَوْتٍ بَارِقِ

~ 25 ~

Eyeballs Laden with Doom

A duckweed pond, dark haunt of ducks
and geese, white-fronts old and young,
black pupils, yellow eyes,[32] other birds
in thick fur coats, honking from spoonlike beaks
like the scratch of reed pens on parchment,
some words tightly spaced, others in the grand style.
I paid them an early visit, before break of day,
before the crow's hoarse caw, with men
carrying pellet pouches and bows,[33]
quick shots with girdle-wrapped grips,
made by an expert fletcher who fitted the pegs
into the lath ends, tying a four-twist string
rolled upward by the roper's hand[34]—bows
that fire bullets like eyeballs laden with doom.
The archers were in position, ready to fire,
arms bared to elbows, their shots sure
to succeed with a true aim. A thundercloud
of death blacked out the sky, and flashes

ذُو فُرَّقٍ مُـرْتَجِسُ ٱلصَّوَاعِقِ
صَكًّا لَهَا بَوَاطِنَ ٱلْعَوَاتِقِ
وَحَيْثُ مُنْتَاطُ ٱلْكُلَى ٱللَّوَاحِقِ
وَلَا يَذَرْنَ صُقُلَ ٱلسَّفَاسِقِ
وَهُنَّ بَيْنَ فَائِظٍ وَفَائِقِ
لَذَّةُ أَصْحَابِي مِنَ ٱلشَّبَارِقِ
وَوَذَرِ ٱلتَّصْفِيفِ وَٱلْوَشَائِقِ
وَدَعْ لِجَهْمٍ لَذَّةَ ٱلزَّرَازِقِ
وَٱلنَّصْبَ لِلْجِمْلَانِ وَٱلْخَرَانِقِ
بَيْنَ طُفُوفِ ٱلنَّجْمِ وَٱلرَّسَاتِقِ
لَا لَذَّةٌ كَلَذَّةِ ٱلْجُلَاهِقِ

of lightning let loose the hail of pellets,
thudding into kidneys and guts. The birds
lay dead or on death's edge. My comrades
wolfed down their kebabs, fillets, and shredded meats.

Let Jahm enjoy casting tiercels and setting traps 29
for bulbuls and hares in meadows and fields—
my passion's hunting with a pellet bow!

~ ٢٦ ~

وقال ينعتها [الرجز]

يَا رُبَّ سِرْبٍ مِنْ إِوَزٍّ رُتَّعِ
فِي صَخِبِ ٱلْحُوتِ بَرُودِ ٱلْمَكْرَعِ
فَهُنَّ بَيْنَ حُوَّمٍ وَوُقَّعِ
مِنْ كُلِّ مَحْبُوكِ ٱلسَّرَاةِ أَدْرَعِ
أَصْفَرِ فَصِّ ٱلْعَيْنِ أَحْوَى ٱلْمَدْمَعِ
مُقَرَّطٍ بِتُومَتَيْنِ أَوْدَعِ
مَوْصُولَةٍ زُجَّتُهُ بِٱلْأَخْدَعِ
عُولِيَ مَتْنَاهُ بِحُبْكٍ أَرْبَعِ
فَهْوَ كَبَيْتِ ٱللُّعَبِ ٱلْمُصَنَّعِ
غَادَيْتُهَا قَبْلَ ٱلْأَذَانِ ٱلْمُسْمِعِ
وَقَبْلَ وَعْوَاعِ ٱلْغُرَابِ ٱلْأَبْقَعِ
بِكُلِّ هَفْهَافِ ٱلْقَمِيصِ شَعْشَعِ
وَشِقَقٍ صُفْرٍ لِذَاذِ ٱلْمَنْزَعِ
مَتَى تُرِيدُ لِينَهَا تُوَضَّعِ
مِنْ غَيْرِ تَخْضِيدٍ وَلَا تَخَشُّعِ
وَفِي مَخَالِي ٱلْأَدَمِ ٱلْمُرَصَّعِ
مُحَدْرَجَاتٌ كَٱلسِّمَامِ ٱلْمُنْقَعِ
مِنْ طِينَةٍ لَمْ تَخْتَلِطْ بِٱلْأَجْرَعِ
وَلَمْ تُخَالِطْ سَبِخًا فَتُودَعِ
حَتَّى إِذَا أَمْكَنَ كُلُّ مَطْمَعِ
وَحَسَرُوا حُرَّ ضَوَاحِي ٱلْأَذْرُعِ

~ 26 ~

Pellets Like Nostrils

In a cold lake where fish splash,
flocks of geese fed at ease,
solid white-fronts swimming
and waddling on its banks,
yellow eyes in black sockets,
shell-white, with silver earrings,
eyebrows joined to necks, backs
covered in four stripes[35]
like a decorated game box.
I visited them before the muezzin,
before the hooded crow's caw,
with nimble men in light tunics
holding yellow bows, a delight
in the draw—when you want
them pliant, set them loose,
they won't crack or embarrass you—
and embossed leather pouches
full of smooth pellets like nostrils
flaring when a nose is flicked,[36]
made of clay that's praised
because it's unmixed with sand
or salty soil. When all was in order
and the archers had rolled up their sleeves
to reveal their fine forearms—

وَلُقِّحَ ٱلرَّمْيُ بِنَزْعٍ مَيْلَعِ
وَجَادَهَا عَارِضُ مَوْتٍ مُفْجِعِ
حَانَتْ مَنَايَا ٱلْبُغْثِ وَٱلْمُوَلَّعِ
وَكُلِّ جَحَّافٍ وَكُلِّ قَعْقَعِ
يَجُرُّ أَثْنَاءَ حَشًى مُقَطَّعِ
فَظَلَّ أَصْحَابِي بِعَيْشٍ خِرْوَعِ
بَيْنَ ٱلنَّشِيلِ ٱلرَّخْصِ وَٱلْمُشَعْشَعِ
فِي مَنْزِلٍ لَيْسَ لَنَا بِمِيدَعِ
بَيْنَ ٱلطُّفَيْفَاتِ وَبَيْنَ لَعْلَعِ
أَحْسَنُ مِنْ نَعْتِ قَلُوصٍ مِيلَعِ
وَوَصْفِكَ ٱلدَّارَ وَذِكْرِ ٱلْمَرْبَعِ
نَعْتُكَ ضَحْضَاحَ إِوَزٍّ شُرَّعِ
مَنْ يُمْتِعِ ٱللهُ بِعَيْشٍ يُمْتَعِ
يَعِشْ بِخَيْرٍ فِي نَعِيمٍ يَرْتَعِ

their swift shots sure to succeed—
when a sudden-death cloud had rained
down upon the birds, it was time
for black ibis and striped geese
to die, cackling and screaming,
convulsed with stomach cramps,
dragging the coils of their shredded
guts. My comrades lived the easy life,
feasting on soft, boiled meat,
quaffing wine mixed with water
between Ṭufayfāt and Laʿlaʿ,
where we wanted for nothing.

Sing not of fleet camels, 31
of lovers' abodes and vernal camps;
sing rather of the lake
where the geese come to drink!
If God has allotted you the good life,
just enjoy it, just relish its splendor.

هـذه قصائده في الطـرد وهي أربع

~ ٢٧ ~

قال ينعت البازي [السريع]

قَدْ أَسْبِقُ ٱلْقَارِبَةَ ٱلْجُونَا   مِنْ قَبْلِ تَأْذِينِ ٱلْمُنَادِينَا
بِكُلِّ مَنْعُوتٍ بِأَنْسَابِهِ   عَلَى عُيُونِ ٱلْأَرْمِنِيِّينَا
رَبِيبِ بَيْتٍ وَأَنِيسٍ وَلَمْ   يُرْبَ بِرِيشِ ٱلْأَبِ مَحْضُونَا
لَمْ يَنْكِهِ جُرْحُ حِيَاصٍ وَلَمْ   يُبْغَ لَهُ فِي ٱلنَّقْلِ تَسْكِينَا
كُرِّزَ عَامٍ صَاغَهُ صَائِغٌ   لَمْ يَدَّخِرْ عَنْهُ ٱلتَّحَاسِينَا
أَلْبَسَهُ ٱلتَّكْرِيزُ مِنْ حَوْكِهِ   وَشْيًا عَلَى ٱلْجُؤْجُؤِ مَوْضُونَا
لَهُ سِنَانٌ عِيجَ مِنْ مَتْنِهِ   تَخَالُ مَحْنَى عَطْفِهِ نُونَا
وَمِنْسَرٌ أَكْلَفُ فِيهِ شَغًا   كَأَنَّهُ عَقْدُ ثَمَانِينَا
فِي هَامَةٍ كَأَنَّمَا قُنِّعَتْ   سِبَّ حِيَالِ ٱلسَّابِرِيِّينَا
وَمُقْلَةٌ أُشْرِبَ آمَاقُهَا   تِبْرًا يَفُوقُ ٱلصَّارِفِيِّينَا
تُطْلِقُ مِنْهُ عِنْدَ إِرْسَالِهِ   عَلَى ٱلْكَرَاكِيِّ دُرَخْمِينَا
دَاهِيَةً تَخْبِطُ أَعْجَازَهَا   خَبْطًا تُحَسِّيهَا ٱلْأَمَرِّينَا
قَدْ مَشَقَتْهُ فِي ٱلْحَشَى مِشْقَةً   أَلْقَتْ مِنَ ٱلْجَوْفِ ٱلْمَصَارِينَا
يَحْمِي عَلَيْهَا ٱلْجَوَّ مِنْ فَوْقِهَا   حِينًا وَيَفِيهَا أَحَايِينَا
يُذِيقُهَا ٱلْمَوْتَ ذُعَافًا فَلَا   يَأْلُو لَهَا مَشْقًا وَتَعْيِينَا

Four Qasidas on Hunting

~ 27 ~

Unharmed by the Needle

A goshawk description:

I'm out here before the black-bellies go to water,
before the muezzin calls,[37] with a highborn gos,
her lineage fully traced by Armenian experts,[38]
manned, not reared under a father's wing,
unharmed by the needle, never calmed
in transport, intermewed—drilled to perfection
by an expert trainer. The molt has patterned
her keel into chain mail, exquisitely crafted;
her spears curve at the tip, hooked like a *nūn*,[39]
her tawny, bucktoothed beak like fingers
making the sign of eighty,[40] her crown
mantled in fine linen,[41] eyeballs washed
with gold dust, a money changer's dreams.

In the cast you drop a bomb on the cranes 11
thwacking into their rear—what bitter pain!—
slicing innards, spilling guts, flying high
to stop their climb; then, in a sudden-death attack—

وَهُنَّ يَرْفَعْنَ صُرَاخًا كَمَا   جَهْوَرَ فِي ٱلشِّعْبِ ٱلْمُلَبُّونَا
فَمُقْعَصٌ أُثْبِتَ فِي سَحْرِهِ   وَخَاضِبٌ مِنْ دَمِهِ ٱلطِّينَا
رُحْنَا بِهَا نَحْمِلُ أَكْبَادَهَا   فِي زَوْرَةٍ عَشْرًا وَعِشْرِينَا
أَعْطَى ٱلْبُزَاةَ ٱللَّهُ مِنْ فَضْلِهِ   مَا لَمْ يُخَوِّلْهُ ٱلشَّوَاهِينَا
لِكُلِّ سَبْعٍ قِسْمَةٌ دُونَهَا   فِي ٱلْقَدْرِ إِنْ فَوْقًا وَإِنْ دُونَا

nonstop slash and thrust. They shriek like pilgrims
shouting in Mecca's vale.[42] Some lie dead,
their lungs pierced; others bloody the mud.

We bring home their livers, ten, twenty, 17
from one sortie. In His bounty, God
gave the gos what He gave not to the peregrine.
To each hunter He allots its special abilities.

~ ٢٨ ~

وقال ينعت الكلب [السريع]

قَدْ أَغْتَدِي وَٱلصُّبْحُ مَشْهُورُ   قَدْ طَلَعَتْ مِنْهُ ٱلتَّبَاشِيرُ
بِمُخْطَفِ ٱلْأَيْطَلِ فِي خَطْمِهِ   طُولٌ وَفِي شِدْقَيْهِ تَأْخِيرُ
عَمَلَّسُ ٱلْعَجْزِ بَعِيدُ ٱلْخُطَى   مُسَلْجَمُ ٱلْمَتْنَيْنِ مِحْضِيرُ
حَتَّى دَعَانَا كُنَّسًا لَمْ يُصَبْ   بِهَا مِنَ ٱلْأَحْدَاثِ مَقْدُورُ
اِقْتَرَنَتْ مِنْ خَشْيَةٍ لِلرَّدَى   عَفَّرَهَا فِي ٱلنَّقْعِ زُنْبُورُ
كَأَنَّهُ سَهْمٌ إِلَى غَايَةٍ   أَوْ كَوْكَبٌ فِي ٱلْأَرْضِ مَحْدُورُ
فَحَانَ مِنْهَا قَرْهَبٌ عُفِّرَتْ   مِنْ بَعْدِهِ عَنْزٌ وَيَعْفُورُ
حَتَّى إِذَا وَالَى لَنَا أَرْبَعًا   وَٱثْنَيْنِ وَٱلْمَجْهُودُ مَوْفُورُ
رُحْنَا بِهِ تَنْضَحُ أَعْطَافُهُ   وَهْوَ بِمَا أَوْلَاهُ مَشْكُورُ
ذُخْرٌ لَنَا فِي لَزْبَةٍ إِنْ أَتَتْ   وَمِثْلُهُ لِلْجُهْدِ مَذْخُورُ

~ 28 ~

Shot to Earth

A dog description:

Dawn had been declared. I crossed[43] through the dark
beside a dog with lean loins, a long muzzle,
a scissor bite, a wolf's croup, a wide stride,
and sword-blade back—in short, a swift runner.
Fate led us to oryx in the cover, still strangers
to Hornet's brutality. In panic they scampered,
two by two. In the dust cloud, Hornet, straight
as an arrow to its target or a star shot
to earth, wrestled them to the ground.
Death came to Old Bull and a doe and a buck,
all harried to extinction. He gave us six,
so we brought him home, his flanks moist,
receiving the thanks he deserved.
This is just the kind of dog you need
in hard times—a fortune in a famine.

~ ٢٩ ~

قال ينعته [المديد]

رُبَّمَا أَغْدُو وَمَعِي كَلْبِي   طَالِبًا لِلصَّيْدِ فِي صَحْبِي
فَسَمَوْنَا لِلْحَزِيزِ بِهِ   فَدَفَعْنَاهُ عَلَى أَظْبِي
فَٱسْتَدَرَّتْهُ فَدَرَّ لَهَا   يَلْطِمُ ٱلرُّفْغَيْنِ بِٱلتُّرْبِ
فَأَدَّرَاهَا وَهْيَ لَاهِيَةٌ   فِي جَمِيمِ ٱلحَاذِ وَٱلْغَرْبِ
فَفَرَى جُمَّاعَهُنَّ حَتْمًا   قُدَّ مَخْلُولَانِ مِنْ عَصْبِ
غَيْرَ يَعْفُورٍ أَهَابَ بِهِ   جَابَ دَفَّيْهِ عَنِ ٱلْقَلْبِ
ضَمَّ لَحْيَيْهِ بِمَخْطِمِهِ   ضَمَّكَ ٱلْكَسْرَيْنِ بِٱلشَّعْبِ
وَٱنْتَحَى لِلْبَاقِيَاتِ كَمَا   كَسَرَتْ فَتْخَاءُ مِنْ لِهْبِ
فَتَعَايَا ٱلتَّيْسُ حِينَ كَبَا   وَدَنَا فُوهُ مِنَ ٱلْعَجْبِ
ظَلَّ بِٱلْوَعْسَاءِ يَنْقُضُهُ   لَذِمًا مِنْهُ عَلَى ٱلصُّلْبِ
تِلْكَ لَذَّاتِي وَكُنْتُ فَتًى   لَمْ أَقُلْ مِنْ لَذَّةٍ حَسْبِي

~ 29 ~

The Grace of an Eagle

Morning hunting trips with dog and friends!
  We'd climb up to Jaggy Rocks and sic
  him on the gazelles, and they'd flirt
  by flicking pebbles against his loins
  as he sped after them.[44] He'd spoil their party
  in the *ḥādh* and *gharb* shrubs,
  splitting them like two thin strips
  cut from Yemeni cloth. But Young Buck
  would egg him on. He'd tear his heart out,
  with his nose in a pincer vise, clasped
  like a broken bone, chasing the does
  with the grace of an eagle in supple
  flight from a crag. Old Bull would trip
  and run out of tricks, our dog's mouth
  nipping at his tail stump. On the sandy plain
  he'd gnaw his loins, crunch his bones.

Those were the days. As a young buck, 11
  I'd never say no to fun!

~ ٣٠ ~

وقال ينعت الفخّ [السريع]

قَدْ كَادَ هٰذَا ٱلْفَخُّ أَنْ يَعْقِرَا　　وَٱحْرَوْرَفَ ٱلْعُصْفُورُ أَنْ يَنْفِرَ
غَيَّبْتُ فِي ٱلتُّرْبِ عَلَيْهِ لَهُ　　بِٱلْمُسْتَوَى خَشْيَةَ أَنْ يَنْقُرَ
لَمَّا رَأَى ٱلتُّرْبَ رَأَى جُثْوَةً　　مَاثِلَةَ ٱلشَّخْصِ فَمَا ٱسْتَنْكَرَ
حَتَّى إِذَا أَشْرَفَهَا مُوفِيًا　　وَعَايَنَ ٱلْحَبَّ لَهُ مُظْهَرَ
خَاطَبَهُ مِنْ قَلْبِهِ زَاجِرٌ　　قَدْ كُنْتُ لَا أَرْهَبُ أَنْ يَزْجُرَ
فَأَعْمَلَ ٱلْفِكْرَ قَلِيلًا فَلَمْ　　يَقْتُلِهِ ٱلرَّحْمٰنُ مَا فَكَّرَ
فَٱحْتَرَبَتْ لَا وَنَعَمْ سَاعَةً　　ثُمَّ تَوَلَّى خَذِلًا مُدْبِرَ
فَضَمَّ كَشْحَيْهِ إِلَى جُؤْجُؤٍ　　كَانَ إِذَا ٱسْتَنْجَدَهُ شَمَّرَ
فَلَمْ يَرُعْنِي غَيْرُ تَدْوِيمِهِ　　آمَنَ مَا كُنْتُ لَهُ مُضْمِرَ
فَٱلرِّزْقُ وَٱلْحِرْمَانُ مَجْرَاهُمَا　　بِمَا قَضَى ٱللّٰهُ وَمَا قَدَّرَ
فَٱصْبِرْ إِذَا ٱلدَّهْرُ نَبَا نَبْوَةً　　فَجُنَّةُ ٱلْحَازِمِ أَنْ يَصْبِرَ
كَمْ مُوسِرٍ أَعْسَرَ فِي بُرْهَةٍ　　وَمُعْسِرٍ فِي مِثْلِهِ أَيْسَرَ

~ 30 ~

His Heart Whispered Caution

A trap net description:

The trap almost worked, but Sparrow refused
the bait hidden in the soil. I feared he'd fly away.
He looked at the soil, saw a mound sticking up,
and, standing by the trap, decided not to worry,
staring at the seed placed out in the open,
but his heart whispered caution (the last thing
I'd planned for!), so he pondered briefly—
surely God in His mercy wouldn't kill him
while he's giving it a thought? He wrestled with yes
and no; then, mind made up, he turned away,
folding his wings to a breast ever ready
to help him escape in time of need. I was dismayed—
his flight had foiled my trap. Failure and success
depend on God's decree—accept it! When Time
delivers a verdict, that's what men do—accept it.
Rich men have woken up poor, and paupers rich!

في جمل مختلفة الأنواع هي بين الصحيح والمنحول

Poems on Various Topics, Some of Which Are Authentic, Others Not

~ ٣١ ~

قال يصف أيره ورواها الناس في وصف الصقر [الرجز]

قَدْ أَغْتَدِي قَبْلَ مَذَادِ ٱلْخَامِسِ
بِضَرِمٍ يَنْقُضُ كَفَّ ٱللَّامِسِ
فِي جِلْدَةٍ تَنْدَى وَحَجْمٍ يَابِسِ
عَلَيْهِ مِنْ مَنْصُوحَةِ ٱلْقَلَانِسِ
قَنْفَاءَ ذَاتِ عَذَبٍ نَوَائِسِ
يَهُوعُ فُوهَا كَهُوَاعِ ٱلْقَالِسِ
تَرَى ٱلرَّدِيفَ فَوْقَهَا كَٱلْقَامِسِ

~ 31 ~

On Fire with Kill Lust

A description of his phallus. Nonexperts identify it as a saker description.

Before the drover takes his camels
to the well, I cross the dark with a raptor
on fire with kill lust, attacking any hand
that touches it: with the glossy sheen
of a date,[45] it's dry and hard when swollen,
protected by a helmet of flesh like a plump,
stubby ear, shooting in spurts. Look—
the passenger mounted upon it bobs
up and down like a pearl diver.

~ ٣٢ ~

وقال يصف الدرهم ورواها الناس في صفة الصقر [الرجز]

لَمْ أَبْكِ رَسْمًا مُقْفِرًا وَدُورَ
تَسْمَعُ لِلصَّعْلِ بِهَا زَمِيرَ
كَقَسِّ دَيْرٍ يَقْرَأُ ٱلزَّبُورَ
لٰكِنْ ظَلِلْتُ مُفْكِرًا شُهُورَ
أَنْعَتُ صَقْرًا يُشْبِهُ ٱلصُّقُورَ
مُظَفَّرًا أَبْيَضَ مُسْتَدِيرَ
وَلِيدَ شَهْرٍ وَاضِحًا مُنِيرَ
تَخَالُهُ فِي قَدِّهِ ٱلْعَبُورَ
مُكَرَّمًا يَجْتَنِبُ ٱلصَّفِيرَ
إِلَّا إِذَا حُرِّكَ أَوْ أُثِيرَ
فَهْوَ صَغِيرٌ يَفْعَلُ ٱلْكَبِيرَ
تَرَى ٱلْحَمَالِيقَ إِلَيْهِ صُورَ
وَٱلصَّيْدُ يَأْتِيكَ بِهِ مَيْسُورَ
يَنْعَشُ ذَا ٱلْحَاجَةِ وَٱلْفَقِيرَ
وَٱلْخَلْقَ قَدْ يَطْلُبُهُ ظَهِيرَ
يَقْتَنِصُ ٱلْأَعْصَمَ وَٱلْقَدُورَ
صَاحِبُهُ مُمْتَلِئٌ سُرُورَ
وَلَا تَرَاهُ فَزِعًا مَذْعُورَ

~ 32 ~

Bright as Canopus

A description of a dirham. The nonexperts identify it as a saker description.

I shed no tears over desert ruins or empty abodes
where you hear the ostrich grumble like a priest
mumbling psalms in a monastery. No, I've been deep
in thought these last few months! I describe a saker
like other sakers: white, round, never bested, shiny
and clean, one month old—look at her: bright as Canopus—
revered, only screeching when moved or scratched.
Though small, she does great things, all eyes trained on her
as effortlessly she hunts for you, bringing wealth
to the poor and needy. All God's creation wants her help:[46]
she'll trap white-leg ibex and fill the pots with meat.
Her owner is flush with joy. Do you ever see him anxious
or sad?[47]

وَلَوْ بَغَى مُرْسِلُهُ ٱلنُّسُورَ
وَٱلْوَحْشَ جَمْعًا أَوْ بَغَى ٱلْعَسِيرَ
لَجَاءَ سَهْلًا سَلِسًا يَسِيرَ
مَا آبَ مَنْ صَادَ بِهِ مَبْهُورَ
مِنْ طَلَبِ ٱلصَّيْدِ وَلَا حَسِيرَ
يُقِيلُ مِنْ عَثْرَتِهِ ٱلْعُثُورَ
بِهِ نَصِيدُ ٱلشَّادِنَ ٱلْغَرِيرَ
مَا هَابَ مَنْ يَمْلِكُهُ ٱلدُّهُورَ

Fly her against vultures and oryx, both at once,
or at the wily wolf, and you'll come home happy with her catch.
Hunt with her and you won't return empty-handed or weary,
winded from chasing game.[48] She helps a man back to his feet
when he's down. She's how we hunt the guileless fawn—
if you possess such a saker, what's there to worry about?

~ ٣٣ ~

وقال ينعت الصولجان إن كان قد قال [الرجز]

قَدْ أَشْهَدُ ٱللَّهْوَ بِفِتْيَانٍ غُرَرْ
مِنْ وَلَدِ ٱلْعَبَّاسِ سَادَاتِ ٱلْبَشَرْ
وَمِنْ بَنِي قَحْطَانَ وَٱلْحَيِّ مُضَرْ
مِنْ كُلِّ مَأْلُوفٍ كَرِيمِ ٱلْمُعْتَصَرْ
زَيَّنَ حُسْنَ وَجْهِهِ طِيبُ ٱلْخَبَرْ
عَلَى جِيَادٍ كَتَمَاثِيلِ ٱلصُّوَرْ
مِنْ كُلِّ طِرْفٍ أَعْوَجِيٍّ قَدْ ضَمَرْ
لَمْ يَكْوِهِ ٱلْبَيْطَارُ مِنْ دَاءِ ٱلْحَمَرْ
جِنٌّ عَلَى جِنٍّ وَإِنْ كَانُوا بَشَرْ
كَأَنَّمَا خِيطُوا عَلَيْهَا بِٱلْإِبَرْ
وَسُمِّرَ ٱلْفَارِسُ فِيهَا فَٱنْسَمَرْ
بَيْنَ رِيَاضٍ مِثْلَ مَوْشِيِّ ٱلْحِبَرْ
مُكَلَّلَاتٍ بِبَهَاءٍ وَزَهَرْ
فَٱنْتَدَبُوا فِي يَوْمِ قُرٍّ وَخَصَرْ
إِذْ ذَرَّ قَرْنُ ٱلشَّمْسِ فِي غِبِّ مَطَرْ
صَوَالِجًا يَصْبُو إِلَيْهَا مَنْ نَظَرْ
مَحْنِيَّةً أَطْرَافُهَا فِيهَا زَوَرْ
قَدَّرَهَا شَابِرُهَا لَمَّا شَبَرْ
فَلَمْ يَعِبْ طُولاً وَلَا شَأْنَ قِصَرْ
وَقَدْ تَنَادَوْا فَتَرَامَوْا بِٱلْأُكَرْ

~ 33 ~

The Gambler Grows Grim

His description of a polo mallet, if indeed it is by Abū Nuwās:

I took part in a game played by noblemen,
scions of ʿAbbās, Qaḥṭān, and Muḍar,
affable patrons and leaders of men,
handsome faces enhanced by their fine names,
astride steeds like mighty monuments,
descended from Aʿwaj, fresh from the trainer,
protected from the farrier by their diet.
They rode like demons mounted on demons,
seemingly stitched and nailed fast
to their horses, coursing through ink-patterned,
tattooed fields bedecked in radiant splendor.
On a cold, wet day, the sun peeking out after rain,
they answered the war cry with mallets
beautiful to behold: their protruding, curved tips[49]
measured precisely by their maker, neither too long
nor too short. After calling to each other,

مُدْمَجَةِ ٱلْأَرْكَانِ مَلْسَاءِ ٱلطُّرَرْ
شَدَّدَ صَفْقَيْ مَتْنِهَا حَشْوُ ٱلشَّعَرْ
أَحْكَمَهَا صَانِعُهَا لَمَّا فَطَرْ
أَلْطَفَ بِٱلْإِشْفَاءِ خَرْزًا إِذْ دَسَرْ
فَلَيْسَ لِلْإِشْفَاءِ بِٱلْجِلْدِ أَثَرْ
يُحْسَبْنَ تُفَّاحًا تَدَلَّى مِنْ شَجَرْ
حَتَّى إِذَا مَا أَغْلَقَ ٱلْقَوْمُ ٱلْخَطَرْ
وَوَكَّلُوا بِٱلْبَزِّ مِقْدَامًا ذَكَرْ
مُجَرَّبًا يَوْمَ ٱلرِّهَانِ ٱلْمُحْتَضَرْ
فَضَّلَهُ حِذْقٌ وَضَرْبٌ مُشْتَهَرْ
وَلَمْ يَجُرْ فِيهِمْ وَلَا ٱلْعَيْنُ فَتَرْ
وَٱسْتَقْدَمَ ٱلْقَوْمَ رَئِيسٌ ذُو خَطَرْ
بِكُرَةٍ دَحَا بِهَا ثُمَّ زَجَرْ
فَٱنْحَدَرَتْ كَٱلنَّجْمِ وَلَّى فَٱنْكَدَرْ
رَفْعًا وَوَضْعًا أَيُّمَا ذَاكَ ٱسْتَقَرّْ
تُدْفَعُ بِٱلضَّرْبِ إِذَا ٱلضَّرْبُ ٱسْتَمَرّْ
تَدَافُعَ ٱلنَّبْلِ بِإِزْعَاجِ ٱلْوَتَرْ
فَكَمْ تَرَى فِيهِمْ حَلِيمًا ذَا وَقَرْ
إِذَا أَجَادَ ٱلضَّرْبَ فَدَّى وَنَعَرْ
وَعَطْعَطَ ٱلْمَرْءُ ٱلَّذِي يَرْجُو ٱلظَّفَرْ
وَٱكْتَأَبَتْ نَفْسُ ٱلَّذِي خَافَ ٱلْغِيَرْ
وَأَيْقَنُوا أَنْ قَدْ عَلَاهُمْ وَقَهَرْ
حَتَّى يَفُوزَ بِٱلرِّهَانِ مَنْ قَمَرْ
يُسَاءُ هٰذَاكَ وَهٰذَاكَ يُسَرّْ
كَذٰلِكَ ٱلدَّهْرُ وَتَصْرِيفُ ٱلْقَدَرْ

they struck the ball back and forth, its sides round
and fringes smooth, both halves hard, stuffed
with hair, crafted to perfection by the artisan's
delicate stitches with his awl, the skin
unmarked by his jabs—you'd think it was an apple
hanging from a tree. When the bets had been placed,
they appointed a brave fellow in charge of the sticks,[50]
no stranger to busy contests, renowned for his guile
and his famous strike,[51] fair to the contestants,
eyes always alert.
A mighty player advanced 32
and with a shout threw a ball high. It fell
like a shooting star. He turned and dipped,
flicked it up and whacked it. The ball landed,
then was further cast and struck during the game,
whirring like an arrow fired from a bow.
Look—so many serious, dignified men swearing
and screaming their approval of a stroke:
the man who thinks he's hit a winner roars;
the gambler, afraid of the debts he'll have to pay,
grows grim—each player knows there must be
a winner who takes the stakes and wins the day.
Until then, some rejoice, others despair.
Such is Time, such are the vagaries of God's decree.

~ ٣٤ ~

وقال يصف اللعب بالطبطاب [الرجز]

وَمَاجِدٍ يَلْعَبُ بِٱلطَّبْطَابِ
بِأَعْقَفٍ كَمَعْقِفِ ٱلْكُلَّابِ
يُغَيِّبُ ٱلْأُكْرَةَ فِي ٱلْحِجَابِ
حَتَّى إِذَا صَارَتْ إِلَى ٱلْمَآبِ
مِنْ قَبْلِ أَنْ تَلْصَقَ بِٱلتُّرَابِ
أَلْحَقَهَا فِي ٱلْجَوِّ بِٱلسَّحَابِ
ثُمَّ نَحَا لِمَنْهَلٍ عُبَابِ
أَخْضَرَ مِثْلَ ٱلسِّلْقِ ذِي حِبَابِ
مُنْفَهِقٍ قَدْ حُفَّ بِٱلرَّوَابِي
بِفِتْيَةٍ مِنْ خَيْرِ مَا أَصْحَابِ
شَبَابِ صِدْقٍ أَيِّمَا شَبَابِ
فَأَبْرَزُوا مَحْنِيَّةَ ٱلْأَصْلَابِ
صُفْرًا كَمَاءِ ٱلذَّهَبِ ٱلْمُذَابِ
مُؤَاتِيَاتٍ لَسْنَ بِٱلصِّعَابِ
يُعْلِنَّ عِنْدَ ٱلنَّزْعِ بِٱنْتِحَابِ
حَنِينَ عَبْرَى حُرَّةٍ كَعَابِ
أَوْجَعَهَا تَفَرُّقُ ٱلْأَحْبَابِ
وَٱلْقَوْمُ فِي ٱلْمَاءِ إِلَى ٱلْأَعْقَابِ
يَسْتَغْرِقُونَ ٱلنَّزْعَ بِٱنْكِبَابِ

~ 34 ~

The Fireball Pitch

A description of a game played with the *ṭabṭāb*:

A champion takes to the field with his club
curved like a spur. He hides the ball in its hijab
until, tossing it up for his serve, he sends it
soaring through the air into the clouds, then heads
for a pond surrounded by hills, where the water
at the rim splashes dark as beet juice,[52]
accompanied by warriors, best of comrades,
good men and true, who brandish their clubs
with curved backs, yellow as molten gold, compliant
not balky, wailing loudly as the game carries on,
like a noble maiden pining for loved ones left behind.
The players are ankle deep in the water, ready
to dive further into the game. The birds[53]

وَٱلطَّيْرُ قَدْ وَلَجْنَ وَسْطَ ٱلْغَابِ
ظُهُورُهَا كَلَامِعِ ٱلزِّرْيَابِ
أَرْجُلُهَا نَاصِعَةُ ٱلْخِضَابِ
مَوْشِيَّةُ ٱلْأَفْخَاذِ وَٱلْأَقْرَابِ
كَنَقْطِكَ ٱلْعَجْمَ عَلَى ٱلْكِتَابِ
نَزَحْنَ عَنْ مَعَايِبِ ٱلْعُيَّابِ
أَيْقَنَّ بِٱلْفُرْقَةِ وَٱلذَّهَابِ
حِينَ رَأَيْنَ ٱلرَّمْيَ ذَا ٱلْتِهَابِ
فَبَعْضُهَا تَرَاهُ ذَا ٱنْصِبَابِ
مِنْقَارُهُ بِٱلدَّمِ ذُو ٱنْثِعَابِ
كَأَنَّمَا يَهْمِلُ مِنْ مِئْزَابِ
فَذَاكَ مَا آخِرَ يَوْمِي دَابِي

are in the reeds, their backs aglow like liquid gold,
their feet dyed dark, their thighs and flanks patterned
in dots as if drawn on a page, fashioned beyond reproach.[54]
When the players saw the fireball pitch, the blood
on the beaks of the clubs was like water from a spout.[55]
What a way to kill time!

~ ٣٥ ~

وقال يصف العنكبوت وصيدها [الرجز]

وَقَانِصٍ مُحْتَقَرٍ ذَمِيمِ
كُدْرِيٍّ لَوْنٍ أَغْبَرٍ قَتِيمِ
مُشْتَبَكِ ٱلْأَعْجَازِ بِٱلْحَيْزُومِ
وَمَخْرَجِ ٱللَّحْظَةِ بِٱلْخَيْشُومِ
أَضْيَقَ أَرْضًا مِنْ مَقَامِ ٱلْمِيمِ
أَوْ نُقْطَةٍ تَحْتَ جَنَاحِ ٱلْجِيمِ
لَيْسَ بِقَعْدِيدٍ وَلَا جَمُومِ
وَلَا عَنِ ٱلْحِيلَةِ بِٱلسَّؤُومِ
لَا يَخْلِطُ ٱلْهِمَّةَ بِٱلتَّنْوِيمِ
مُنْخَفِضًا فِي كَنَفِ ٱلنَّعِيمِ
بَيْنَ نِتَاجَيْ حَبَشٍ وَرُومِ
فِي ظُلَلِ ٱلذُّرَّةِ وَٱلْعُلْجُومِ
كَأَنَّمَا دَبِيبُهُ فِي ٱلنِّيمِ
دَبِيبُ خَمْرٍ بُزِلَتْ خُرْطُومِ
أَسْرَعُ مِنْ كَرَّةِ طَرْفٍ يُومِي
أَوْ نَهْضَةٍ تَنْهَضُ فِي نَؤُومِ
أَشْجَعُ مِنْ ذِي لِبَدٍ هَضِيمِ
حَتَّى ٱحْتَوَى عَالِيَةَ ٱلتَّمِيمِ
بُؤْسَى لَهُ مِنْ هَالِكٍ مَعْدُومِ

~ 35 ~

Luxuriating in His Web

A description of the hunting skills of the spider:

The hunter—this mean and despicable trifle,
the color of dark, muddy water, with its tiny
back and chest, and its mouth and nose smaller
than the support of a *mīm* or the dot
under the loop of a *jīm*.[56] Neither a coward
nor a hothead, this thing embraces deceit
in pursuit of gain, ever awake, luxuriating in his web,
surrounded by the offspring of Ethiopians
and Romans[57] in those shady corners
where ants and frogs thrive. Faster than a wink
or waking with a jolt, this thing scurries about
like a heady wine spouting from an amphora
when broached. Braver than the ravenous, thick-
maned lion, this thing dominates the uplands
of the Tamīm. What a vicious thing, this hunter!
I wish it didn't exist!

جمل من الطرديّات منسوبة في النسخ إلى أبي نواس لم يروها عنه الرواة

A Series of Poems Attributed to Abū Nuwās in the Manuscripts but Not Recorded by the Experts on His Verse

نعت الكلب وهو ثمان وعشرون أرجوزة

~ ٣٦ ~

قال ينعته [الرجز]

قَدْ أَغْتَدِي وَٱللَّيْلُ فِي ٱدْهِمَامِهِ
لَمْ يَحْسُرِ ٱلصُّبْحُ دُجَى ظَلَامِهِ
بِسَاهِمٍ يَمْرَحُ فِي إِدَامِهِ
مُزَبْرَجِ ٱلْمَتْنِ وَفِي خِدَامِهِ
مِثْلَ بَدِيعِ ٱلْعَصْبِ فِي إِحْكَامِهِ
كَأَنَّ خَطَّيْ جَانِبَيْ لِثَامِهِ
مِنْ مُؤْخِرِ ٱلْخَدِّ إِلَى قُدَّامِهِ
خَطٌّ مُبِينُ ٱلنَّقْشِ فِي إِعْجَامِهِ
أَجْرَاهُمَا بِٱلْعُودِ مِنْ أَقْلَامِهِ
لَا يَأْمَنُ ٱلْوَحْشِيُّ مِنْ عُرَامِهِ
يَعُدُّ يَوْمَ ٱلدَّجْنِ مِنْ أَيَّامِهِ
فَصَادَ وَٱلْمَقْرُورُ فِي أَهْدَامِهِ
قَبْلَ ٱنْتِبَاهِ ٱلْحُرِّ مِنْ مَنَامِهِ
اِبْنَ فَلَاةٍ ظَلَّ مِنْ آرَامِهِ
ثُمَّ ٱنْتَحَى فِي سَنَنَيْ جَمَامِهِ
لِنَاشِطٍ يَدْفَعُ عَنْ أَخْلَامِهِ

Dog Descriptions: Twenty-Eight *Urjūzah*s

~ 36 ~

His Malignity

As dawn unpeeled layer after layer
of the pitch-black night, I crossed the dark
accompanied by a hound, lean and swift
as an arrow, lively in his leather collar,
with brindled back and well-built shanks
clothed in a dyed Yemeni weave,
his muzzle between nose and cheek
like a reed pen's stroke, fine and bold.
The oryx can't flee his malignity. Let it rain—
he knows today's the day he'll prevail.
In the chill of night, we shivered in our rags,
the sun's heat asleep. He hunted the bull,
this son of the desert, out all night,
far from his harem. In a double burst of energy,
he sped at a feisty oryx defending the coverts,

فَظَلَّ يَفْرِي مُلْتَقَى خِصَامِهِ
مِنْ خَلْفِهِ طَوْرًا وَمِنْ أَمَامِهِ
كَأَنَّهُ فِي ٱلْكَرِّ وَٱقْتِحَامِهِ
ضَرْبُ فَتَى شَيْبَانَ فِي إِقْدَامِهِ
مِنْ خَبْطِهِ ٱلنَّحْرَ وَمِنْ عِذَامِهِ
حَتَّى هَوَى يَفْحَصُ فِي رَغَامِهِ
مُنْقَلِبَ ٱلرَّوْقِ عَلَى أَزْلَامِهِ
يَا لَكَ مِنْ غَادٍ إِلَى حِمَامِهِ

biting at his legs and loins—now in front,
now behind, now wheeling and charging,
lunging and darting at his chest
like a champion sword fighter. The bull
sped off, a dust cloud in his trail, horns
aimed at the dog's arrow-thin legs,
but today was his day to die!

~ ٣٧ ~

وقال ينعته [الرجز]

قَدْ أَغْتَدِي فِي فَلَقِ ٱلصَّبَاحِ
بِمُطْعَمٍ يُوجِزُ فِي سَرَاحِ
مُؤَيَّدٍ بِٱلنَّصْرِ وَٱلنَّجَاحِ
غَذَتْهُ دَايَاتٌ مِنَ ٱللِّقَاحِ
فَهْوَ كَمِيشٌ ذَرِبُ ٱلسِّلَاحِ
لَا يَسْأَمُ ٱلدَّهْرَ مِنَ ٱلضُّبَاحِ
مُنَجَّدٍ يَأْشَرُ لِلصَّبَاحِ
مَا ٱلْبَرْقُ فِي ذِي عَارِضٍ لَمَّاحِ
وَلَا ٱنْقِضَاضُ ٱلْكَوْكَبِ ٱلْمُنْصَاحِ
وَلَا ٱنْبِتَاتُ ٱلْحَوْأَبِ ٱلْمُنْدَاحِ
حِينَ دَنَا مِنْ رَاحَةِ ٱلْمُتَّاحِ
أَجَدُّ فِي ٱلسُّرْعَةِ مِنْ سِرْيَاحِ
يَكَادُ عِنْدَ ثَمَلِ ٱلْمِرَاحِ
يَطِيرُ فِي ٱلْجَوِّ بِلَا جَنَاحِ
إِذَا سَمَا ٱلْحَائِلُ لِلْأَشْبَاحِ
يَفْتَرُّ عَنْ مِثْلِ شَبَا ٱلرِّمَاحِ
فَكَمْ وَكَمْ ذِي جُدَّةٍ لِيَاحِ
وَنَازِبٍ أَعْفَرَ ذِي طِمَاحِ
غَادَرَهُ مُضَرَّجَ ٱلصِّفَاحِ

~ 37 ~

Drunk on Energy

Dawn split the sky. I crossed the dark,
out on the plain with a dog fed on his prey.
Blessed by God with success, suckled
on camel's milk, bold with lethal weapons,
never weary of Fox's yelp, with a battle-
hardened veteran's gusto for the dawn chase,
like lightning bursts in cloud banks,
like blazing star screams, like a bucket
plunging down a well when the rope snaps
as you bend to drink—Locust outstrips
them all and, wingless, drunk on energy,
seems to fly. At the brow of the hill,
the oryx fled from his scorpion-sting
spears. So many dusty bulls in rut,
all piss and grunts; so many oryx,
black stripes agleam on white hides,
lying dead in the dirt, flanks dyed in blood.

~ ٣٨ ~

وقال ينعته [الرجز]

قَدْ أَغْتَدِي مَعَ ٱلْقَنِيصِ ٱلْمُدْلِجِ
بِنَاطِحٍ وَعَاطِفٍ وَدُمْلُجِ
بِكُلِّ مَحْبُوكٍ قَرَاهُ مُدْمَجِ
مُحَنَّبٍ أَضْلَاعُهُ مُفَرْزَجِ
مِنَ ٱلسَّلُوقِيَّاتِ غَيْرِ أَحْبَجِ
وَصَادِقِ ٱلنَّظْرَةِ مِثْلِ ٱلْأَبْلَجِ
بِذِي سِلَاحٍ كَٱلزِّجَاجِ ٱلزُّجُجِ
وَيُؤْيُؤٍ كَٱلْحَجَرِ ٱلْمُدَحْرَجِ
وَزُرَّقٍ أَبْيَضَ غَيْرِ كُوبَجِ
قُرْنِصَ فِي بُرْدِ حِبَالٍ تَوَّجِي
رَحْبِ ٱلذِّرَاعِ ظَهْرُهُ كَٱلْمُدْبَجِ
ذِي مِنْسَرٍ أَعْقَفَ مِثْلِ ٱلْمِنْسَجِ
كَأَنَّمَا جَلَّى بِعَيْنَيْ زُمَّجِ
آنَسَ بَيْنَ شُبْرُمٍ وَعَرْفَجِ
وَبَيْنَ سِدْرٍ مُورِقٍ وَعَوْسَجِ
حُبَارَيَاتٍ كَٱلدُّجَاجِ ٱلدُّجَّجِ
يَتْبَعْنَ خَطْوَ خَرَبٍ سَفَنَّجِ
أَجْفَلَ مِثْلِ ٱلسَّاجِسِيِّ ٱلْأَخْرَجِ
مِنْهُ بِرِيشِ طَائِرٍ مُدَرَّجِ
وَٱنْسَلَّ مِنْ كَفِّ وَصِيفٍ أَدْعَجِ
مُجَرَّبٍ لِصَيْدِهِ مُدَرَّجِ

~ 38 ~

Quick as a Landslide

I crossed the dark in the company
of an expert night huntsman,
with Omen, Doe Neck, and Bracelet,
their finely welded backs like twisted
ropes and their ribs well-sprung.
Brightly colored[58] hungry salukis,
true gazehounds, eyes well spaced.
I also brought a saker armed with iron-
tipped lances; a merlin, as quick
as a landslide; and a white Tawwajī gos,
kept in the mews wrapped
in a gown of ropes,[59] not a small tarsell,[60]
but with wide sails, a brocaded back,
a beak curved like a weaver's knife,[61]
and the stare of an eagle.
Amid the spiny bushes, 14
the leafy lotes, and desert thorns,
the saker sighted some houbaras
like raspy chickens crowded thick
behind an ostrich-quick male
whose stately feather ruff
would shame a fleecy ram![62]
She flew from the fist of a dark-
eyed trainer well versed in how she hunted.

فَصَلَّ رَأْسَ ٱلْخَرَبِ ٱلسَّفَنَّجِ
بِضَرْبَةٍ مِنْ طَائِرٍ بِبَرْدَجِ
شَاهٍ مِنَ ٱلطَّيْرِ عَتِيقِ ٱلْمَخْرَجِ
فَلَفَّهُنَّ صَقْرُنَا لَمْ يُنْهَجِ
لَفًّا كَأَمْثَالِ ٱلْكِبَاشِ ٱلثَّوْأَجِ
لَمْ يُنْجِهِنَّ مِنْهُ شَوْكُ ٱلْمَوْلَجِ
ثُمَّ صَفَرْنَا بِٱلظِّبَاءِ ٱلنُّفَّجِ
وَٱلْعَلْهَبَاتِ وَٱلنِّعَاجِ ٱلنُّعَّجِ
بِكُلِّ ضَأْنٍ بِدَمٍ مُضَرَّجِ
مِنْ كُلِّ رِئْمٍ مُرْشِقٍ وَعَوْهَجِ
كَأَنَّهُنَّ فِي ٱلنِّجَاءِ ٱلْمُرْهِجِ
ثُمَّ ٱسْتَلَبْنَا مِقْوَدَاتِ ٱلْأَحْرُجِ
وَقَالَ بِسْمِ ٱللهِ كُلُّ مُرْتَجِ
وَٱنْصَاعَ كُلُّ مُحْصَرٍ مُحَرَّجِ
سَفًّا يَطِيرُ فِي ٱلرِّيَاحِ ٱلنُّضَّجِ
وَٱنْصَعْنَ فِي كُلِّ طَرِيقٍ أَعْوَجِ
مُسَجَّحَاتٍ وَٱلْفِجَاجِ ٱلْفُجَّجِ
فَهُنَّ بَيْنَ مُقْعَصٍ وَنُشَّجِ
فَلَمْ نَزَلْ بَيْنَ طَبِيخٍ مُنْضَجِ
وَبَيْنَ خَامِيزِ ٱلْمُتُونِ ٱلرَّخْتَجِ
بِكُلِّ أَبْزَارٍ وَخَلٍّ سِفْتَجِ
وَفِي شِوَاءٍ طَيِّبٍ مُلَهْوَجِ
ثُمَّ ٱنْصَرَفْنَا بِصُيُودِ ٱلْبُنَّجِ
وَبِٱلظِّبَاءِ ٱلْعَافِرَاتِ ٱلنُّعَّجِ
كَأَنَّمَا رُحْنَا بِهِ مِنْ كُرْبَجِ

The swift houbara's skull imploded
under her strike. My saker boasts
the finest pedigree, a queen
among captive birds! With no loss
of fuel, she corralled her quarry
like bleating rams—
even a covert of thorns offered
no safety. We whistled her to attack
the darting *ẓaby*s—the big-necked bulls,
the comely does, the deer dyed dark as blood,[63]
the soft-eyed, long-necked gazelles,
plump as if living under clouds
rich with rain. We removed the cowrie collars
from the dogs.[64] Eagerly we shouted,
"In the Name of God!" The famished hounds
flew from their shackles at the speed
of hellfire winds.[65] The game bolted.
Some ran hard on twisting paths,
some took to the knock-kneed hills,
some died on the spot, others bleated
in fear.
        We enjoyed our stew well done.
Others ate spicy jellied loin with sharp
vinegar and pungent meats grilled rare.
We headed home with our spoils of dusty,
comely *ẓaby*s and lovely does,
as if we'd just bought them at market.

~ ٣٩ ~

وقال ينعته [الرجز]

قَدْ أَغْتَدِي قَبْلَ ٱنْشِقَاقِ ٱلنُّورِ
وَٱللَّيْلُ مُرْخٍ هُدُبَ ٱلسُّتُورِ
وَقَارِيَاتُ ٱلطَّيْرِ فِي ٱلْوُكُورِ
بِمُخْطَفِ ٱلْجَنْبَيْنِ وَٱلْخُصُورِ
مُلَاحَكِ ٱلْأَرْسَاغِ وَٱلْفُقُورِ
أَسْوَدَ أَوْ ذِي بَلَقٍ مَشْهُورِ
مُحَرَّجٍ بِٱلْوَدْعِ وَٱلسُّيُورِ
بَيْنَ صَرِيفِينَ فَأَعْلَى ٱلدُّورِ
زُيِّنَ بِٱلتَّلْوِيحِ وَٱلضُّمُورِ
حَتَّى إِذَا كَانَ مَعَ ٱلسُّفُورِ
عَنَّ لَنَا لِلْقَدَرِ ٱلْمَقْدُورِ
مُرْهَفَةُ ٱلْأَعْجَازِ وَٱلصُّدُورِ
مِثْلَ ٱرْفِضَاضِ ٱللُّؤْلُؤِ ٱلْمَنْثُورِ
وَقَدْ رَعَتْ فِي بَارِضِ ٱلنُّؤُورِ
فِي رَوْضَةٍ نَأَتْ عَنِ ٱلْوُعُورِ
وَٱلْحَزْنِ وَٱلصَّمَّانِ وَٱلصُّخُورِ
وَجَادَهَا ٱلنَّوْءُ بِذِي دُرُورِ
مِنَ ٱلسَّحَابِ خَمِلٍ مَطِيرِ
حِينَ كَسَاهَا شِيَةَ ٱلْحَبِيرِ
كَذَاكَ دَأْبُ ٱلْخَمْسَةِ ٱلشُّهُورِ
فَآضَ مِثْلَ ٱلْجَنْدَلِ ٱلْمَنْقُورِ

~ 39 ~

In Cowrie Collar

Before the light burst from the dark veil of night
and the pin-tails left their nests, I crossed the dark
between Ṣarīfūn and High Homes with a hound—
his flanks well defined, his loins a lean arch,
his hocks let down, his vertebrae firm, black
or dark-spotted, in cowrie collar and leather leash,
a famed beauty of a dog, starved till he became
solid as wood.
                    At dawn, Fate called. We spotted oryx
with slender haunches and chests, scattered about
like loose pearls, grazing on new shoots of *na'ūr*
in a meadow far from the rugged lava tracts
and rock flats.[66] For five months the field had been clad
in a two-tone robe by the season's generous
cloudbursts. The dog stood like a chiseled stone,

فَشَدَّ فِيهَا شَدَّةَ ٱلْمُغِيرِ
أَوْ مِثْلَ شَدِّ ٱلْحَنَقِ ٱلْمَوْتُورِ
فَرَدَّ أُولَاهَا عَلَى ٱلْأَخِيرِ
وَلَبَّسَ ٱلتَّحْقِيبَ بِٱلتَّصْدِيرِ
ثُمَّ ٱنْتَحَى لِسَلْهَبٍ دَرِيرِ
يَهْوِي عَلَى مُنْخَرِقِ ٱلدَّبُورِ
فَعَاقَبَ ٱلْإِلْهَابَ بِٱلضُّبُورِ
كَٱلدَّلْوِ خَانَتْهَا ٱلْقُوَى فِي ٱلْبِيرِ
تَمْصَحُ بِٱلطَّرْفِ مِنَ ٱلْهُمُورِ
حَتَّى إِذَا صَارَ إِلَى ٱلْكُرُورِ
عَلَّقَهُ بِلَهْذَمٍ مَطْرُورِ
مُفَرِّقٍ مَجَامِعَ ٱلسُّحُورِ
وَعَابِطَاتٍ لِلْجُلُودِ زُورِ
تَخَالُ مِنْهُنَّ شَبَا ٱلْأُظْفُورِ
مِثْلَ سِنَانِ ٱلْحَرْبَةِ ٱلْمَطْرُورِ
لَمْ يَقِهَا ٱللَّهُ مِنَ ٱلْمَحْذُورِ
ثُمَّ أَجَالَ فِي ٱقْتِنَاصِ ٱلْحُورِ
مُشَمِّرًا وَأَيَّمَا تَشْمِيرِ
فَوَرَدَتْ مَوْرِدَ لَا مَصْدُورِ
فَهُنَّ بَيْنَ فَائِظٍ مَنْحُورِ
وَذِي رِمَاقٍ بِٱللِّوَى مَبْقُورِ
فَرَدَّ قَبْلَ ٱلْأَيْنِ وَٱلْفُتُورِ
عِشْرِينَ عُلْجُومًا إِلَى يَعْفُورِ
مَخْضُوبَةَ ٱلْأَطْرَافِ وَٱلنُّحُورِ

then charged into battle, an avenging fury. Rounding up
the oryx at the front of the charge, he pushed
them back among the stragglers, then, in a sprint
that pulled his girth hard against his brisket,[67]
he lunged at lively Bighorn. Riding the gusts
of the west wind, he dashed like wildfire,
then pounced hard, fast as a bucket
falling from a snapped well rope, water
sloshing from its lip. Bighorn wheeled to attack,
but the dog skewered him with his own sharp spearhead,
parting lungs from ribs, tearing at his skin with brute claws—
look—you'd think his nails were lance points.
God did not protect the oryx from terror!

Then he turned to hunt the houri-eyed *ẓaby*s 38
and pushed them hard. There was no escape—
some lay dead, necks torn open; others gasped
their last breath, disemboweled at Dune's Edge.
Before he tired, he brought back twenty big gazelles
and a young buck, their hooves and breasts dyed red.

قُلْ لِظِبَاءٍ بِٱلْحَزِيزِ صُورِ
إِلَيْهِ مِنْ خِلَاطِهِ نَفُورِ
هَيْهَاتَ لَا نَجَاةَ مِنْ زُنْبُورِ
فَٱنْجِدِي إِنْ شِئْتِ لَا بَلْ غُورِي
بَذَاكَ لَا بِٱلرَّمْيِ لِلطُّيُورِ
وَدَلَجٍ فِي غَلَسِ ٱلْبُكُورِ
لِلْبَرْزِ فِي ٱلْآجَامِ وَٱلدُّبُورِ
أَقْطَعُ مَا عَمَّرْتُ مِنْ دُهُورِي
يَا لَكَ يَوْمًا جَامِعَ ٱلسُّرُورِ

Say to the shy *ẓaby*s at Ḥazīz, too coy to mix with him,
"No chance! You can't escape Hornet in upland or valley."

Who needs to shoot pellets at birds, running for thickets
and sown fields in the dark while dawn peeks on?
Hunting like this is how I'd pass my life. What a day—full of joy!

~ ٤٠ ~

وقال ينعته [الرجز]

قَدْ أَغْتَدِي قَبْلَ غُدُوِّ ٱلثَّعْلَبِ
وَقَبْلَ تَأْوِيبِ ٱلْقَطَا ٱلْمُقَرِّبِ
بِضَامِرِ ٱلْخَصْرِ نَبِيلِ ٱلْمَنْكِبِ
أَبْيَضَ أَوْ أَحْمَرَ لَوْنَ ٱلْمُذَهَّبِ
يَرْنُو بِعَيْنَيْ حَيَّةٍ فِي مَرْقَبِ
وَرَاءَ جَفْنَيْ حُوَّلِيٍّ قُلَّبِ
فِي هَامَةٍ كَٱلْحَجَرِ ٱلْمُذَرَّبِ
مَا كَانَ إِلَّا لَمَعَانُ ٱلثَّعْلَبِ
وَجَوْلَةَ ٱلْوَحْشِ بِأَعْلَى ٱلسَّبْسَبِ
حَتَّى ٱنْثَنَى مُخْتَضِبَ ٱلْمُلَبَّبِ
بِتِسْعَةٍ فِي عَقْدِ شَاوٍ مُلْهَبِ
لَمْ يُزْرَ بِٱلْكَلْبِ وَلَمَّا يُتْعَبِ
وَعَاشِرٍ أَنْفَذَهُ بِمِخْلَبِ
فَٱلْقَوْمُ أَضْيَافٌ كَثِيرُو ٱلنُّصُبِ
بِرَوْضَةٍ خَضْرَاءَ رَيَّا ٱلْمِذْنَبِ
يُسْقَوْنَ مِنْ رَاحٍ عَتِيقٍ أَصْهَبِ
تَرْكُضُ فِي ٱلْكَأْسِ ٱرْتِكَاضَ ٱلْجُنْدَبِ
بُورِكَ فِي ٱلْكَلْبِ وَفِي ٱلْمُكَلِّبِ

~ 40 ~

A Viper's Cunning Eyes

I crossed the dark, before the fox and the fleet grouse
were out, with an arch-loined, sharp-shouldered dog,
white, or rather light red, the color of gilt cloth,
his head like a sharp-pointed stone, staring out from a knoll
with a viper's cunning eyes.
                                        At the top of the plain, 8
a flash of fox, a charge of oryx. Then a wildfire race,
the dog's brisket dyed dark with blood. In a perfect display
of his skills, he chased down nine with no signs of fatigue—
the tenth he dispatched with his claws.
                                                    My guests dined well 14
in a lush field by a brook, sipping fiery red wine,
bubbles dancing in the cup like locusts.

Blessed be dog and trainer! 18

~ ٤١ ~

وقال ينعته [الرجز]

قَدْ أَذْعَرُ ٱلْعُصْمَ مَعَ ٱلْأَسْحَارِ
عِنْدَ ٱشْتِبَاكِ ٱللَّيْلِ وَٱلنَّهَارِ
بِأَكْلُبٍ صَادِقَةِ ٱلْحِضَارِ
شَوَازِبٍ مُخْطَفَـــةٍ ضَوَارِ
كَانَ ٱقْتِنَاؤُهَا عَنِ ٱخْتِبَارِ
مِنْ كُلِّ أَذْفَى مُوثَقِ ٱلْفَقَارِ
أَسِيلِ مَجْرَى ٱلطَّوْقِ وَٱلْعِذَارِ
أَبْيَضَ أَوْ أَحْمَرَ كَٱلدِّينَارِ
كَأَنَّمَا يَفْتَرُّ عَنْ شِفَارِ
مَا كَانَ إِلَّا لَمْحَةُ ٱلصُّوَارِ
وَجَوْلَةُ ٱلْأَوْعَالِ بِٱلصَّحَارِي
حَتَّى ٱنْثَنَى مُخْتَضِبَ ٱلْأَظْفَارِ
بِأَرْبَعٍ أُثْبِتْنَ فِي ٱلْإِحْضَارِ
بِمُرْهَفَاتٍ كَمُدَى ٱلْجَزَّارِ
وَخَامِسٍ مُنْفَرِجِ ٱلصِّدَارِ
لَمْ يُنْجِهِ ٱلْخَوْفُ مِنَ ٱلْأَقْدَارِ
فَكَانَ مَا ٱصْطَادَ عَلَى ٱلْوَقَارِ
خَمْساً مَضَى فِيهَا بِلَا ٱنْبِهَارِ
بُورِكَ فِي ٱلْكَلْبِ وَفِي ٱلزُّوَّارِ

~ 41 ~

Fierce Daggers

Day was trapped in night's snare.
In the dark I terrified stripe-legged
oryx with hounds of savage speed
and strength—natural hunters, lean
and slim, purchased with care,
humpbacked dogs with welded spines,
thin of collar and muzzle, white
or gold-coin red, fierce daggers
lurking in their smiles.
A glimpse of the herd.
A charge of oryx in the desert plain.
He returned, toes dyed, four felled
in a cavalry charge, slain by fangs
like a butcher's cleaver, a fifth lying dead,
her snood ripped apart—fear
couldn't save her from Fate. His pride intact,
not even out of breath, he killed five.

Blessed be dog and guests!

~ ٤٢ ~

وقال ينعته [الرجز]

قَدْ أَذْعَرُ ٱلْأَرْنَبَ فِي ٱبْتِكَارِهَا
عِنْدَ تَغَنِّي ٱلطَّيْرِ فِي أَشْجَارِهَا
بِعَبْلَةِ ٱلزَّوْرِ عَلَى ٱضْطِمَارِهَا
مَعْصُوبَةِ ٱللَّحْمِ عَلَى ٱقْوِرَارِهَا
كَأَنَّمَا خِيطَ عَلَى أَقْطَارِهَا
مَا بَيْنَ أُذْنَيْهَا إِلَى أَظْفَارِهَا
قُوهِيَّةٍ تَغْلُو عَلَى تُجَّارِهَا
بَيْضَاءَ أَوْ صَفْرَاءَ فِي ٱحْمِرَارِهَا
كَأَنَّمَا تَحْنُو عَلَى آثَارِهَا
ثِنْتَيْ شَرَارٍ ذَكَوَا مِنْ نَارِهَا
إِذَا رَأَتْهَا أَرْنَبٌ فِي دَارِهَا
لَمْ يُنْجِهَا مِنْهَا أَخُو حِذَارِهَا
مَا كَانَ إِلَّا ٱلرَّهْجُ مِنْ غُبَارِهَا
وَعَطْفَةُ ٱلْغُضْفِ عَلَى آثَارِهَا
حَتَّى ٱنْثَنَتْ تَمْرَحُ فِي شَوَارِهَا
مُحْمَرَّةَ ٱلزَّوْرِ عَلَى ٱصْفِرَارِهَا
مِنْ خَمْسَةٍ لَمْ تَنْجُ مِنْ شِفَارِهَا
بُورِكَ فِيهَا سَاعَةَ ٱخْتِيَارِهَا

~ 42 ~

A Spout of Dust

While the birds sang in the trees
at break of day, I brought panic
to the hare with a deep-brisketed dog,
her flesh lean and muscled, so slim
her neck and toes seem sewn
to her flanks when she runs,
white or yellowish red, the color
of costly Qūhī cloth. Double sparks
blazed over her tracks. When the hares
in their homes spotted her, all hiding
was in vain. A spout of dust—
the drop ears turning in the hares'
tracks and returning with a jaunty air,
five held in her dagger teeth,
her golden brisket bloodied red.

Blessed the day I picked her! 18

~ ٤٣ ~

وقال ينعته [الرجز]

أَنْعَتُ كَلْبًا كَامِلًا فِي قَدِّهِ
أَتْلَعَ سَبْطَ ٱلْخَلْقِ غَيْرَ جَعْدِهِ
أَمْعَنَ هَرْتُ شِدْقِهِ فِي خَدِّهِ
كَٱلْمِقْوَدِ ٱلْمَجْدُولِ فِي مُمْتَدِّهِ
حَتَّى إِذَا ٱلصُّبْحُ بَدَا مِنْ غِمْدِهِ
صَبَّحْتُ وُرْدَ ٱلضَّأْنِ قَبْلَ وِرْدِهِ
فِي سَبْسَبٍ رَحْبِ ٱلْفَضَاءِ جَرْدِهِ
وَهُنَّ فِي ٱلْمَنْصَفِ مِنْ مُعْتَدِّهِ
كَمَجْمَعِ ٱلْفُرْسِ بِدَسْتَبَنْدِهِ
حَتَّى إِذَا ٱنْصَاعَ تُجَاهَ قَصْدِهِ
وَرَاحَ غَيْرَ يَائِسٍ مِنْ بُعْدِهِ
خَلَّيْتَهُ كَٱلسَّهْمِ مِنْ سَكْبَنْدِهِ
تُخْرِجُهُ حَاجَتُهُ مِنْ جِلْدِهِ
فَصَادَنَا قَبْلَ بُلُوغِ جَهْدِهِ
كَبْشًا وَأَيْضًا نَعْجَةً مِنْ بَعْدِهِ
وَثَالِثًا عَفَّرَهُ فِي شَدِّهِ
فَآبَ مَجْهُودًا بِيُمْنِ جَدِّهِ
قَدْ نَالَنَا مِنْ عَيْشِنَا بِرَغْدِهِ
ذَاكَ بِشُكْرِ رَبِّنَا وَحَمْدِهِ

~ 43 ~

Hands Clasped in a Persian Dance

I sing of a perfectly built, long-necked,
slim-bodied, short-haired dog, his cheek
cut in two by a thin, deep jaw stretched
like a twisted collar. As dawn unsheathed
its blade, I raided the red deer
before the herd began to move
waterward, gathered in a circle
like hands clasped in a Persian dance.
The dog realized they were grazing
in the midst of a bare plain and sped off straight
at his target, distance no problem,
like an arrow in flight, so hungry
he seemed to leave his skin behind.
Before he reached his limit, he killed
a buck and a doe, then raced to fell
a third, lying in the dust. Exhausted,
he brought home his share of good fortune—
his ease keeps us alive! God be praised!

~ ٤٤ ~

وقال ينعته [الرجز]

أَنْعَتُ كَلْباً أَهْلُهُ فِي خِصْبِ
إِذَا ٱلسِّنُونَ وَاتَـرَتْ بِجَدْبِ
قَاتَهُمُ ٱلْكَلْبُ بِحُسْنِ ٱلْكَسْبِ
فَقَدْ أَحَبُّوهُ بِكُلِّ ٱلْقَلْبِ
حُبَّ ٱلْبَنِـينَ لِبَقَـاءِ ٱلْأَبِ
لَوْ مَلَكُوا دَفْعَ قَضَـاءِ ٱلرَّبِّ
لَدَافَعُوا عَنْهُ جَلِيـلَ ٱلْخَطْبِ
زَيَّنَـــهُ ٱللّٰهُ بِأُذْنٍ شَـطْبِ
وَمِخْطَـمٍ سَهْـلٍ وَزَوْرٍ رَحْبِ
مُضْطَمِرَ ٱلْكَشْحِ وَسَاعِ ٱلْوَثْبِ
إِذَا ٱلظِّبَاءُ عَرَّدَتْ فِي ٱلسُّهْبِ
أَنْحَى لَهَـا مِنْـهُ بِشَـدٍّ لَهْبِ
يَجْمَعُ بَيْنَ شَـرْقِهَا وَٱلْغَـرْبِ
بِمَـائِرِ ٱلْخَصْرِ دَرِيـرِ ٱلْعَقْبِ
حَتَّى تَـرَى أُمَّ ٱلرَّشَـا ٱلْأَقَبِّ
مَعْقُولَةَ ٱلظِّلْفِ بِسَحْقِ ٱلتُّرْبِ
نَاهِيكَ يَوْمَ فَاقَةٍ مِنْ كَلْبِ

~ 44 ~

God-Given Beauty

I sing of a dog whose family enjoys plenty
in years of hunger, fed on his prey.
They love him with all their heart,
like sons wishing their father longevity.
They hold him so dear they would repeal
our Lord's decree if this were a possibility.
He has a God-given beauty: a soft, plush ear,
a flat muzzle, a deep brisket, a lean flank,
and a pounce of great range.
                                        *Ẓaby*s fled 11
across the soft ground—in a burst of fire,
he attacked from the side, rounding them up,
east and west, with a swerve of his hips
and fleet hocks. Look—there's the mother
of a slim fawn, hobbled in the bare soil.
What a dog to own in a time of famine!

~ ٤٥ ~

وقال ينعته [الرجز]

أَنْعَتُ كَلْبًا لَقِنَ ٱلنُّحَاسِ
مَحْسُورَ أَقْطَارِ شُؤُونِ ٱلرَّاسِ
يُدِيرُ فِي وَقْبَيْنِ ذَا ٱنْخِفَاسِ
طَمَّاحَتَيْنِ كَلَظَى ٱلْمِقْبَاسِ
مِثْلَ ٱحْوِرَارِ ٱلشَّادِنِ ٱلْمَيَّاسِ
مُسَلَّكَ ٱلْخَلْقِ كَغُصْنِ ٱلْآسِ
نِعْمَ ٱلْخَلِيلُ وَٱلْأَخُ ٱلْمُوَاسِي
مِنْ غَيْرِ مَا بَيْعٍ وَلَا مِكَاسِ
كَمْ تَيْسِ رَمْلٍ لَاحَ فِي ٱلْكِنَاسِ
عَفَّرَهُ بِجَانِبَيْ أَوْطَاسِ
لَمْ يُعْطَ إِلَّا مِثْلَهُ ٱلنُّوَاسِي

~ 45 ~

Slim as a Myrtle Twig

I sing of a dog with a sharp mind,
his head nothing but bones, the sutures
of his skull visible through the skin.
His restless firebrand eyes burn deep
in their sockets with a shy fawn's glossy gaze,
his body slim as a myrtle twig.
He's generous and true, a fine comrade.
We don't haggle over his wares—
sand-dune bucks sprung from cover
felled on the slopes of Awṭās.
He earns the choice raisins we feed him![68]

~ ٤٦ ~

وقال ينعته [الرجز]

أَنْعَتُ كَلْبًا مُرْهَفًا خَمِيصَا
ذَا شِيَةٍ مَا عَدِمَتْ وَبِيصَا
تَخَالُ فِي أَجْفَانِهِ فُصُوصَا
أُدِّبَ حَتَّى أَحْكَمَ ٱلتَّقْنِيصَا
وَعَرَفَ ٱلْإِيحَاءَ وَٱلْعَوِيصَا
بُورِكَ كَلْبًا نَهِمًا حَرِيصَا
هَتَّكَ عَنْ حُجْبِ ٱلظِّبَى ٱلْقَمِيصَا
فَمُحِّصَتْ آرَابُهَا تَمْحِيصَا
حَتَّى تَرَى غَالِيَهَا رَخِيصَا
تَمْنَحُهَا ٱلطَّارِينَ وَالشُّخُوصَا
أَضْحَى بِهِ مَالُ لَهُ مَخْصُوصَا
لَمْ يَرَ مِنْ عَيْشٍ بِهِ تَنْغِيصَا

~ 46 ~

Gems in Bezels

I sing of a dog lean as an arrow,
his belly hungry, a bright sheen to his coat.
Look—his eyes are gems in bezels.
Trained to be a prize hunter,
he knows all the secret codes and commands.
A keen dog, blessed with a wolf bite,
he violates the *ẓaby*s, tears their veils
from their gowns, picks their limbs
clean of flesh; you'd think meat
this rare is now the common fare[69]
offered to visitors and strangers.
Of game he soon amasses his own fortune—
hardship's a thing he'll never know.

~ ٤٧ ~

وقال ينعته [الرجز]

أَعْدَدْتُ كَلْبًا لِلطِّرَادِ فَظَّا
إِذَا عَدَا مِنْ لَهَبٍ تَلَظَّى
وَجَاذَبَ ٱلْمِقْوَدَ وَٱسْتَلَظَّا
كَأَنَّ شَيْطَانًا بِهِ أَلَظَّا
يَكُظُّ أَسْرَابَ ٱلظِّبَاءِ كَظَّا
حَتَّى تَرَاهَا فِرَقًا تَشَظَّى
يُحْرِزُ مِنْهَا كُلَّ يَوْمٍ حَظَّا
حَتَّى تَرَى جَمِيعَهَا مُفْتَظَّا

~ 47 ~

Fueled by Hunger

I ready a brutal dog for the hunt,
his fiery pace fueled by hunger.
He rears and tugs on the leash
as if harried by a pitiless demon.
The *ẓaby*s pant in panic.
Look—they bolt, but he wins the day.
The herds lie spattered on the ground
like water spilled from a camel's gut.[70]

~ ٤٨ ~

وقال ينعته [الرجز]

أَنْعَتُ كَلْبًا قُلَّبِيًّا سَلْطَا
أَعْدَلُ حُكْمَيْهِ إِذَا تَمَطَّى
أَنْ يَعْبِطَ ٱلْأَرْضَ ٱلْفَضَاءَ عَبْطَا
كَانَ ٱقْتِنَاءَ مُقْتَنِيهِ سَبْطَا
تَخَالُهُ يَخْطُو إِذَا تَخَطَّى
عَلَى أَسَاطِينَ أُجِيدَتْ خَرْطَا
مِنْ مَرْمَرٍ يَلْقُطُهُنَّ لَقْطَا
مُضْطَمِرَ ٱلْخَلْقِ رَشِيقًا سَبْطَا
يَعُطُّ أَجْلَادَ ٱلظِّبَاءِ عَطَّا
كَأَنَّ حَجَّامًا يُجِيدُ ٱلشَّرْطَا
حُكِّمَ فِي أَجْلَادِهَا فَٱشْتَطَّا

~ 48 ~

Two Verdicts

I sing of a most able dog, all bones—
his owner practically gave him away!
He delivers two verdicts. The first one is just—
to stretch into a run and kick up
the flatland dust. Picture him striding
along on those lank marble pillars he lifts
with care, lean-bodied, arrow-thin,
short-haired. He shreds *ẓaby* skins
with ease, like a barber deft with a razor—
his second, far more brutal verdict.

~ ٤٩ ~

وقال ينعته [الرجز]

لَمَّا تَبَدَّى ٱلصُّبْحُ مِنْ حِجَابِهِ
وَٱنْعَدَلَ ٱللَّيْلُ إِلَى مَآبِهِ
خَرَّطَهُ ٱلْقَانِصُ وَٱغْتَدَى بِهِ
فِي مِقْوَدٍ يَرْدَعُ مِنْ جِذَابِهِ
يُصِرُّهُ طَوْرًا عَلَى ٱسْتِصْعَابِهِ
وَتَارَةً يَنْصَبُّ لِٱنْصِبَابِهِ
كَأَنَّمَا يَفْتَرُّ مِنْ أَنْيَابِهِ
عَنْ مُرْهَفَاتِ ٱلنَّصْلِ أَوْ حِرَابِهِ
كَأَنَّ عَيْنَيْهِ إِذَا رَأَى بِهِ
فَصَّا عَقِيقٍ قَدْ تَقَابَلَا بِهِ
مُنْسَدِلَ ٱلزَّوْرِ لَدَى تَلَبَابِهِ
يَرْثِمُ أَنْفَ ٱلْأَرْضِ مِنْ ذَهَابِهِ
حَتَّى إِذَا ٱسْتَشْرَفَ أَوْ حَاذَى بِهِ
بَعْدَ ٱنْخِزَارِ ٱلطَّرْفِ وَٱنْقِلَابِهِ
بِرَوْضَةِ ٱلْقَاعِ إِلَى أَعْجَابِهِ
ذَا أُشُرٍ قَدْ عَنَّ فِي أَسْرَابِهِ
أَرْسَلَهُ كَٱلسَّهْمِ إِذْ عَلَا بِهِ
يَسْبِقُ طَرْفَ ٱلْعَيْنِ فِي ٱلْتِهَابِهِ
شَدًّا بِبَطْنِ ٱلْقَاعِ مِنْ إِلْهَابِهِ
يَكَادُ أَنْ يَنْسَلَّ مِنْ إِهَابِهِ
كَلَمَعَانِ ٱلْبَرْقِ فِي سَحَابِهِ

~ 49 ~

Eyes Like Moonstones

Dawn lifted her veil and night slunk home.
The hunter muzzled his dog and departed.
The collar, tight when he pulled, loose
when he let up, kept the dog from tugging.
His smile revealed teeth as sharp
as arrowheads or assegais, his eyes stared
like moonstones, his brisket sat low
at the neck, his feet broke the face
of the earth. The hunter scoured the dunes
and spotted Old Bull up ahead in a meadow,
proud among his herds. He sicced
the dog, an arrow shot high from a bow,
scorching the flatlands faster than the eye
can see, nearly leaving his skin behind,
a lightning bolt exploding from a rain cloud.

حَتَّى إِذَا مَا كَادَ أَوْ حَاذَى بِهِ
نَادَاهُ يَا أَبْعَدَ مَا نَأَى بِهِ
فَٱعْتَابَهُ عَلَقَيْنِ فِي ٱغْتِصَابِهِ
حَتَّى إِذَا عَفَّرَهُ هَاهَا بِهِ
فَٱنْصَاعَ لِلصَّوْتِ ٱلَّذِي يُدْعَى بِهِ

He's nearly there; now he's on him!
The hunter shouted, "Whoa, too far!"
rebuking him for a double lunge.[71]
The bull was felled. The hunter hallooed
and the dog jumped at his call.

~ ٥٠ ~

وقال ينعته [الرجز]

لَمَّا رَأَيْتُ ٱللَّيْلَ قَدْ تَصَرَّمَا
عَنِّي وَعَنْ مَعْرُوفِ صُبْحٍ أَشْيَمَا
خَرَجْتُ أَقْتَادُ أَقَبَّ سَلْجَمَا
مُلَاحَكَ ٱلْأَضْلَاعِ سَلْطًا سَلْطَمَا
وَذَاتَ شَدٍّ تُورِثُ ٱلطَّرْفَ ٱلْعَمَى
قَدْ صَاغَهَا صَائِغُهَا فَأَحْكَمَا
أَحْكَمَ مِنْهَا مَتْنَتَيْهَا وَٱلْفَمَا
وَزَيَّنَ ٱلْمُؤْخَرَ وَٱلْمُقَدَّمَا
فَهْيَ عَرُوفٌ لِلَّذِي تَكَلَّمَا
تَأْتِي ٱلَّذِي قَالَ وَمَا إِنْ نَغَّمَا
مِرْجَمَةٌ تَتْلُو عَسُولًا مِرْجَمَا
حَتَّى ذَعَرْنَا ذَا كِنَاسٍ أَرْثَمَا
فَغَاوَرَاهُ ٱلشَّدَّ شَأْوًا مُفْعَمَا
يَنْتَسِجَانِ ثَوْبَ دَجْنٍ أَقْتَمَا
إِنْ هَبَطَا وَعْثًا دَمِيثًا أَصْرَمَا
أَوْ مَعَجَا فِي ٱلْقُفِّ مَعْجًا أَضْرَمَا
فِي جَانِبَيْهِ مَرْوُهُ ٱلْمُخَذَّمَا
كَأَنَّ كَلْبَيْنَا إِذَا مَا ٱنْهَزَمَا
سَهْمَا رَسِيلَيْنِ أَرَادَا عَلَمَا
حَتَّى ٱسْتَفَاآهُ وَمَا إِنْ عَتَّمَا
وَعَطَّطَا أَدِيمَهُ وَعَجَّمَا

~ 50 ~

Rapid-Fire Arrows

Displeased with me and the gift of day, night
withdrew, leaving a tiny mole on dawn's cheek.
I fetched the harness of an arch-loined dog
with well-sprung ribs, lean and long, and a bitch
so fast she's blinding,[72] perfectly honed
by her trainer, her spine well knit,
her muzzle taut, her front and back exquisite.
Loyal and true, pounding the ground with her heavy
paws, she's quick to react to whatever you say
or sing.

In a fast raid, a torrent of a race, 11
we startled White Lip the oryx in his covert.
The dogs wove a robe of gloom, kicking up
the soft sand, kindling crops of *marw*
on rocky banks, shooting like rapid-fire
arrows in a contest.[73] He was their spoil.
Without delay, his skin was torn and chewed.

وَطَالَمَا وَطَالَمَا وَطَالَمَا
قَدْ أَثْكَلَا وَأَيَّمَا وَأَيَّمَا
أَجَلْ وَكَمْ قَدْ أَحْسَنَا وَأَنْعَمَا
رَأَيْتَ ذَاكَ ٱلْعَيْشَ وَٱلتَّنَعُّمَا
لَا ٱلرَّبْعَ جَادَتْهُ أَهَاضِيبُ ٱلسَّمَا
وَلَا بُكَاءَ كُلْثُمٍ وَتُكْتَمَا
وَلَا حُمُولَ ٱلْحَيِّ وَلَّتْ زِيَمَا
بَكَتْ جُفُونِي يَوْمَ أَبْكِيهُمْ دَمَا

So many fawns so quickly orphaned!
Yes, these dogs have done me many a good deed—
I know this is the good life, not that spring camp
in the rain, nor those tears for Kulthūm and Tuktam,
nor those camels and the tribe's silent goodbye
that sad day my eyes wept tears of blood.

~ ٥١ ~

وقال ينعته [الرجز]

لَمَّا رَأَيْتُ ٱللَّيْلَ مُنْشَقَّ ٱلْحُجُبْ
عَنْ سَائِلِ ٱلْغُرَّةِ مَشْهُورِ ٱلنُّقَبْ
نَاهَضْتُ عُصْمَ ٱلْوَحْشِ بِٱلْغُضْفِ ٱلْغُضُبْ
مِنْ كُلِّ أَحْوَى ٱللَّوْنِ مُبْيَضِّ ٱللَّبَبْ
يَهْتَزُّ فِي ٱلْمِشْيَةِ عِنْدَ ٱلْمُنْجَذَبْ
هَزَّكَ فِي ٱلْكَفِّ حُسَامًا ذَا شُطَبْ
كَأَنَّمَا يَطْرِفُ مِنْ بَيْنِ ٱلْهُدُبْ
بِجَمْرَتَيْ نَارٍ بِكَفِّ مُحْتَطِبْ
مَا كَانَ إِلَّا جَوْلَةُ ٱلْأَرْوَى ٱلسَّغِبْ
وَوَثْبَةُ ٱلتَّيْسِ بِأَنْوَاعِ ٱلْحَدَبْ
حَتَّى ٱنْثَنَى مُخْتَضِبًا وَمَا ٱخْتَضَبْ
مِنْ مَغْرِزِ ٱلزَّوْرِ إِلَى عَجْبِ ٱلذَّنَبْ
بِتِسْعَةٍ أَحْرَزَهَا بِلَا تَعَبْ
وَعَاشِرٍ أَثْبَتَهُ فِي ٱلْمُنْقَلَبْ
بِمُرْهَفَاتٍ سَمْهَرِيَّاتٍ سُلُبْ
يَنْشِطُ أُذْنَيْهِ بِهَا عِنْدَ ٱلطَّلَبْ
نَشْطَ أَشَافِي ٱلْخَرْزِ أَثْنَاءَ ٱلْقِرَبْ
فَٱلْقَوْمُ مِنْ مُنْتَشِلٍ أَوْ مُسْتَلِبْ
بَيْنَ رِيَاضٍ ذَاتِ وَشْيٍ مُؤْتَشَبْ
يُسْقَوْنَ مِنْ رِيقَةِ مَسْطُوحٍ أَزِبْ
بِمَاءِ مُزْنٍ سَالَ مِنْ خَصْرَيْ تَعِبْ
بُورِكَ مِنْ كَلْبٍ كَرِيمِ ٱلْمُنْتَهَبْ

~ 51 ~

Sharp Samharī Spears

Night's headscarf was torn. That famous
beauty, the sun, shone from behind her veil.
I roused the white-leg deer with angry drop-eared dogs,
their black chests spotted white, tugging on the leash
and quivering in the hand like broad-ridged
swords, their eyes ablaze as if from below the fringe
of a gown, like a torch in an arsonist's hand.
Tired *ẓabys* fled and the buck sprang across the dunes.
The dog returned, dyed red from brisket top
to tail tip—full of energy, he had felled nine gazelles.
On the way back, a tenth was skewered
by his sharp Samharī spears—deadly weapons
that in the chase pierced his ears with stitch
holes punched by an awl in a waterskin.[74]
In fields of patterned plants, some of the troop
started looting the pot; others snatched meat,
sipping from the bulging skins a wine as sharp as saliva,[75]
mixed with pure rain drained from the belly of a cloud.

Blessed be the noble dog who gives us his spoils![76] **22**

~ ٥٢ ~

وقال ينعته [الرجز]

لَمَّا تَخَطَّى ٱللَّيْـلُ وَٱبْيَضَّ ٱلْأُفُقْ
وَٱنْجَابَ وَجْهُ ٱللَّيْلِ عَنْ وَجْهِ ٱلطُّرُقْ
بَاكَرَنِي سَهْـلُ ٱلْمُحَيَّـا وَٱلْخُلُقْ
نَـدْبٌ إِذَا ٱسْتَنْـدَبْتَـهُ شَهْـمٌ لَبِقْ
يَـدْعُو إِلَى ٱلصَّيْـدِ كَبَرْقٍ يَا تَلِقْ
بِأَكْلُبٍ غُضْفٍ صَحِيحَاتِ ٱلْحَدَقْ
مِنْ أَصْفَـرِ ٱللَّوْنِ وَمُبْـيَضٍّ يَقَقْ
كَأَنَّمَا أُذْنَاهُ مِنْ بَعْضِ ٱلْخِـرَقْ
لَوْ يَلْصَقُ ٱلْخَـدَّ بِأُذْنٍ لَٱلْتَصَقْ

~ 52 ~

Ears Like Rags

Taking his leave, night made an about-face.
The sky grew white. The trails shone bright.
I had an early visit from a comrade, right
for the job at hand—noble, clever, ready for the fight.
"To the hunt!" he shouted. "Quick, hurry up!
Bring on the drop-ears, yellow and snow-white,
with jaws of steel and ears like rags stuck to their cheeks."

~ ٥٣ ~

وقال ينعته [الرجز]

لَمَّا غَدَا ٱلثَّعْلَبُ فِي ٱعْتِدَائِهِ
وَٱلْأَجَلُ ٱلْمَقْدُورُ مِنْ وَرَائِهِ
صَبَّ عَلَيْهِ ٱللَّهُ مِنْ بَلَائِهِ
سَوْطَ عَذَابٍ صُبَّ مِنْ سَمَائِهِ
تَرَى لِمَوْلَاهُ عَلَى جِرَائِهِ
تَحَدُّبَ ٱلشَّيْخِ عَلَى أَبْنَائِهِ
يُكِنُّهُ بِٱللَّيْلِ فِي غِطَائِهِ
يُوسِعُهُ ضَمًّا إِلَى أَحْشَائِهِ
وَإِنْ غَدَا جُلِّلَ فِي رِدَائِهِ
مِنْ خَشْيَةِ ٱلطَّلِّ وَمِنْ أَنْدَائِهِ
يَضِنُّ بِٱلْأَرْذَلِ مِنْ أَطْلَائِهِ
ضَنَّ أَخِي عَكْلٍ عَلَى عَطَائِهِ
يَقْنَعُ بِسْمِ ٱللَّهِ فِي إِشْلَائِهِ
تَكْبِيرَةً وَٱلْحَمْدُ مِنْ دُعَائِهِ
حَتَّى إِذَا مَا ٱنْشَامَ فِي مُلَائِهِ
وَصَارَ لَحْيَاهُ عَلَى أَنْسَائِهِ
وَلَيْسَ يُنْجِيهِ عَلَى دَهَائِهِ
تَنَسُّمُ ٱلْأَرْوَاحِ فِي ٱنْبِرَائِهِ
خَضْخَضَ ظُنْبُوبَيْهِ فِي أَمْعَائِهِ
وَشَدَّ نَابَيْهِ عَلَى عِلْبَائِهِ

~ 53 ~

Stalked by Fate

As he set off on his patrol, Fox was stalked by Fate.
God rained down His scourge,
heaven's whip-crack of destruction.[77]
Look at the owner 5
fussing over his pups like an old man
tending to his sons. He wraps the dog in his sheet
at night, holding him tight, folding him in his cloak
when they go out, afraid of the early dew and damp,
cherishing even the runt of the litter like a pauper
hoarding a gift.
The hunt was on. He shouted 13
the dog's name, then "In the Name of God!"
"God is Almighty!" and "Praise God!"[78]
Fox was engulfed in the dust cloud, jaws
snapped at his tendons—no caution, no wary sniff
of the wind, no trick could save him. Claws
ripped into his guts, teeth sank into his neck

كَسَدِّكَ ٱلْقُفْلَ عَلَى أَشْبَائِهِ
كَأَنَّمَا يَطْلُبُ فِي عِفَائِهِ
دَيْناً لَهُ لَا بُدَّ مِنْ قَضَائِهِ
فَفَحَصَ ٱلثَّعْلَبُ فِي دِمَائِهِ
يَا لَكَ مِنْ غَادٍ إِلَى حَوْبَائِهِ

like a bolt clicking into place, as if the hound demanded his debt be paid in fur. Fox's blood flowed, his life surrendered to a fine dog.

~ ٥٤ ~

وقال ينعته [الرجز]

لَمَّا غَدَا ثَعْلَبٌ فِي سَفْحِ ٱلْجَبَلْ
صِحْتُ بِكَلْبِي هَا فَرَاحَ كَٱلْبَطَلْ
كَلْبٌ جَرِيءُ ٱلْقَلْبِ مَحْمُودُ ٱلْعَمَلْ
مُؤَدَّبٌ لَهُ ٱلْكِلَابُ كَٱلْخَوَلْ
فَجَاذَبَ ٱلْمِقْوَدَ كَفِّي وَحَمَلْ
وَطَرَدَ ٱلثَّعْلَبَ طَرْدًا مَا بَطَلْ
وَمَرَّ كَٱلصَّقْرِ عَلَى ٱلصَّيْدِ ٱشْتَمَلْ
فَلَفَّهُ لَفًّا سَرِيعًا لِلْأَجَلْ
يَا لَكَ مِنْ كَلْبٍ إِذَا صَادَ عَدَلْ

~ 54 ~

A Saker Stoop

Fox popped up on the slope. I shouted,
"Over there!" My dog prepared for battle—
bravehearted, praised for his feats,
well trained: compared to him, other hounds
are mere chattel. He tugged on the leash,
then attacked. The hunt was a success.
With a saker stoop on quarry, he caught Fox.
A swift toss, then death. What a fine hunter!

~ ٥٥ ~

وقال ينعته هذا كلب لسعته حيّة فمات فرثاه [الرجز]

يَا بُؤْسَ كَلْبِي سَيِّدَ ٱلْكِلَابِ
قَدْ كَانَ أَغْنَانِي عَنِ ٱلْعُقَابِ
وَكَانَ قَدْ نَابَ عَنِ ٱلْقَصَّابِ
وَعَنْ شِرَائِي جَلَبَ ٱلْأَجْلَابِ
بَيْنَ ٱلظِّبَاءِ ٱلْعُفْرِ وَٱلْكِلَابِ
وَكُلِّ شِصٍّ طَالِعٍ وَثَّابِ
يَخْتَطِفُ ٱلْقُطَّانَ فِي ٱلرَّوَابِي
كَٱلْبَرْقِ بَيْنَ ٱلنَّجْمِ وَٱلسَّحَابِ
كَمْ مِنْ غَزَالٍ لَاحِقِ ٱلْأَقْرَابِ
ذِي جَيْئَةٍ صَعْبٍ وَذِي ذَهَابِ
أَشْبَعَنِي فِيهِ مِنَ ٱلْكَبَابِ
خَرَجْتُ وَٱلدُّنْيَا إِلَى تَبَابِ
بِهِ وَكَانَ عُدَّتِي وَنَابِي
أَصْفَرَ قَدْ ضُرِّجَ بِٱلْمَلَابِ
كَأَنَّمَا يُدْهَنُ بِٱلزِّرْيَابِ
فَبَيْنَمَا نَحْنُ بِهِ فِي ٱلْغَابِ
إِذْ بَرَزَتْ كَالِحَةُ ٱلْأَنْيَابِ
رَقْشَاءُ جَرْدَاءُ مِنَ ٱلثِّيَابِ
كَأَنَّمَا تَنْظُرُ مِنْ نِقَابِ
فَعَلَّقَتْ عُرْقُوبَهُ بِنَابِ

~ 55 ~

My Yellow Prince

A threnody for a dog that died from a snakebite:

I've lost the prince of dogs!
He was better than an eagle—
I needed no butcher
to sell me camel meat in hard times:
dusty *ẓaby*s, dogs,[79] wily game
springing from cover—he'd snatch
all these hill dwellers, a lightning bolt
flashing between grass and cloud,
giving me my fill of roast meat—
lean-hipped gazelles, hard,
mazy runners.
We'd gone out 12
to hunt. My world collapsed—
I relied on my yellow prince,
saffron-dyed as if washed in gold.
We were in the bush. A sinuous,
speckled snake, eyes framed
in a niqab, showed her fangs
and bit his heel at the tendon.

لَمْ تَـرَلِي حَقًّا وَلَمْ تُحَابِ
لَا أُبْتُ لَا أُبْتُ بِلَا عِقَابِ
حَتَّى تَذُوقِي أَوْجَعَ ٱلْعَذَابِ

That pitiless judge showed me no mercy.
Snake, if ever I come back,
I'll make you taste bitter pain!

~ ٥٦ ~

وقال ينعته ورواها له سليمان بن خلصة وابن الداية [الرجز]

يَا رُبَّ خَرْقٍ فَنَازِحٍ جَدِيبِ
أَخْلَصَهُ ٱلسَّحَابُ بِٱلصَّبِيبِ
غَزَوْتُهُ بِمُخْطَفِ ٱلْوُثُوبِ
مُضَمَّرِ ٱلْكَشْحَيْنِ كَٱلْيَعْسُوبِ
مُصَدَّرٍ مُلَاءِمِ ٱلْعُرْقُوبِ
كَأَنَّمَا يَفْغُرُ عَنْ قَلِيبِ
أَوْ عَنْ وِجَارِ ضَبُعٍ وَذِيبِ
يَعْلُو ٱلْإِكَامَ وَذُرَى ٱلْكَثِيبِ
وَتَارَةً يَنْحَطُّ فِي ٱلْغُيُوبِ
كَعَوْمِ سُفْنِ ٱلْبَحْرِ فِي ٱلْجَنُوبِ
رَأَى ظِبَاءً ذُعَّرَ ٱلْقُلُوبِ
نَائِيَةً عَنْ نَظَرِ ٱلْمَهِيبِ
فَٱعْتَامَهَا بِٱلشَّدِّ ذِي ٱللَّهِيبِ
كَأَنَّهُ فِي شِرَّةِ ٱلْهَبُوبِ
تَهْوِي بِهِ خَافِيَتَا رَقُوبِ
مُعْتَمِدًا لِتَيْسِهَا ٱلْمَهِيبِ
فَصَكَّهُ بِزَوْرِهِ ٱلرَّحِيبِ
صَكًّا هَوَى مِنْهُ إِلَى شَعُوبِ

~ 56 ~

An Avenging Fury

Sulaymān ibn Khalṣah and Ibn al-Dāyah both attribute this piece to Abū Nuwās.

I raided parched deserts revived by rain clouds,
with a dog lank in leap and lean in flank,
a king bee,[80] yellow, with a white blaze on his chest,
hocks let down, mouth like a well or the den of a hyena
or wolf, able to climb hilltops and dune crests or sail
into low scrublands like a ship in a south wind.
In the distance, he saw timid *ẓaby*s trying to hide
from their fear, then, faster than an angry tornado,
shot toward them, stooping like an alert bird on the wing.
He headed for Old Bull, feared by all. Stunned by the attack,

فَقَضْقَضَ ٱلْعَجْبَ إِلَى ٱلظُّنْبُوبِ
وَٱنْتَهَسَ ٱلْأَرْفَاغَ بِٱلنُّيُوبِ
يَهْوِي بِهِ صَكًّا عَلَى ٱلْجُيُوبِ
كَثَائِرٍ أُمْكِنَ مِنْ مَطْلُوبِ
يَا لَكَ مِنْ ذِي حِيلَةٍ كَسُوبِ

the bull toppled over, his bones crunched from tail
to shin, his flesh torn clean off. It was a stoop, a thwack,
a heart-stop, an avenging fury. Such a wily hunter!

~ ٥٧ ~

وقال ينعته [الرجز]

يَا رُبَّ ثَوْرٍ بِمَكَانٍ قَاصِي
ذِي زَمَعٍ دُلَامِصٍ دَلَّاصِ
بَاتَ يُرَاعِي ٱلنَّجْمَ مِنْ خَصَاصِ
صَبَّحْتُهُ بِضُمَّرٍ خِمَاصِ
لَاحِقَةٍ أَطْبَاؤُهَا شَوَاصِي
فَهُنَّ بَعْدَ ٱلْحُضُرِ ٱلنَّصْنَاصِ
مِنْهُ لَهَا حَيْثُ يَكُونُ ٱلْخَاصِي
يَكْشِرُ عَنْ نَابٍ لَهُ فَرَّاصِ
أَرْنَبَةً سَوْدَاءَ كَٱلْعَنَاصِي
بِهَا يُعَاطِي وَبِهَا يُعَاصِي
يَصِيدُنَا بِٱلْقُرْبِ وَٱلْأَقَاصِي
كُلَّ سَمِينٍ دَهِنٍ رَقَّاصِ

~ 57 ~

His Teeth Bared

In a far-flung place, Strong Leg[81] the bull, his coat
glinting like chain mail, grazed on rain-soaked grass.
I attacked early with lean, hungry bitches,
bursting with energy like full waterskins, their teats
taut and thin. A hard run—now, right on top of him,
they tried to geld him. Heeding, then ignoring the dogs,
he snapped at them, teeth bared between black lips
like wisps of hair on a bald head. Near and far,
the dogs danced and darted at the bulls.

~ ٥٨ ~

وقال ينعته [الرجز]

يَا رُبَّ ظَبْيٍ بِمَكَانٍ خَالِي
صَبَّحْتُهُ وَٱللَّيْلُ ذُو أَهْوَالِ
بِأَغْضَفٍ غُذِّيَ بِحُسْنِ حَالِ
مُسَوَّدِ ٱلْعَمِّ كَرِيمِ ٱلْخَالِ
أُعْطِيَ تَمَامَ ٱلْقَدِّ وَٱلْجَمَالِ
قَلَّدْتُهُ قِلَادَةَ ٱلْأَعْمَالِ
يَجُولُ فِي ٱلْمِقْوَدِ كَٱلْمُخْتَالِ
هِجْنَا بِهِ فَهَاجَ لِلنِّزَالِ
وَآنَسَ ٱلظَّبْيَ بِتَلٍّ عَالِي
فَٱنْسَلَّ قَبْلَ سَاعَةِ ٱلْإِرْسَالِ
وَمَرَّ يَتْلُوهُ وَلَمْ يُبَالِ
بِٱلْحَزْنِ وَٱلسَّهْلِ وَبِٱلرِّمَالِ
أَكْرِمْ بِهٰذَا ٱلْكَلْبِ مِنْ مُحْتَالِ
أُتِيحَ حَتْفَ ٱلظَّبْيِ وَٱلْأَوْعَالِ

~ 58 ~

Proud on the Leash

Night was a sea of fears. In empty regions
I attacked the *ẓaby*s with Drop Ear, raised
like a lord, princes on his father's side,
nobles on his mother's, his perfect physique
enhanced by grace. I fitted his work collar
and he swaggered, proud on the leash.
We goaded him on, priming him for battle.
He spotted a *ẓaby* on a high hill, then, sicced
too soon, gave chase, without a care whether
he ran on sand or hard ground.[82] "Praise me,
wily dog that I am! I'm death to *ẓaby*s and deer!"

~ ٥٩ ~

وقال ينعته [الرجز]

يَا دِبْقُ يَا خَيْرَ ٱلْكِلَابِ أَنْتَا
أَنْتَ ٱلَّذِي كُلَّ ٱلْكِلَابِ سُدْتَا
إِنْ أَصْلَدَتْ يَوْمًا فَمَا أَصْلَدْتَا
أَوْ جَبُنَتْ يَوْمًا فَمَا جَبُنْتَا
يَا رُبَّ سِرْبٍ آمِنٍ صَبَّحْتَا
قَبْلَ طُلُوعِ ٱلْفَجْرِ حِينَ رُعْتَا
ظِبَاءَهُ وَٱلشَّاءَ قَدْ ذَعَرْتَا
هٰذَا وَكَمْ مِنْ أَيِّلٍ طَلَبْتَا
ذِي ثِقَةٍ بِنَفْسِهِ تَرَكْتَا
يَرْكَبُ فِي رَوْقَيْهِ إِذْ أَبْغَتَّا

~ 59 ~

Face Down on Their Horns

Fetch,[83] you're the prince of dogs!
Other dogs may fail to blaze—not you!
Other dogs may shrink in fear—not you!
Before dawn, you attack the herds
safe at rest, terrorizing *ẓaby*s and deer,
then chase ibex, bold and beautiful—your blitz
leaving them face down on their horns.

~ ٦٠ ~

وقال ينعته [الرجز]

قَدْ طَالَمَا أَفْلَتِّ يَا ثُعَالَا
وَطَالَمَا وَطَالَمَا وَطَالَا
جُلْتِ بِكَلْبِي يَوْمَكِ ٱلْأَهْوَالَا
مَاطَلْتِ مَنْ لَا يَسْأَمُ ٱلْمِطَالَا
حَتَّى إِذَا ٱلْيَوْمُ حَدَا ٱلْآصَالَا
أَتَاكِ حَيْنٌ يَقْدُمُ ٱلْآجَالَا

~ 60 ~

Slip and Slide

You were able to slip and slide,
Mrs. Fox, for such a long time,
making my dog run futile lap
after lap all day, refusing to pay
your debt to my relentless piper—
then, as day urged evening on,
Death brought an end to your life.

~ ٦١ ~

وقال ينعته [الرجز]

وَبَلَدٍ عَارٍ مِنَ ٱلسُّكَّانِ
مُمْتَنِعِ ٱلْجَوِّ مِنَ ٱلرُّكْبَانِ
نَاهَضْتُهُ وَهْنًا مَعَ ٱلْأَذَانِ
بِشَائِكِ ٱلْأَنْيَابِ وَٱلْبَنَانِ
كَأَنَّ تَحْتَ مُلْتَقَى ٱلْأَجْفَانِ
مِنْهُ إِذَا أَثَارَ كَوْكَبَانِ
أَوْ جَمْرَتَانِ تَتَأَلَّقَانِ
لَا بَلْ هُمَا فَصَّانِ مِنْ عِقْيَانِ
يَصْنَعُ فِي ٱلضَّأْنِ وَغَيْرِ ٱلضَّأْنِ
صَنِيعَ لَيْثِ ٱلْغَابِ فِي ٱلْأَقْرَانِ
فَكَمْ وَكَمْ مِنْ تَيْسِ رَمْلٍ ثَانِي
جَرَّعَهُ كَأْسًا مِنَ ٱلذَّيْفَانِ
بِمُرْهَفَاتٍ عَبْلَةِ ٱلْبَوَانِي
أَعَدَّهَا ٱلْقَانِصُ لِلضِّيفَانِ
يَقْوَى إِذَا مَا ٱعْتَرَّ جَادَ ثَانِي
فَٱصْطَادَ قَبْلَ أَوْبَةِ ٱلنُّدْمَانِ
عِشْرِينَ مِنْ بَكْرٍ إِلَى عَوَانِي
فَٱلْقَوْمُ أَضْيَافُ غَنِيٍّ غَانِي
بَيْنَ أَبَارِيقَ إِلَى كِيزَانِ
يُسْقَوْنَ مِنْ حَمْرَاءَ كَٱلدِّهَانِ
عَلَى أَقَاحٍ وَعَلَى جَوْذَانِ
بُورِكَ فِي ٱلْكَلْبِ وَفِي ٱلْفِتْيَانِ

~ 61 ~

Death's Poison

An uninhabited, impassable valley—
which I raided at the dawn call to prayer
with a thorn-toothed, sharp-nailed
dog, whose stares burn like stars
or coals—no, like glinting gold nuggets—
and who treats oryx and game with a lion's
disdain for rivals, making the buck
of the sand dunes drink deep of Death's
poison, raked by the sharp claws and thick legs
trained by the hunter so the dog
can welcome its guests to their ends.
A strong beast, giving double what's asked,
he felled twenty does and nannies,
before the return of the carousers,
guests of a lavish host, sipping flame-
red[84] wine from jugs and cups
amid chamomile and lily.
Blessed 22
be my dog, blessed be my comrades!

~ ٦٢ ~

وقال ينعته وأثبتها له سليمان بن سخطة [الرجز]

أَقُولُ لِلْقَانِصِ حِينَ غَلَّسَا
وَٱلصُّبْحُ فِي ٱلظَّلَامِ مَا تَنَفَّسَا
يَقُودُ كَلْبًا لِلطِّرَادِ أَطْلَسَا
لَمْ يُلْفَ عَنْ فَرِيسَةٍ تَحَوَّسَا
مَا رَشَقَ ٱلظِّبَاءَ إِلَّا قَرْطَسَا
وَرَّثَهُ ٱلنَّجْدَةَ مِمَّا أَسَّسَا
أَبٌ وَخَالٌ لَمْ يَزَلْ مُرَأَّسَا
تَخَالُهُ ٱلْعَيْنُ لِمَنْ تَفَرَّسَا
فِي حَوْمَةِ ٱلطَّرْدِ هُمَامًا أَشْرَسَا
إِنْ هَمَّ بِٱلشِّدَّةِ يَوْمًا غَلَّسَا
فَأَعْدَمَ ٱلْخِزَّانَ مِنْهُ ٱلْأَنْفُسَا
حَتَّى لَقَدْ أَبْكَى ٱلْقِنَانَ ٱلطُّمَّسَا
بُورِكَتْ قَنَّاصًا سَلِيلًا أَخْنَسَا
فَكَمْ رَأَيْنَا ضَاوِيًا مُهَلِّسَا
يَشْكُو إِذَا لَاقَاكَ جَدًّا أَتْعَسَا
أَصْبَحَ مِنْ كَسْبِكَ قَدْ تَكَرْدَسَا

~ 62 ~

Strong Like the Lion

This poem is attributed to Abū Nuwās by Sulaymān ibn Sakhṭah.

There was not a whisper of dawn in the murk.
In the black of night, the hunter brought a dark dog
to the kill, a hound no prey had withstood—
one look at the *ẓaby*s and he hits his target,
heir to the courage and royalty of two princes,
father and uncle. In the heat of the chase,
the expert eye[85] can tell he's a fierce warrior
in battle at night's end. He deprives the desert
jacks of their souls, moving the distant mountains
to tears.[86] I said to the houndman, "Good luck
on the hunt! Be strong, like the lion! We know
of many hungry hunters who bewail their luck
and in the morning wince at your success."

نعت الفهد خمس أرجوزات

~ ٦٣ ~

قال ينعته [الرجز]

قَدْ أَغْتَدِي وَٱلشَّمْسُ فِي حِجَابِهَا
مَسْتُورَةٌ لَمْ تَبْدُ مِنْ جِلْبَابِهَا
لَمْ يَقْطَعِ ٱللَّيْلُ عُرَى أَطْنَابِهَا
وَلَمْ تَبَرَّجْ حَاسِرًا مِنْ بَابِهَا
مِثْلَ ٱلْكِعَابِ ٱلرُّودِ فِي نِقَابِهَا
فِي فِتْيَةٍ لَا مَذْقَ فِي أَنْسَابِهَا
مَعْرُوفَةٍ بِٱلْفَضْلِ فِي آدَابِهَا
مِنْ هَاشِمٍ فِي ٱلسِّرِّ مِنْ لُبَابِهَا
نَائِلُهَا سَحٌّ عَلَى طُلَّابِهَا
تَنْفِي بِهِ ٱلْعُسْرَةَ عَنْ أَصْحَابِهَا
كَنْزُ ٱلتُّقَى وَٱلْبِرِّ فِي لُبَابِهَا
إِلَى قُرَى بَرْبَرَ فِي ٱخْتِضَابِهَا
وَغَيْرَ وَقْتِ ٱلْخِصْبِ مِنْ جَدَابِهَا
بِفَهْدَةٍ بُورِكَ فِي جَلَّابِهَا
سَقْيًا لَهَا وَلِلَّذِي غَدَا بِهَا

Cheetah Descriptions: Five *Urjūzah*s

~ 63 ~

Full of Spirit

Night was encamped, and the sun, still wrapped
in her jilbab, had not yet appeared in all her finery,
concealed in hijab and niqab like a modest girl.
Among men renowned for their generous deeds,
men of spotless ancestry from Hāshim's inner circle,
heroes who rain gifts on petitioners, who treasure
piety in their hearts, keep poverty from their comrades,
spreading prosperity as far as the Berber villages
and depriving the dry season of its drought,
I crossed the dark accompanied by a cheetah.
Blessed be her trapper! God cherish her
and her handler! Look at how she sits so tall
upon her mount, like a mighty forest lion,

رَاكِبَةً تَخْتَالُ فِي رِكَابِهَا
كَأَنَّهَا بَعْضُ لُيُوثِ غَابِهَا
تَرْنُو بِعَيْنٍ خِلْتُ مِنْ أَثْقَابِهَا
ضِرَامَ نَارٍ طَارَ مِنْ لُعَابِهَا
كَأَنَّمَا ٱلنُّمْرَةُ فِي ٱقْتِرَابِهَا
رَقْمُ دَيَابِيجَ عَلَى أَثْوَابِهَا
مُخْطَفَةُ ٱلْكَشْحَيْنِ فِي ٱضْطِرَابِهَا
كَأَنَّهَا ٱلْقَنَاةُ فِي ٱنْتِصَابِهَا
وَٱلْحَيَّةُ ٱلرَّقْطَاءُ فِي ٱنْسِيَابِهَا
وَسُرْعَةُ ٱلْعُقَابِ فِي ٱنْصِبَابِهَا
وَتَارَةً كَٱللَّيْثِ فِي وِثَابِهَا
مُعْفِيَةُ ٱلسَّائِسِ مِنْ عِتَابِهَا
نَزَّاهَةٌ لِنَفْسِهَا عَنْ عَابِهَا
فَأَبْصَرَتْ مِنْ حَيْثُ يَمَّمْنَا بِهَا
عُفْرَ ٱلظِّبَاءِ وَهْيَ فِي أَسْرَابِهَا
تَرْتَعُ فِي ٱلْمَرْتَعِ مِنْ جَنَابِهَا
تُوَاتِئُ ٱلْأَجْيَادَ مِنْ رِقَابِهَا
فَأَقْبَلَتْ تَمْرَحُ فِي جِذَابِهَا
حَتَّى إِذَا مَا كُتِّبَتْ رَمَى بِهَا
فَذَهَبَتْ تَنْسَلُّ فِي طِلَابِهَا
تَأْكُلُ وَجْهَ ٱلْأَرْضِ فِي ذَهَابِهَا
فِي ٱلصَّحْصَحَانَاتِ وَفِي أَطْرَابِهَا
فَلَوْ تَرَى ٱلْفَهْدَةَ فِي ٱلْتِهَابِهَا
وَشِدَّةِ ٱلْعُنْفِ إِذَا ٱغْلَوْلَى بِهَا

with eyes whose stare's so bright I think of sparks
shooting from a blazing fire. Up close,
her spots resemble figures embroidered
on silk cloth. With a ripple of back muscle
she prowls, then stands straight as a javelin,
like a speckled snake in her slinky sidewinding,
boasting an eagle's speed in flight, followed
by a lion's pounce. Shame is something
she can't stand, as her handler knows.
We sharpened her sight to spot herds
of dusty *ẓaby*s grazing in their fields, necks
slack with ease. She advanced, full of spirit,
tugging at her leash. The *ẓaby*s stood
in squadron formation. Sicced, she sprinted
into the chase, devouring the face of the earth
as she raced through the flatland and tender grass.
If only you'd seen her blistering speed,

فِي نَأْيِهَا عَنْهُنَّ وَٱقْتِرَابِهَا
تَكَادُ أَنْ تَخْرُجَ مِنْ إِهَابِهَا
فَجُلْنَ وَٱعْصَوْصَبْنَ فِي ٱعْصِيصَابِهَا
فَٱلْوَيْلُ مِنْهُنَّ لِمَنْ يَصْلَى بِهَا
إِذْ أَدْرَكَتْهُنَّ بِلَا إِتْعَابِهَا
فَأَقْبَلَتْ حَطْمًا عَلَى أَصْلَابِهَا
وَعَرَضَتْهُنَّ عَلَى عَذَابِهَا
بَيْنَ شَبَا مِخْلَبِهَا وَنَابِهَا
يَا حُسْنَ مِهْنَانَةَ فِي ٱخْتِضَابِهَا
مِنْ صَائِكِ ٱلْأَوْدَاجِ وَٱنْسِحَابِهَا
فَلَوْ تَرَاهَا وَهْيَ فِي ٱنْكِبَابِهَا
مِنْ نَهْشِهَا لِلَّحْمِ وَٱسْتِلَابِهَا
كُلٌّ يُفَدِّيهَا لَدَى أَرْبَابِهَا
تَفْدِيَةَ ٱلْعَرُوسِ فِي أَحْبَابِهَا
فِي مَدْحِهَا طَوْرًا وَفِي خِطَابِهَا
فَنَحْنُ فِي عَيْشٍ مِنَ ٱكْتِسَابِهَا
وَلَذَّةٍ وَنَعْمَةٍ نُعْنَى بِهَا
بَيْنَ قُدُورٍ جَمَّةٍ نُؤْتَى بِهَا
وَبَيْنَ خَامِيزٍ وَمِنْ كَبَابِهَا
مِنْ فَضْلِ مَا تُجْدِي عَلَى أَصْحَابِهَا

her pace in pursuit, her brutal assault
—as if she'd left her skin behind in her wake!
They stampeded, bewailing their comrades
trapped in the clutches of the cheetah.
With no sign of fatigue, she attacked,
crushing spines, slashing with claw
and fang. How magnificently Mihnānah
sauntered, dyed in thick heart spurts
of gore! If only you'd seen
how she crunched the flesh and tore off
the skin! In the presence of her owner,
she was feted in panegyrics and speeches
fit for a bride. Thanks to her labors,
we're spoiled, living the high life—
teeming pots of stew, chilled broth,
and kebabs laid out before us.
What a generous feast for her comrades!

~ ٦٤ ~

وقال ينعته [الرجز]

قَدْ أَغْتَدِي وَٱلصُّبْحُ مِثْلَ ٱلْمَحْضِ
أَبْيَضُ أَشْبَاهُ مُلَاءِ ٱلرَّحْضِ
بِصَارِمٍ ذِي شِرَّةٍ مِرَضِّ
لِلصَّيْدِ إِذْ لَاقَى بِوَلْقٍ مَضِّ
فَهُنَّ صَرْعَى بِجَنُوبِ ٱلْقَضِّ
بِمَيِّتٍ وَجَاثِمٍ لَمْ يَقْضِ

~ 64 ~

A Vicious Cheetah

Dawn as milky white
as a threadbare robe.
I crossed the dark
with a vicious cheetah
whose fierce swipe
crushes prey
on the battle ground—
the dead lay scattered
south of the Pebbles;
the rest gave up the ghost.

~ ٦٥ ~

وقال ينعته [الرجز]

قَدْ أَغْتَدِي وَٱللَّيْلُ فِي ٱسْوِدَادِهِ
مُعْتَكِرًا مِنْ طُولِ سَرْمِدَادِهِ
وَذُو ٱلنُّعَاسِ فِي كَرَى رُقَادِهِ
مُسْتَقْبِلًا نَوْمًا عَلَى وِسَادِهِ
يَسْتَقْصِرُ ٱللَّيْلَ عَلَى ٱمْتِدَادِهِ
غُدُوَّ مَنْ قَدْ لَجَّ فِي ٱرْتِيَادِهِ
ثُمَّ ٱغْتَدَى وَذَاكَ مِنْ رَشَادِهِ
بِصَحْبِهِ وَفَهْدِهِ وَزَادِهِ
مُشْتَبِكًا بِٱلصُّمِّ مِنْ جَلْمَادِهِ
وَقَبْلَ رِيِّ ٱلطَّرْفِ مِنْ رُقَادِهِ
بِشَاذِرٍ بِنَاظِرٍ وَقَّادِهِ
يَخَالُ ذُو ٱلْفِطْنَةِ فِي ٱجْتِهَادِهِ
مَا بَيْنَ رُسْغَيْهِ إِلَى أَعْضَادِهِ
مَا شَنَّجَ ٱلشَّانِجُ مِنْ أَمْسَادِهِ
يَلْطَأُ بِٱلدَّقْعَاءِ فِي ٱرْتِدَادِهِ
حَتَّى إِذَا آنَسَ مِنْ أَجْنَادِهِ
غَفْلَةَ سَاهٍ لَجَّ فِي مُرَادِهِ
يَعْبَثُ بِٱلرُّجَاجِ فِي أَجْلَادِهِ
كَأَنَّهُ إِذْ لَجَّ فِي كِيَادِهِ
مُحْتَسِبٌ لِلْأَجْرِ فِي جِهَادِهِ
يُحْضِرُ مَا صَادَ عَلَى فَهَّادِهِ

~ 65 ~

Like a Fond Father

While the drowsy sleeper welcomed
another dream to his pillow, deeming
the long night too short, I started out
across a darkness, confused by its sheer expanse.
Before there's enough light for the groggy eye
to see (it's the right way to proceed!),
the serious hunter[87] breaks camp with his cheetah,
his comrades, and camel loads of supplies.
With me I brought a bellicose beast
whose eyes blazed—to see him hunt,
the expert imagines that palm
fibers, puckered by a rope maker,
stretch from his wrist to his patella.
Zigging then zagging, he stalked
low to the barren ground. The herd
paid no heed—he rushed his target,
toyed with it, tossing its skin
to and fro, devoted to the ambush
like a holy man hoping to earn his reward

تَحَنُّنَ ٱلشَّيْخِ عَلَى أَوْلَادِهِ
فَلَيْسَ يَغْدُو مَعَهُ بِزَادِهِ
كَفَاهُ أَنْ يَنْصِبَّ فِي تَرْدَادِهِ
لِطَلَبِ ٱلْأَرْزَاقِ فِي ٱجْتِهَادِهِ
يُفَقِّئُ ٱلْأَعْيُنَ مِنْ حُسَّادِهِ

in Heaven. Like a fond father
fussing over his children, he yielded
his catch to his handler. On the hunt
the cheetah needs no supplies—he just longs
to be sicced. His hard work earns him
his keep, blinding the evil eye.

~ ٦٦ ~

وقال ينعته [الرجز]

قَدْ أَغْتَدِي وَٱللَّيْلُ فِي سَوَادِهِ
بِسَبْسَبٍ مُفْضٍ إِلَى وِهَادِهِ
تَرَى ٱلْوُحُوشَ فِي ذُرَى نِجَادِهِ
كَٱلْوَرَقِ ٱلْغَضِّ عَلَى أَعْوَادِهِ
وَافَيْتُهُ فَكُنْتُ مِنْ عُوَّادِهِ
إِذْ حَثْحَثَ ٱللَّيْلُ إِلَى وِسَادِهِ
فَأَظْهَرَ ٱلْفَجْرُ سَنَا ٱمْتِدَادِهِ
وَأَبْرَقَ ٱلْإِشْرَاقُ مِنْ عِمَادِهِ
كَمَشْرَفِيٍّ سُلَّ مِنْ غِمَادِهِ
فَأَقْبَلَ ٱلْوَحشُ عَلَى ٱتِّئَادِهِ
يَقْدُمُهُ ٱلظَّبْيُ إِلَى وِفَادِهِ
مُنْفَرِدًا يَدْنُو إِلَى وِرَادِهِ
فَكَانَ حَتْفُ ٱلنَّفْسِ فِي ٱنْفِرَادِهِ
لَمَّا رَآه ٱلْفَهْدُ فِي صِفَادِهِ
قَطَّعَ مَا وُكِّدَ مِنْ أَعْقَادِهِ
وَأُرْعِبَ ٱلْمُخِيفُ مِنْ إِرْعَادِهِ
وَخَافَ أَنْ يُبْدِيهِ مِنْ مَعَادِهِ
فَأَطْلَقَ ٱلْكَفَّيْنِ مِنْ كُدَّادِهِ
وَأَسْرَعَ ٱلنَّهْضَةَ فِي ٱشْتِدَادِهِ
كَٱلْبَرْقِ يَغْشَاكَ عَلَى بِعَادِهِ
أَوْ كَوْكَبٍ يَنْقَضُّ فِي ٱتِّقَادِهِ

~ 66 ~

Numbers Became Foreign

I crossed the black of night into the desert
gullies where—look!—the deer
stood out on the hilltops like new buds
on a branch. I had often visited the site.
I arrived as night made its way to bed,
dawn's brightness stretching out, and the sun
climbing bright like a Mashrafī blade drawn
from its sheath. Slowly they advanced,
led by a lone *ẓaby* to the water hole
in the uplands—but solitude tempts death.
The shackled cheetah spotted the deer
and tore his rope apart. A thunderclap—
the terrified buck bellowed the alarm.
The cheetah, fearing an attack on his return,
redoubled his efforts, shifting into high gear—
a lightning bolt out of the blue,
an exploding supernova, a wrecking ball

أَوْ فِهْرِ صَخْرٍ زَلَّ عَنْ أَوْتَادِهِ
فَكَانَ ذَا دُونَ مَدَى ٱجْتِهَادِهِ
فَٱخْتَرَمَ ٱلْحَبَّةَ مِنْ فُؤَادِهِ
بِسَاعِدٍ ضُبِّرَ فِي أَزْنَادِهِ
كَلَاعِبٍ بِٱلْجَوْزِ فِي نِقَادِهِ
ثُمَّ ٱنْثَنَى لِلْجَمْعِ بِٱحْتِيَادِهِ
كَمَاهِدٍ يَدْنُو إِلَى مِهَادِهِ
فَغَافَصَ ٱلْهَارِبَ مِنْ عَرَادِهِ
وَٱخْتَطَفَ ٱلْمُفْرَدَ فِي إِفْرَادِهِ
كَحَارِفٍ بِٱللَّيْلِ مِنْ حِرَادِهِ
فَأَغْرَبَ ٱلْإِحْصَاءَ مِنْ عِدَادِهِ
وَأَنْوَرَ ٱلْأَلْسُنَ فِي إِحْمَادِهِ
مُجَلَّلًا بِٱلضِّعْفِ مِنْ أَبْرَادِهِ
كَأَنَّهُ قَيْصَرُ فِي أَجْنَادِهِ
يَحْدُو بِهِ لِلطَّرَبِ ٱلْمُعْتَادِهِ
مُغَرِّدٌ تَخَالُ فِي تَغْرَادِهِ
أَصْوَاتَ زِيرِ ٱلْعُودِ مِنْ عَوَّادِهِ
مُكَرَّمُ ٱلنِّسْبَةِ فِي أَجْدَادِهِ
مُوَفَّقٌ لِلرُّشْدِ مِنْ سَدَادِهِ

swung loose.[88] Still going full tilt,
he ripped out the bull's heart
with a swipe of his hard-boned arm,
as if toying with a walnut before cracking its shell.
To corral them, he doubled back, avoiding them,
stretched down low as if unfurling a rug,
ambushing runners in flight, snatching any solitary deer,
like a lone artisan laboring through the night.
Numbers became foreign, lost their meaning.
Exhausted by the hunt, wrapped in his cloak
like Caesar among his troops, he was praised
in a procession led by a singer who sang
his shrill tune to the lute's top string.
Flawless in his decisions, the scion of noble
ancestors, this cheetah's success comes from God.

~ ٦٧ ~

وقال ينعته [الرجز]

لَمَّا طَوَى ٱللَّيْلُ حَوَاشِي بُرْدِهِ
عَنْ وَاضِحِ ٱللَّوْنِ نَقِيٍّ وَرْدِهِ
نَادَيْتُ فَهَّادِي بِرَدِّ فَهْدِهِ
نِدَاءَ مَنْ جَادَ لَهُ بِوُدِّهِ
فَجَاءَ يُزْجِيهِ عَلَى سَمَنْدِهِ
أَصْفَرَ أَحْوَى بَيْنَ بَزِّ زَرْدِهِ
وَاخِدَ قَدٍّ فِي ٱكْمِلَالِ قَدِّهِ
قُلْتُ ٱرْتَدِفْهُ فَٱنْثَنَى لِزَنْدِهِ
تَكَفِّيَ ٱلطِّفْلِ لِدَعْوَى حَدِّهِ
مَا كَانَ إِلَّا نَظْرَةٌ مِنْ بَعْدِهِ
وَنَظْرَةٌ أُخْرَى بِأَدْنَى جُهْدِهِ
حَتَّى أَرَانَا ٱلْعِينَ دُونَ وِرْدِهِ
مُطَّرِدًا يَعْدُو بِشَفْرَيْ عِدِّهِ
فَٱنْصَاعَ مُرْقَدًّا عَلَى مُرْقَدِّهِ
كَأَنَّهُ حِينَ ٱنْبَرَى فِي شَدِّهِ
وَٱمْتَدَّ لِلنَّاظِرِ فِي مُرْتَدِّهِ
كَوْكَبُ عِفْرِيتٍ هَوَى لِعَدِّهِ
كَمَا ٱنْطَوَى ٱلْعَاقِدُ مِنْ ذِي عَقْدِهِ
خَمْسِينَ عَقْدًا بِيَدَيْ مُعْتَدِّهِ
حَتَّى ٱحْتَوَى ٱلْعَيْرَ وَلَمَّا يُرْدِهِ
فَنَحْنُ أَضْيَافُ حُسَامَيْ غِمْدِهِ
فِيمَا ٱشْتَهَيْنَا مِنْ ذَوَاتِ طَرْدِهِ

~ 67 ~

An Infant's Angry Howl

Night lifted its cloak, red gleamed bright.
I called out for the cheetah master.
My cheetah, his perfect physique wrapped
in his protective cloak, arrived on an isabelline steed.
"Let him ride behind me," I said. He recoiled,
displaying his rage with an infant's angry howl.
Sweeping the far horizon, he spotted
black-eyed oryx in a line on the pool's lip,
well within his range this side of the water hole.
In leaps and bounds, he was off like a shot
and his prey burst into flight. Pared back,
at full stretch, in high gear, he darted here
and there in front of us like a star
fired at an ifrit, swooping into his run
like a man making the finger sign
for the number fifty[89]—until the buck
was on the verge of death.[90] We ate our fill
of meat, the spoils of his sawtooth hunt.

نعت البازي وهو عشر أرجوزات

~ ٦٨ ~

قال ينعته [الرجز]

قَدْ أَغْتَدِي وَٱللَّيْلُ قَدْ حَدَا بِهِ
لِسَانُ نُورٍ سُلَّ مِنْ قِرَابِهِ
كَٱلْحَبَشِيِّ ٱفْتَرَّ عَنْ أَنْيَابِهِ
سُوقُ ٱلنَّدَى وَٱلْمَجْدِ عِنْدَ بَابِهِ
إِذَا يُبَاعُ شَرَفٌ أَغْلَى بِهِ
بِتَوَّجِيِّ ٱلْجِنْسِ فِي ٱنْتِسَابِهِ
لَا يَطْمَعُ ٱلْعَائِبُ فِي مَعَابِهِ
بِحُضْرَةٍ مِنْهُ وَلَا ٱغْتِيَابِهِ
كَأَنَّ جَادِيًّا عَلَى ٱقْتِرَابِهِ
بِمَنْهَلٍ مُلْتَحِفٍ بِغَابِهِ
ٱلْبُلْقُ وَٱلْخُضْرُ مَعًا تَرْعَى بِهِ
قَدِ ٱكْتَسَيْنَ ٱلْأَمْنَ فِي جَنَابِهِ
حَتَّى إِذَا أَمْكَنَهُ دَحَا بِهِ
فَٱنْسَابَ يُلْقِي ٱلرِّيشَ فِي ٱنْسِيَابِهِ
تَخَالُهُ ٱلْخَطَّافَ فِي ذَهَابِهِ
حَتَّى إِذَا مَا قُلْتَ قَدْ حَاذَى بِهِ

Goshawk Descriptions: Ten *Urjūzah*s

~ 68 ~

A Swift in Flight

Night was chased by a tongue of light,
a flash of white teeth in a negus's smile,
whose court is a bazaar of gifts and glory
where honor fetches a high price.
I crossed the dark with a Tawwajī gos
on the glove, beyond reproach
whether or not seen in action.
As she approached, saffron light washed
a water hole thick with bushes where birds,
dark and piebald, fed in the safety
of the pond. They were within her reach,
an outpouring of speed, a rush of feathers—
picture a swift in flight. "She's there!"

دَوَّمَ أَعْلَى ٱلرَّأْسِ لِٱنْقِلَابِهِ
نَفَّرَهُ ٱلسَّائِسُ لِٱقْتِرَابِهِ
فَٱنْصَبَّ مُشْتَاقًا إِلَى ٱكْتِسَابِهِ
يَسْبِقُ شَأْوَ ٱلرِّيحِ فِي ٱنْصِبَابِهِ
فَعَفَّرَ ٱلْأَخْضَرَ فِي أَسْرَابِهِ
بِشَثْنَةٍ تَغْرَقُ فِي إِهَابِهِ
فَرَجَّعَ ٱلطَّيْرَ عَلَى أَعْقَابِهِ
مِنْ هَوْلِ مَا عَايَنَ مِنْ إِلْهَابِهِ
فَرَدَّهُ ٱلذُّكَاءُ مِنْ شِهَابِهِ
مُنْخَرِقًا يَخْرُجُ مِنْ جِلْبَابِهِ
حَتَّى إِذَا مَا صَادَ فِي حِسَابِهِ
عَشْرًا وَعَشْرًا كُلُّهَا وَالَى بِهِ
مَالَ إِلَى ٱلْبُسْتَانِ فِي أَصْحَابِهِ
فَظَلَّ فِي ٱلنِّعْمَةِ مِنْ إِيَابِهِ
بَيْنَ نَشِيلِ ٱلطَّيْرِ أَوْ كَبَابِهِ
يَكْسُو لُحُومَ ٱلطَّيْرِ مِنْ شَرَابِهِ
أَعْتَقَ مَا يُدْخَرُ مِنْ أَعْنَابِهِ
تَمَّتْ لَنَا ٱلنِّعْمَةُ مِنْ أَطْرَابِهِ

you shout. She rings overhead, then turns back.
Panicked by her attack, the leader flees.
Lusting for victory, swooping faster
than the wind, she fells the dark bird
amid his flock, a lion's lethal claw sunk
in his flesh, then rounds up the birds
terrified at the sight of this fireball,
as the sun blazed through a torn jilbab.
At the count, a full twenty were killed
in her attack. Her owner went to the garden
where his blissful comrades fed on the spoils
of her lavish hunt—boiled fowl and kebabs,
doused with wine from ancient vines.[91]

~ ٦٩ ~

وقال ينعته [الرجز]

قَدْ أَغْتَدِي وَٱللَّيْلُ كَٱلْمِدَادِ
وَٱلصُّبْحُ يَنْفِيهِ عَنِ ٱلْبِلَادِ
طَرْدَ ٱلْمَشِيبِ حَالِكَ ٱلسَّوَادِ
غُدُوَّ بَاغِي قَنَصٍ مُعْتَادِ
فِي فِتْيَةٍ مِنْ مَعْشَرٍ أَنْجَادِ
هُمْ غِيَاثُ ٱلسَّنَةِ ٱلْجَمَادِ
إِذْ ضَنَّ ذُو ٱلْإِرْفَادِ بِٱلْإِرْفَادِ
وَٱنْحَجَرَ ٱلْحَاضِرُ بَعْدَ ٱلْبَادِي
وَقَدْ حَدَا بِٱلْمُعْضِلَاتِ حَادِي
حَتَّى يُحِلُّوا لَزْبَةَ ٱلشِّدَادِ
بِٱلْخَيْلِ وَٱلْكِلَابِ وَٱلْفِهَادِ
وَتَوَّجِيٍّ طَيِّعِ ٱلْقِيَادِ
جَلَّ عَنِ ٱلصِّفَاتِ وَٱلْأَنْدَادِ
مُقَابَلِ ٱلْخَالَاتِ وَٱلْأَجْدَادِ
ذِي حَجَنَاتٍ صِدْقَةٍ شِدَادِ

~ 69 ~

We Unleashed Destruction

I crossed the inky night, its darkness dispatched
by the sun like black hairs routed by the gray
—early, as is the hunter's wont, amid a group
of brave Najdī comrades,[92] like welcome rain clouds
in times of drought when the generous
turn stingy and friends hide out at home[93]
and calamities, like camels, come in droves.

We stopped and unleashed destruction—
horses, dogs, cheetahs, and a Tawwajī gos,
easy on the jess. An incomparable bird,
peerless, a true pedigree,[94] wielding
grappling hooks, battle-hardened, true.

~ ٧٠ ~

وقال ينعته [الرجز]

قَدْ أَغْتَدِي وَٱللَّيْلُ ذُو لَوْنَيْنِ
بِأَصْلَتِيٍّ غَـائِـرِ ٱلْعَيْنَيْنِ
كَأَنَّمَا يَنْظُـرُ مِنْ قَلْتَيْنِ
وَقَانِصٍ أَخْفَى مِنَ ٱلْجَدَّيْنِ
يَقِيهِ بِٱلْكُمِّ مِنَ ٱلْبَرْدَيْنِ
فَصَادَنَا قَبْلَ ٱلْوَنَى وَٱلْأَيْنِ
وَقَبْلَ أَنْ يَرْتَدَّ طَرْفُ ٱلْعَيْنِ
تِسْعِينَ تَدْرُوجاً وَبَطَّتَيْنِ
مِنْ قَبْلِ أَنْ تُبَيِّنَ ٱلْخَيْطَيْنِ

~ 70 ~

A Fencing Master

I crossed the two-toned night with a gos
on the glove, a fencing master,
her sunken eyes like two rock pools,
beside a huntsman of unknown lineage
who protects her in his sleeve from the cold
night and day. Before the onset of fatigue,
before we could see clearly,
before she could untangle the threads
of dawn and dusk,[95] she killed
two ducks and ninety coursers.

~ ٧١ ~

وقال ينعته [الرجز]

كَمْ غُدْوَةٍ هِجْتُ مِنَ ٱلرُّقَادِ
تَحْمِلُ يُسْرَايَ طَوِيلَ ٱلْهَادِي
مُدَوَّرَ ٱلْهَامَةِ فِي ٱشْتِدَادِ
أَسْوَدَ رِيشِ ٱلظَّهْرِ وَٱلْأَوْتَادِ
زَيَّنَ خَدَّيْهِ إِلَى ٱلْأَلْغَادِ
خَطَّانِ بَرَّاقَانِ مِنْ سَوَادِ
مُدَوِّمًا فِي ٱلْجَوِّ ذَا إِصْعَادِ
وَعَيْنُهُ خَوْصَاءُ لِٱرْتِيَادِ
فَلَيْسَ يُنْجِي مِنْهُ طَيْرَ ٱلْوَادِي
تَضَعْضُعٌ مِنْهُ وَلَا تَنَادِي
دُونَ جِلَادٍ أَيَّمَا جِلَادِ
بِسَبِطَاتٍ لَيْسَ بِٱلْجِعَادِ
تَقْتَلِعُ ٱلْأَحْشَاءَ بِٱلْأَكْبَادِ
إِذَا ٱنْتَحَى لِطَائِرٍ غَرَّادِ
عَنْهُ إِذَا لَاقَاهُ ذَا ٱنْحِيَادِ
بَطَّنَهُ بِسُحُمٍ حِدَادِ
إِذَا تَفَلَّى رَجْعَةَ ٱلْمَرَادِ
تَرَى عَلَى مَنْكِبِهِ ٱلْمَيَّادِ
بِظَاهِرِ ٱلزَّوْرِ إِلَى ٱلْفُؤَادِ
خَطَّ دَمٍ كَهَيْئَةِ ٱلنِّجَادِ

~ 71 ~

A Streak of Blood

It was early morning. Gone was sleep.
Perched on my left hand, Long Neck,
with her dark sails and wing bolts
and two bright black streaks
from throat to cheek,[96] moved her head
intently. She towered, then circled:
her sunken eyes had spotted quarry.
The wadi's birds could not escape
with kowtows or shrieks. Only combat
counted—and what combat! Her repeated
hair-thin pounces scooped out livers and guts.
She aimed for a blissful warbler:
it was smashed by a blacksmith's hammer.
Back she flew, a rebel jinni.[97] Look—
on her proud shoulder, from keel to heart,
lies a sword strap, a streak of blood.

~ ٧٢ ~

وقال ينعته [الرجز]

أَعْدَدْتُ لِلصَّيْدِ بَعِيدَ ٱلْمُسْتَهَمْ
مُجْتَمِعَ ٱلْخَلْقِ لَهُ لَحْمٌ زِيَمْ
مَا مِثْلُهُ فِي عَرَبٍ وَلَا عَجَمْ
لَهُ جَنَاحَانِ وَرَأْسٌ كَٱلرَّجَمْ
إِذَا تَتَلَّتْهُ ٱلْبُزَاةُ وَٱعْتَزَمْ
زَادَ عَلَيْهَا بِٱلْجَمَالِ وَٱلْكَرَمْ
فَهُوَ مِنَ ٱلْعُجْبِ بَعِيدُ ٱلْمُخْتَطِمْ
يَصِيدُنَا وَهُوَ نَشِيطٌ مَا سَئِمْ
ثَمَانِيًا وَأَرْبَعًا وَمَا عَتَمْ

~ 72 ~

A Tombstone Head

I readied for the hunt a single-minded gos
without peer among Arabs and non-Arabs.
She has well-wrought, muscled flesh,
strong wings, and a tombstone head.
Other hawks try to pester her with strife,
but she indulges them, her proud beak
raised high, surpassing them in decorum
and pride. Running on full, off the block,
no sign of fatigue, she killed eight, then four!

~ ٧٣ ~

وقال ينعته [الرجز]

أَحْسَنُ مِنْ ذِكْرِ ٱلشَّجَا مِنَ ٱلشَّجِي
وَطَلَلٍ كَٱلْأَتْحَمِيِّ ٱلْمُنْهَجِ
غُدُوُّ خِرْقٍ أَحْوَذِيٍّ مُدْلِجِ
قَبْلَ ٱبْتِسَامٍ مِنْ صَبَاحٍ أَبْلَجِ
يَصِيدُ أَحْوَى ٱللَّوْنِ دُونَ ٱلدَّيْزَجِ
أَقْمَرَ بُطْنَانَ ٱلْجَنَاحِ أَخْرَجِ
وَسُهْرَدَازِ ٱللَّوْنِ أَوْ سَبَهْرَجِ
مُطَرَّقِ ٱلرِّيشِ عَلَى تَدَرُّجِ
كَحُبُكٍ مِنْ زِبْرِجٍ مُزَبْرَجِ
مُقَابَلٍ فِي نَسَبٍ مِنْ تَوَّجِ
تَمَّتْ لَهُ بَرَاثِنٌ كَٱلْعَوْسَجِ
عَلَى جَذَامِيرَ لَهُ لَمْ تَفْحَجِ
عَنْ سَبْطَةٍ لِلْكَفِّ لَمْ تُشَنَّجِ
مُنْتَصِبِ ٱلْهَادِي بِخَلْقٍ مُدْمَجِ
وَنَظَرٍ يَقْذِفُ بِٱلتَّوَهُّجِ
كَشَرَرٍ مِنْ قَبَسِ ٱلْمُؤَجَّجِ
كَأَنَّمَا يَلْمَحُ عَنْ فِيرُوزَجِ
أَكْلَفَ مِنْ مَنْسِرِهِ ٱلْمُحَمْلَجِ
حَلِيمِ حَمْلٍ فِي ٱلطِّرَادِ أَهْوَجِ
تَرَى لَهُ ظَهْرًا كَظَهْرِ ٱلْمِحْلَجِ
وَهَامَةً مَلْمُومَةً لَمْ تُخْلَجِ
عَلَى صَلًا مِثْلِ ٱلرِّتَاجِ ٱلْمُتَّجِ

~ 73 ~

An Arsonist's Fuse

Don't complain about being choked with tears
at the sight of some dumb campsite
like an old *atḥamī* robe! Far better to cross
the dark, before the smile of early light,
with a swift, sharp-witted comrade,
hunting brown, almost ash-colored, larks,
their underwing coverts dusty white,
with a *suhradāz,* or rather a *sabahraj* gos,
her sleek feathers tightly packed in layers,
clad in a finely woven gem-worked gown.
She's from Tawwaj, with truly noble pedigrees,
and sports full-grown boxthorn-needle
pounces on tight-bunched stumps with long toes
that give no release, a splendid neck poised
above her welded physique, and blazing eyes
spitting sparks like an arsonist's fuse,
a glance bright as turquoise, above the tawny bellows
of her beak. She's bold yet patient in attack.
Look—her back resembles a carder's tabletop.
Her solid crown fixes on prey and her spine
is as studded as a strong door. On the trainer's

كَأَنَّهُ عَلَى يَدِ ٱلْمُهَجْهِجِ
فُوَيْقَ قَفَّازٍ لَهُ مُدَمَّجِ
طَالِبُ ثَأْرٍ غَيْرُ ذِي تَحَرُّجِ
كَأَنَّهُ مُطَوَّقٌ بِدُمْلُجِ
بَعَثْتُهُ قَبْلَ ٱلصَّبَاحِ ٱلْأَدْعَجِ
وَقَبْلَ أَصْوَاتِ ٱلدَّجَاجِ ٱلدُّجَّجِ
بِكُلِّ مُعْتَادِ ٱلْقَنِيصِ مُمْعَجِ
بِمَكْرُمَاتٍ جَدُّهُ مُتَوَّجِ
فَكَمْ أَفَاءَ كَدُّهُ مِنْ تَدْرُجِ
وَمِنْ إِوَزٍّ نَافِرٍ وَحُبْرُجِ
مَرَّ عَلَى إِجِّرِيَا لَمْ يُعَرِّجِ
وَشَاحِجٍ وَوَدَّ أَنْ لَمْ يَشْحَجِ
مُخَرَّقٍ أَمْعَاءُهُ مُضَرَّجِ
فَرَاحَ فِي ٱلْمِخْلَاةِ لَمْ يُنَجْنِجِ
إِلَّا بِصَكٍّ ضَرِمٍ مُسْتَدْرَجِ
إِلَى بَنِي لَهْوٍ كَرِيمِ ٱلْمُدْلِجِ
عَلَى نِتَاجٍ لِلْمَنَى لَمْ يُنْتَجِ
فَكَمْ تَرَى مِنْ مُشْتَوٍ مُلَهْوَجِ
وَمُنْضِجٍ مِنْهُمْ وَغَيْرِ مُنْضِجِ
يَنْشُلُهُ عَلَى أَبِي ٱلْمُفَرَّجِ
عَلَى مُدَامٍ كَسِرَاجِ ٱلْمُسْرِجِ
مُدَامِ خَلٍّ طَيِّبٍ مُطَبْهَجِ
فِي ٱلشَّمْسِ فَرَّاجُ لِأَمْرٍ مُرْهِجِ
يُقِيمُ دَرْءَ ٱلْمَائِدِ ٱلْمُعَوَّجِ
أَسْمِجْ بِمَنْ عَابَ ٱلْمُدَامَ أَسْمِجِ

gloved hand, she seems to rage, on fire
with vengeance, her neck as if armlet clad.
Before the gray dawn, before the hens began
to scrabble, I flew her at swift quarry,
her fortune crowned with victories. Her triumphs
included coursers, houbaras, and swift geese—
for her custom is to fly straight, not to swerve.
The crows soon repented of their caws.
Guts were scooped, blood was spilled.
In swift and decisive thwacks, her prey
was taken unawares,[98] one by one. She returned
to the feed pouch, to the night's noble hosts,
sons of pleasure enjoying all the unborn flights
of this brood of birds.[99] Many roasted the meat
then scoffed it down, others waited
for portions more fully done, some filched bits
from the pot, feeding their fellow feasters,[100]
gaily drinking a fine vintage, lamplight-bright,
a sharp, sweet-scented, tangy pickle of a wine.
At the break of day, a fine young youth
brought great relief to one of the drinkers
by bending him over and slipping it in.[101]
How despicable are the enemies of wine!

~ ٧٤ ~

وقال ينعته [الرجز]

آلَفُ مَا صِدْتُ مِنَ ٱلْقَنِيصِ
بِكُلِّ بَازٍ وَاسِعِ ٱلْقَمِيصِ
ذِي بُرْنُسٍ مُذَهَّبٍ رَصِيصِ
وَهَامَةٍ وَمَنْسِرٍ حَصِيصِ
وَجُؤْجُؤٍ عُولِيَ بِٱلتَّدْلِيصِ
مُدَبَّجٍ مُعَيَّنِ ٱلْفُصُوصِ
عَلَى ٱلْكَرَاكِي نَهِمٍ حَرِيصِ
آنَسَ عِشْرِينَ بِذَاتِ ٱلْعِيصِ
فَٱنْسَلَّ مِنْ شِكَارِهِ ٱلْمَحُوصِ
وَٱنْقَضَّ يَهْوِي وَهْوَ كَٱلْوَبِيصِ
دَانَى جَنَاحَيْهِ عَلَى نَصِيصِ
فَأعْتَامَ مِنْهَا كُلَّ ذِي خَمِيصِ
فَقَدَّهُ بِمِخْلَبٍ قَنُوصِ
فَكَمْ ذَبَحْنَا ثَمَّ مِنْ مَوْقُوصِ
وَكَمْ لَنَا فِي ٱلْبَيْتِ مِنْ مَقْصُوصِ
مُعَدَّةٍ لِلشَّيِّ وَٱلْمَصُوصِ

~ 74 ~

At a Scorching Pace

My favorite food is the game I've hunted
with my keen, broad-mail-shirted gos
clad in a well-made gold-stitched hood,
with her crown and hairless beak, a keel
sheathed in glinting chain mail like brocade
set with gold nuggets. She's trained
to kill cranes. At Wood Pond twenty
were sighted. She slipped from the sewn
leash, swooping like a lightning bolt, wings
close to the ground at a scorching pace,
choosing the lean-bellies—cranes sliced
by a hunter's talons, necks snapped,
butchered for kebabs and pickled meat.

~ ٧٥ ~

وقال ينعته [الرجز]

يَا رُبَّ بَازٍ فَازَ بِٱلْمَنَاقِبِ
مُعَافِرٍ مُنَاجِزٍ مُحَارِبِ
فَوْقَ ٱلشِّمَالِ كَٱلْأَمِيرِ ٱلرَّاكِبِ
يَبِينُ فِيهِ كَرَمُ ٱلْمَنَاسِبِ
لِلنَّاظِرِ ٱلْعَالِمِ بِٱلْمَعَايِبِ
عَيْنَانِ كَٱلتِّبْرِ ٱلْمُصَفَّى ٱلذَّائِبِ
كَأَنَّمَا فِي ٱلزَّوْرِ وَٱلتَّرَائِبِ
مِنْهُ وَتَحْتَ مُنْحَنَى ٱلْمَنَاكِبِ
تَعْلِيقُ رَاآنٍ بِكَفِّ كَاتِبِ
يَحُثُّ عِنْدَ رَغْبَةِ ٱلْمُطَالِبِ
قَوَادِمًا تَحْكِي مَدَارِي كَاعِبِ
رُحْنَا بِهِ غِبَّ سَمَاءٍ صَائِبِ
وَٱلطَّيْرُ لَمْ يَنْهَضْنَ لِلْمَكَاسِبِ
مِنْ لَثَقِ ٱلْأَنْدَاءِ وَٱلْهَوَاضِبِ
إِذْ عَنَّ سِرْبُ خَصِبَ ٱلْمَسَارِبِ
حَبَارِجٌ يَرْتَعْنَ فِي ٱلسَّبَاسِبِ
مِثْلَ ٱلنَّعَامِ ٱلْجُفَّلِ ٱلْخَوَاضِبِ
فَشَدَّ مِثْلَ ٱلثَّائِرِ ٱلْمُحَارِبِ
مُبَاغِتًا لِلطَّيْرِ ذَا تَجَارِبِ
مُشَرِّدًا فِي ٱلْبِيدِ لِلْهَوَارِبِ
فَخَيَّطَ ٱلْحُبْرُجَ بِٱلْمَخَالِبِ

~ 75 ~

The Cavalry Charge

A gos with all the fighting skills: hand-to-hand
combat, the cavalry charge, the assegai thrust.
Like an emir mounted on his steed, she's carried
on the left hand, her eyes like molten gold,
with two *rā*'s drawn by a scribe on her mail,
gorge, and the curve of her wrist. Put to the task,
she beat her wings like combs in a girl's hair.
We brought her back. No birds were flushed—
the ground was wet from the heavy rains.
Then a flock was sighted in lush fields—
houbara cocks feeding on the open plain,
big and speedy like ostriches reddened by rut.
What a veteran! In a burst, she caught them off guard,
an avenging fury scattering them in flight

حَتَّى تَوَارَتْ غَيْرَ قِيلِ ٱلْكَاذِبِ
فِي صَحْفَةِ ٱلزَّوْرِ إِلَى ٱلرَّوَاجِبِ
بُورِكَ مِنْ مُرَافِقٍ مُصَاحِبِ

across the desert, her pounces stitching holes
in one big male, sunk toe-deep in his breast!

What a blessed comrade in arms, how true to her aim! 24

~ ٧٦ ~

وقال ينعته [الرجز]

وَمَنْهَلٍ نَاءٍ عَنِ ٱلْمَرَاصِدِ
وَرَدْتُهُ قَبْلَ ٱلْحَمَامِ ٱلْوَارِدِ
وَقَبْلَ أَنْ تَطْرِفُ عَيْنُ ٱلرَّاقِدِ
بِضَارِيَيْنِ ٱسْتُمِيَا لِلصَّائِدِ
قَدْ عُوِّدَا صَيْدَ قَطَا ٱلْمَوَارِدِ
وَٱلْبَطَّ وَٱلنُّجَّامَ فِي ٱلصَّيَاخِدِ
لَيْثَانِ عِنْدَ ٱلْقَنْصِ وَٱلتَّجَالُدِ
إِذَا ٱسْتَحَاطَا بِغَدِيرٍ حَاشِدِ
وَٱعْتَقَبَا مِنْ هَابِطٍ وَصَاعِدِ
قُلْتَ وَقَدْ مَالَا عَلَى ٱلرَّوَاكِدِ
دَلْوَانِ جَالَا فِي رِشَاءٍ وَاحِدِ
رَافِدُ بَازِيَّيْنِ أَيُّ رَافِدِ
قَدْ أَمِنَا ٱلْإِقْتَارَ فِي ٱلشَّدَائِدِ
زَيْنَانِ لِلْمَوْلَى وَلِلسَّوَاعِدِ
حِرْصُهُمَا لِلصَّيْدِ حِرْصُ ٱلْوَالِدِ
عَلَى بَنِيهِ عِنْدَ كَسْبٍ جَاهِدِ
أُبْتُ وَفِي كَفِّي مِنَ ٱلْفَوَائِدِ
صَيْدُهُمَا مِنْ طَارِفٍ وَتَالِدِ
فَٱلْحَمْدُ لِلّٰهِ ٱلْعَزِيزِ ٱلْوَاحِدِ

~ 76 ~

Lion's Pounce

I visited a water hole far from the watchtowers
before the pigeons arrived,[102] before the insomniac
rubbed his eyes, with two carefully chosen
hawks, both skilled in lion's pounce and maul,
seasoned hunters of ducks and sandgrouse
at pools, or geese basking in the sun's rays.
Circling a crowded pond, they climbed
then swooped by turns, diving at their drowsy
quarry. "They're two buckets tied to one well
rope!" you shout.[103] What a gift they are
when food proves scarce; no need for their owner
to rely solely on camel milk.[104] They care
for the hunt as a father cares for his sons
with the sweat of his brow. I came home,
my hands full of all the precious morsels
they'd hunted.[105] Praise the One True God!

~ ٧٧ ~

وقال ينعته [الرجز]

كَمْ غُدْوَةٍ صِدْتُ عَلَى نَشَاطِ
بِتَوَّجِيٍّ مُعْفِقِ ٱلْأَشْـــرَاطِ
يَلْمَـحُ فَوْقَ أَثَـرِ ٱلْخَيَّـاطِ
بِـمُقْـلَةٍ قَلِيـلَةِ ٱلسِّقَـاطِ
آنَسَ سِـرْبًا مِنْ قَطًـا فُـرَّاطِ
بِٱلْمَـرْبَإِ ٱلْمُوفِي عَلَى ٱلْأَغْوَاطِ
بَيْنَ ٱلْقُبَـيْبَاتِ وَذِي أَرَاطِي
بِـهِ ٱلْقَطَـا وَأُبَّـدُ ٱلْغَطَـاطِ
فَوْضَى وَكُلُّ خَرِبٍ مُشْتَـاطِ
أَعْـرَفُ ذِي بَـرَاثِنٍ سِبَـاطِ
حَـتَّى إِذَا أَصْبَـحَ بِٱلْغَطَـاطِ
قَبْـلَ وُكُورٍ أَوَّلِ ٱلْفُـرَّاطِ
آنَسَ سِـرْبًا زَهِـمَ ٱلْآبَـاطِ
فَٱنْقَضَّ سَامِي ٱلطَّرْفِ فِي ٱخْتِلَاطِ
يَرْكُضُ مِنْ حِرْصٍ عَلَى ٱلْخِلَاطِ
فَظَـلَّ يَفْـرِسْـنَ بِٱلْبَلَاطِ
ثَقْفًـا إِذَا سَاوَرَ ذَا ٱعْتِبَـاطِ
يَـرْأَسُ فَوْقَ مَوْضِعِ ٱلْعِـلَاطِ
ضَـرْبَ ٱلْأَمِـيرِ أَعْيُنَ ٱلْأَنْبَـاطِ
بَيْنَ خُفَـافَـيْنِ وَذِي سِمَـاطِ

~ 77 ~

A Deft Butcher

Early, energetic hunts with a Tawwajī
gos rounding up all the feeble birds.
Above her tailored coat, a keen eye
that never errs burns bright.
From the rise above the meadows
between Qubaybāt and Arṭāh Wood,
she spots the scouts of a flock
of sandgrouse next to the twitchy pin-tails
scattered here and there, and the skittish
crested houbara, blindingly quick.
With her hair-thin pounces, she raids
the pin-tails before even the scouts
are awake, spotting a plump-thighed
flock and swooping, head high
in the confusion, tucking in her wings
to move among them, and, like a deft
butcher, slicing and dicing them
on the ground, smiting their necks crosswise
as the emir smote the Nabataean nobles
between Khufāfān and Dhū Simāṭ.[106]

نعت الزرّق وهو ثلاث أرجوزات

~ ٧٨ ~

قال ينعته [الرجز]

قَدْ أَغْتَدِي وَٱللَّيْلُ فِي ظُلْمَتِـهِ
كَطُـرَّةِ ٱلْبُـرْدِ فِي عَطْفَتِـهِ
بِـزُرَّقٍ نَاهِيـكَ فِي سُـرْعَتِـهِ
مَوْشِيَّـةٍ ضَـاحِيَتَـا دَفَّتِـهِ
كَأَنَّمَـا يَنْظُـرُ مِنْ مُقْـلَتِـهِ
مِنْ جَمْـرَةٍ شُبَّتْ لَدَى نَظْرَتِـهِ
يَـرْقُـدُ إِثْـرَ ٱلطَّيْرِ فِي كَرَّتِـهِ
كَٱلْكَوْكَبِ ٱلْمُنْقَضِّ فِي رَجْمَتِـهِ
فَصَـادَنَا وَهُوَ عَلَى حِـدَّتِـهِ
خَمْسِـينَ مُحْصَـاةً لَدَى دَفْعَتِـهِ
لَمْ يَنْقُصِ ٱلْإِلْهَابُ مِنْ مَيْعَتِـهِ
شَيْئًـا وَلَا ٱلْأَنْدَابُ مِنْ شِرَّتِـهِ
تَعْنُو لَهُ ٱلطَّـيْرُ لَدَى لَحْظَتِـهِ
رُحْنَا بِهِ وَٱلصَّيْـدُ مِنْ هَيْئَتِـهِ
لَمْ تَنْقُصِ ٱلْفَتْرَةُ مِنْ شَهْوَتِـهِ
مِنْ نَهَـمِ ٱلْحِـرْصِ وَلَا لَذَّتِـهِ

Tiercel Goshawk Descriptions: Three *Urjūzah*s

~ 78 ~

Built for the Kill

As the night lay curled in darkness
like the fringe of a *burd*, I made my way
with the swiftest of tiercels,
his sails patterned, his eyes
blazing like burning coals. His attack
on prey is as quick as a comet unleashed
on a jinni. Keeping his edge, he killed
fifty, tallying another at every strike.
Like a forest fire his pace blazed.
His malice couldn't be appeased
by the wounds he inflicted—the birds
cowered and submitted at the mere sight of him.
We brought him home. Built for the kill,
his desire, his greed, his elation
were unaffected by the battle's end.

~ ٧٩ ~

وقال ينعته [الرجز]

قَدْ أَغْتَدِي وَٱللَّيْلُ فِي ذِي قَارِهِ
بِزُرَّقٍ إِقْلَاقِ بَازِيَارِهِ
اِخْتَارَهُ ٱلْقَانِصُ مِنْ أَطْيَارِهِ
يَنْقَضُّ فِي ٱلْجَوِّ عَلَى ذِمَارِهِ
وَيَخْطِفُ ٱلْبُنَيَّ مِنْ قَرَارِهِ
أَدَّبَهُ ٱلْقَيْنُ بِحَرِّ نَارِهِ

~ 79 ~

Destroyer of Nests

Night was covered in pitch.
I crossed the dark
with a tiercel on the glove,
his handler's darling,
singled out by the hunter
from all his other birds.
As if wrought by a smith
in the fires of his furnace,
he swoops on his dominions—
destroyer of nests.

~ ٨٠ ~

وقال ينعته [الرجز]

قَدْ أَغْتَدِي بِسُفْرَةٍ مُعَلَّقَهْ
فِيهَا ٱلَّذِي تُرِيدُهُ مِنْ مَرْفَقَهْ
مَعْ بَازِيَارٍ رَافِعٍ فِي ٱلْمِنْطَقَهْ
مِنْ جَانِبَيْ قَبَائِهِ وَٱلْفَرَّقَهْ
مُبْتَكِرًا بِزُرَّقٍ أَوْ زُرَّقَهْ
وَصَفْتُهُ بِصِفَةٍ مُصَدَّقَهْ
كَأَنَّ عَيْنَيْهِ بِحُسْنِ ٱلْحَدَقَهْ
نَرْجِسَةٌ نَابِتَةٌ فِي وَرَقَهْ
ذُو مَنْسِرٍ مُخْتَضِبٍ بِعَلَقَهْ
كَأَنَّهُ رَامِشْنَةٌ مُخَلَّقَهْ
فِي كَفِّ خَوْدٍ طِفْلَةٍ أَوْ مِعْلَقَهْ
كَمْ وَزَّةٍ صِدْنَا بِهِ وَلَقْلَقَهْ
وَكَمْ خَشَنْشَارٍ وَكَمْ مِنْ لَقْلَقَهْ
وَصَيْدُ دُرَّاجٍ بِهِ وَخِرْنِقَهْ
وَشِيقَةٍ فِي حَائِرٍ مُفَرَّقَهْ
سِلَاحُهُ فِي لَحْمِهَا مُفَرَّقَهْ
ثُمَّ ٱنْصَرَفْنَا بِكَرِيمِ ٱلْمَصْدَقَهْ

~ 80 ~

Clotted Blood

I crossed the dark with a tied pouchful
of food, a trap box,[107] and a falconer
by my side, shirt tucked into his belt,
out hunting with a tiercel or a kite—
let me describe him to a tee!
Lovely, lustrous eyes like narcissi
on their leaves, his beak, dark with clotted blood,
like a smooth-worn ladle or a trowel
in a girl's hand. So many geese, storks,
khashanshārs, francolins, and leverets
has he felled, so many gadwalls scattered
in ponds,[108] so many holes has he driven
into flesh. How gladly we traveled
in the retinue of such a generous patron!

نعت الصقر وهو ثلاث أرجوزات

~ ٨١ ~

قال ينعته [الرجز]

يَا رُبَّ لَيْلٍ كَجَنَاحِ ٱلنَّاعِقِ
قَدْ خُضْتُهُ قَبْلَ طُلُوعِ ٱلشَّارِقِ
بِأَجْدَلٍ يَفْهَمُ نُطْقَ ٱلنَّاطِقِ
مُلَمْلَمِ ٱلْهَامَةِ فَخْمِ ٱلْعَاتِقِ
طَبٍّ بِصَيْدِ ٱلسَّانِحَاتِ حَاذِقِ
أَقْنَى ٱلْمَخَالِيبِ طَلُوبٍ مَارِقِ
كَأَنَّهَا نُونَاتُ كَفِّ مَاشِقِ
لَمْ يَخْلُ مِنْ صَبٍّ إِلَيْهِ شَائِقِ
وَعَاشِقٍ جَاوَزَ حَدَّ ٱلْعَاشِقِ
حَتَّى بَدَا ضَوْءُ صَبَاحٍ فَاتِقِ
مِثْلَ تَبَدِّي ٱلشَّيْبِ فِي ٱلْمَفَارِقِ
فَنَجَمَتْ لِلَحْظِ عَيْنِ ٱلرَّامِقِ
عَشْرٌ مِنَ ٱلْإِوَزِّ فِي غَلَافِقِ
فَمَرَّ كَٱلرِّيحِ بِعَزْمٍ صَادِقِ
حَتَّى دَنَا مِنْهَا دُنُوَّ ٱلسَّارِقِ
ثُمَّ عَلَا بِجَنَاحٍ خَافِقِ

Saker Descriptions: Three *Urjūzah*s

~ 81 ~

An Expert Surgeon

I've waded through many a raven-wing night
before sunrise with a saker in yarak,
her crown rock-hard, her wrist thick,
fluent in words. She's an expert
surgeon specialized in footing sprung
does with her scalpels curved
like a calligrapher's round *nūn*s.
She has a devoted troop of admirers
whose love knows no bounds.

Dawn streaked the gloom, a shock
of white hair on a dark head.
A side glance from her sharp eye
spotted ten geese in a duckweed pond.
She raked away on a true course,
a puff of wind, creeping like a thief.
With a flick of wing, she was on them,

يَضْرِبُ أَجْوَازَ ٱلْحَشَا مِنْ حَالِقِ
كَمَا سَمِعْتَ رَجَزَ ٱلصَّوَاعِقِ
فَطَفِقَتْ مِنْ هَالِكٍ أَوْ فَائِقِ
وَحَسَرَ ٱلْقَوْمُ إِلَى ٱلْمَرَافِقِ
فَنَحْنُ فِي مُلَهْوَجٍ وَلَاحِقِ
وَشَارِبٍ رَاحًا كَلَمْعِ ٱلْبَارِقِ
فَٱلْحَمْدُ لِلّٰهِ ٱلْوَهُوبِ ٱلرَّازِقِ

ripping the guts from a nimble bird
in a display of rhyming thunder—
many perished; others flew away.
The troop rolled up their sleeves,
some falling on their food,
others cooking it just right. Some
drank wine, sheet-lightning bright.
Praise God, the Generous Provider!

~ ٨٢ ~

وقال ينعته [الرجز]

قَدْ أَغْتَدِي قَبْلَ مُنَى أَصْحَابِي
بِتَوَّجِيٍّ خَالِصِ ٱلْأَنْسَابِ
مُقَابَلٍ فِي ٱلْحَسَبِ ٱللُّبَابِ
إِذْ عَنَّ لِي سِرْبٌ مِنَ ٱلْأَسْرَابِ
تَرَبَّعَتْ مَوَاضِعَ ٱلسَّحَابِ
مِنْ كُلِّ هَجْلٍ طَيِّبِ ٱلرَّوَابِي
كَأَنَّمَا لُفِّعَ بِٱلْمُلَابِ
حَتَّى إِذَا أَفْضَتْ بِذِي ٱلْأَرْبَابِ
سَاوَرَهَا كَقَبَسِ ٱلشِّهَابِ
يَعْمَلُ فِي ٱللَّبَّاتِ وَٱلْآهَابِ
كَشَفْرَةِ ٱلْجَزَّارِ أَوْ قَصَّابِ

~ 82 ~

A Lush Field

I crossed the dark, earlier than my comrades would like,
with a pure Tawwajī saker on the glove, both pedigrees
noble. A herd of does appeared. They'd spent the spring
in rain country, amid steep valleys and sandy banks
scented with saffron. They reached a lush field
and the saker exploded like a supernova,[109] hacking at breasts
and hides, a slaughterhouse butcher wielding his cleaver!

~ ٨٣ ~

وقال ينعته [الرجز]

لَمَّـا رَأَيْتُ ٱللَّيْـلَ قَدْ تَحَسَّـرَ
مُنْضَرِجًا لِلصُّبْحِ حِينَ أَسْفَـرَ
يَحْتَثُّ مِنْـهُ ٱلتَّالِيَاتِ ٱلْغُـبَّرَ
نَبَّهْتُ خِرْقًا لَمْ يَكُنْ عَـذَوَّرَ
أَبْلَجَ فَضْفَاضَ ٱلْقَمِيصِ أَزْهَـرَ
سَقَتْهُ كَفُّ ٱللَّيْلِ أَكْوَاسَ ٱلْكَرَى
فَقَامَ وَٱللَّيْلُ يُبَارِي ٱلسَّحَـرَ
فِيهِ وَمَا ٱلْتَاثَ وَلَا تَكَرْكَـرَ
بِأَسْفَعِ ٱلْخَـدَّيْنِ طَـاوٍ أَمْغَـرَ
عَارِي ٱلظَّنَابِيبِ إِذَا تَغَشْمَـرَ
شَـدَّ بِهَـا حَوْزَتَـهُ فَأُظْفِـرَ
مُتَّخِذًا إِحْـدَى يَـدَيْـهِ مِنْـبَرَ
يَنْهَمُـهُ بِٱلنَّبْضِ إِنْ تَـأَطَّـرَ
أَوِ ٱسْتَحَالَ شَبَحًا أَوْ صَرْصَـرَ
رَهْبَـةَ أَنْ يَجْتَـذَّ مِنْـهُ ٱلْخِنْصِرَ
حَتَّى إِذَا رَاخَى ٱلْمِقَـاطَ ذَمَّـرَ
فَصَادَ فِي شَوْطَيْهِ حِينَ أَظْهَرَ
عَشْرًا وَعِشْرِينَ وَخَمْسَ عَشَـرَ
لَاقَيْنَ مِنْـهُ دَوْسَرِيًّا مِدْسَـرَ
إِذَا تَعَـالَيْـنَ عَـلَا فَشَمَّـرَ
وَإِنْ تَحَـدَّرْنَ لَهُ تَحَـــدَّرَ

~ 83 ~

Our Fierce Lancer

I saw night shed her cloak as dawn
shooed away the lagging stars.
I roused a loyal comrade of mine,
gracious, generous, and bright,
but still drunk with sleep.
When day finally wrested him
from the grip of night, he stood
up straight on his own two feet.
On his left hand, as if on a pulpit,
stood a rufous saker, her cheeks
stippled black, her best maneuver
the belly truss,[110] binding to with bare arms
as she wreaks havoc. She was roused
by her handler with a tug on the ties
should she shy, stare after quarry, or click,
bent on nipping his finger. His calls
urged her on when he released the jess.
After noon and her second cast, the tally
reached ten, fifteen, twenty birds, fallen
in their battles with our fierce lancer.
If they sped up, she flew faster; if they dove,

كَحَجَرِ ٱلْقَذَّافِ صَكًّا مِطْحَرَ
فَكَمْ تَـرَى مِنْ خَـرَبٍ مُجَوَّرَ
إِذَا سَـمَا لِنَهْضَـةٍ تَعَفَّـرَ
أَنْحَى لَهُ مَخَالِبًا وَمِنْسَـرَ
يَتْرُكُ مَنْ صَادَفَهُ مُشَرْشَرَ
ثُمَّتَ رَاحَ سَامِيًا مُصَدَّرَ
تَخَالُ أَعْلَى زَوْرِهِ مُعَصْفَـرَ
مِنْ صَائِكِ ٱلْأَوْدَاجِ أَوْ مُمَغَّـرَ
تُقْفِيهِ مِنْهَا كُلَّمَا تَخَيَّـرَ
حَبَّ ٱلْقُلُوبِ وَٱلْغَرِيضَ ٱلْأَحْمَرَ

she did too, her thwacks like a ballista's boom.
Look at the mighty male houbaras
lying there in the dust, speared by her full-
frontal charge, all talons and slicing beak!
High-flying, she returned, her mail soaked,
her gorge dyed saffron or ochre by clots
of spurted blood. We gave her first pick:
the juicy black flesh of a heart.

نعت الشاهين وهو أربع أرجوزات

~ ٨٤ ~

قال ينعته [الرجز]

قَدْ أَغْتَدِي وَٱللَّيْلُ دَاجٍ عَسْكَرُهْ
وَٱلصُّبْحُ يَفْرِي جِلْدَهُ وَيَدْحَرُهْ
كَٱللَّهَبِ ٱلْمُؤْتَجِّ طَارَ شَرَرُهْ
بِأَحْجَنِ ٱلْكُلُّوبِ أَقْنَى مَنْسِرُهْ
مُعَاوِدِ ٱلْإِقْدَامِ حِينَ تَذْمُرُهْ
أَحْوَى ٱلظُّهَارِ جَسِدٌ مُعَذَّرُهْ
كَأَنَّمَا زَعْفَرَهُ مُزَعْفِرُهْ
لَا يُوئِلُ ٱلْأَبْغَثَ مِنْهُ حَذَرُهْ
حِينًا يُسَامِيهِ وَحِينًا يُدْجِرُهْ
يَهْوِي لَهُ مَخَالِبًا تُشَرْشِرُهْ
طَوْرًا يُفَرِّيهِ وَطَوْرًا يَنْقُرُهْ
وَٱلسِّرْبُ لَا يَنْفَعُهُ مَا يَسْتُرُهْ
مِنَ ٱلْإِوَزِّ ٱلْخَانِسَاتِ تَقْفُرُهْ
صَكًّا إِذَا جَدَّ بِهِ تَقَدُّرُهْ
كَطَالِبِ ٱلْوِتْرِ أُطِلَّتْ ثُؤَرُهْ
أَوْ كَمُحِلِّ ٱلنَّذْرِ كَانَ يَنْذِرُهْ

Peregrine Descriptions: Four *Urjūzah*s

~ 84 ~

No Refuge in Fear

Night's troops, billeted in their camps,
were driven away, routed by dawn's
flame bursts and spitting sparks.
I crossed the dark with a peregrine,
her spurs curved, her beak hooked,
a bold jouster who always answers the call,
her dark beams bloody at the hood
brace, the color of deep saffron.

The ibis found no refuge in fear. 8
She ringed high, confusing it,
then stooped and, tearing and piercing,
trussed it with sharp talons.
Nor did camouflage help the flock
of geese in cover. They were outwitted
in flight. A thwack, then boom,
like a man finally sating his bloodlust
as he carries out his oath of revenge.

~ ٨٥ ~

وقال ينعته [الرجز]

قَدْ أَغْتَدِي وَٱللَّيْلُ بَادٍ غُرَّتُهْ
بِسَوْذَنِيقٍ لَا تُذَمُّ صُحْبَتُهْ
مَحْمُودَةٍ رَوْحَتُهُ وَغَدْوَتُهْ
مُضَرَّجٍ حَوْبَاؤُهُ وَلَبَّتُهْ
يَنْفُذُ حِضْنَيْ كُلِّ وَادٍ مُقْلَتُهْ
لَا تَسْبِقُ ٱلْوَثْبَةَ مِنْهُ نَظْرَتُهْ
مَذْرُوبَةٍ سِلَاحُهُ وَعُدَّتُهْ
خَذَّامَةٍ تَثْنِي ٱلْخَذَامَ نَهْشَتُهْ
مُسْتَوْفِزٍ عَلَى ٱلسِّمَاكِ قُبَّتُهْ
حَتَّى إِذَا ٱسْتَافَ وَلَاحَتْ بُغْيَتُهْ
طَأْمَنَ مِنْ رَأْسٍ عَظِيمٍ جُثَّتُهْ
وَعُنُقٍ طَالَ وَوَافَتْ زُبْرَتُهْ
فَجَالَ كَٱلْبَرْقِ ٱللَّمُوحِ جَوْلَتُهْ
لِخُزَزٍ لَا يُرْقَيَنَّ وَهْلَتُهْ
حَتَّى تَلَاقَاهُ ٱعْتِسَافًا خُطْفَتُهْ
وَخُزَزٌ عَنَّ فَلَاحَتْ صَفْحَتُهْ
قُضَّ عَلَيْهِ لَيْسَ يُثْنَى قَضَّتُهْ
غَائِبَةٌ فِي مَتْنِهِ دَابِرَتُهْ
ضِرْغَامَةٌ غَصْبُ ٱلنُّفُوسِ هِمَّتُهْ

~ 85 ~

Deadly Weapons

In the early gleam of day,
I crossed the dark with my comrade,
a white peregrine beyond reproach,
praised for her forays at dawn
and dusk, a *sawdhanīq* with her blood-
smeared mail, her eyes
penetrating a wadi's every corner,
her attack faster than a glance.
She's fitted with deadly weapons,
her fierce bite ripping flesh
apart—over and over again.
On her block, like a lord in his tent,
she stood ready. She sensed,
then homed in on the quarry,
moving her mighty head, long neck,
and sturdy wrists. She wheeled
like a lightning bolt, in pursuit of a jack—
fear was a useless talisman.
They met in a brutal snatch.
Up popped a second jack, showing its flank.
One bind was enough, her spur sunk
in its back—like a grisly lion,
she lives to take lives.

~ ٨٦ ~

وقال ينعته [الرجز]

قَدْ أَغْتَدِي فِي حَالِكٍ بَهِيمِ
أَحْوَى ٱلْهَذَالِيلِ قَوَامِ ٱلنِّيمِ
إِلَّا سِبَاقَ سَاطِعٍ طَمِيمِ
فِي ٱلْأُفُقِ ٱلشَّرْقِيِّ كَٱلْبَرِيمِ
بِخُلُجِ ٱلْمَطْلُوبِ مُسْتَدِيمِ
لَا فَائِتٍ خَوْفًا وَلَا مَحْرُومِ
أَحَمَّ مِثْلَ ٱلْحَجَرِ ٱلْمَلْمُومِ
مِنْ تَوَّجٍ فِي نَفْسِهَا ٱلْكَرِيمِ
شَاكِي ٱلسِّلَاحِ أَحْجَنِ ٱلْخُرْطُومِ
إِمَالَةَ ٱلْكَاتِبِ عَطْفَ ٱلْمِيمِ

~ 86 ~

Arms at the Ready

On a night as black as a neem tree
blocking out the sun, with a quick ray
of light threading through the eastern sky,
I crossed the dark, a peregrine on the glove.
Refused nothing, she spears her target
every time, patient not to overshoot.
A Tawwajī purebred, she's black,
she's brick-hard, arms at the ready,
her beak hooked like the loop of a *mīm*.

~ ٨٧ ~

وقال ينعته [الرجز]

أَنْعَتُ شَاهِينًا بِكَفٍّ حَاذِقِ
بِصَيْدِهِ وَلِعْبِهِ مُطَابِقِ
غَدَا بِهِ كَٱلْأَمْغَرِ ٱلسُّوذَانِقِ
أَسْفَعَ ذَا قَوَادِمٍ عَتَائِقِ
صُمٍّ صِلَابٍ لَيْسَ بِٱلرَّقَائِقِ
وَلَا عِرَاضٍ لَا وَلَا دَقَائِقِ
كَأَنَّ بَيْنَ ذَنَبٍ وَعَاتِقِ
مِنْ صَدْرِهِ جَنْدَلَةُ ٱلْمَجَنِقِ
مُفَرْوَزٍ مِنْ غَيْرِ مَا دُنْبَالَقِ
مُدَوِّمٍ يَحُومُ غَيْرَ خَافِقِ
غَدَا بِهِ أَزْهَرُ ذُو قَرَاطِقِ
مُنْتَطِقٍ بِأَكْرَمِ ٱلْمَنَاطِقِ
ذُو خَدَمٍ مِنْ عِلْيَةِ ٱلْهَبَائِقِ
وَذُو صِحَابٍ سَادَةٍ بَطَارِقِ
أَبْنَاءُ فَرْعٍ سَابِقٍ لِسَابِقِ
بُلْجُ ٱلْوُجُوهِ طَيِّبِي ٱلْخَلَائِقِ
ذُو مَنْصِبٍ فِي ٱلْمَكْرُمَاتِ سَابِقِ
مِنْ أَصْلِ فَرْعٍ فِي ٱلسَّمَاءِ سَامِقِ
أَكْرَمُ مُلْتَفٍّ عَلَى ٱلنَّمَارِقِ
كَٱلْبَدْرِ أَوْ مِثْلَ ٱلصَّبَاحِ ٱلْفَالِقِ
لَمَّا بَدَتْ بِٱلْأَشْهَبِ ٱلسَّمَالِقِ

~ 87 ~

Thunderbolt Quick

I sing of a peregrine perched on the glove
of a wily handler expert at his trade. Brought
out early, she's like a saker, ochre and dappled
black, her exquisite beams full-summed
and hard, neither slender, wide, nor fine,
clad in her tasseled cloak from wrist to tail.
Her mail is as hard as a trebuchet's stone. She circles
and waits on without a flap of her wings.
A bright falconer, tunic tied with a charming belt,
left early with her, amid a retinue of fine servants
and comrades, patrician lords of noble origin
with pleasant natures and handsome looks.
The finest ever to sit in a saddle, he shone
bright as a full moon or the sun at the crack
of dawn, a man of many great deeds, his roots
a tree of glory raised high in the sky.
A leveret, a fine, fat female, appeared on the plain.

عِكْرِشَةٌ مِنْ أَسْمَنِ ٱلْخَرَانِقِ
ضَمَّ جَنَاحَيْهِ لَهَا مِنْ حَالِقِ
وَٱنْقَضَّ يَهْوِي كَٱنْقِضَاضِ ٱلصَّاعِقِ
كَأَنَّمَا ٱلدَّمُ بِرِيشٍ لَاصِقِ
صَمْغٌ عَلَيْهِ أَوْ غَرًا كَرَاتِقِ
فَٱنْزَهَقَتْ خَشْيَةَ مَوْتٍ زَاهِقِ
مِثْلَ نَجَاءِ ٱلْمُخْطِرِ ٱلْمُسَابِقِ
تَأْمُلُ أَنْ تَلْجَا إِلَى مَخَافِقِ
مَوَاكِبٍ لِلرَّمْلِ ذِي ٱلْأَبَارِقِ
وَعَرْفَجِ ٱلْوَعْسَاءِ وَٱلشَّقَائِقِ

The peregrine folded her wings, racing from a height,
stooping at top speed, thunderbolt quick,
the blood sticking to her feathers like resin
or a cloudy wisp of glue. Afraid of instant death,
the hare leapt away and ran as if competing
in a race, seeking safety in the mirages
on the flats near the stony sands
or among the *ʿarfaj* trees on the hills.

نعت اليؤيؤ وهو أرجوزتان

~ ٨٨ ~

قال ينعته [الرجز]

وَيُؤْيُؤٍ أَسْفَعَ كَٱلدِّينَارِ
أَدْكَنَ قَدْ وُشِّيَ بِٱحْمِرَارِ
بِنُقَطٍ لَوَائِحٍ صِغَارِ
حُرٍّ يُقِرُّ أَعْيُنَ ٱلْأَحْرَارِ
كَأَنَّ عِشْرَيْهِ لَدَى ٱلْمَطَارِ
سُودُ مَدَارِي ٱلْخُرُدِ ٱلْعَذَارِي
يَصْمُدُ لِلْهَدَاهِدِ ٱلْكِبَارِ
فَمَا تَرَاهُ أَعْيُنُ ٱلنُّظَّارِ
مِنْ طَائِرٍ قَدْ سَاحَ فِي ٱلْقِفَارِ
حَتَّى يَقُدُّ ثَبَجَ ٱلْفَقَارِ
يَعْتَامُهُ بِصَارِمٍ بَتَّارِ
مُوَائِلٌ يَلُوذُ بِٱلْفِرَارِ
يُنْشِبُهُ فِي ظُفُرِ ٱلْمِقْدَارِ

Merlin Descriptions: Two *Urjūzah*s

~ 88 ~

Dinar Gold

A merlin, dappled black, dinar
gold, rufous, tattooed red
with shiny spots, a noble sight
for noble eyes, her beams in flight
like iron combs fixed in a girl's
raven hair. The merlin flies
straight at a group of hoopoes.
The onlookers catch a glimpse—
a bird rocketing across the plain—
then she shreds the hoopoe's spine,
slicing bechins with her blade.
Another hoopoe takes flight—
to be pierced by the talons of Death.

~ ٨٩ ~

وقال ينعته [الرجز]

وَمُغْتَــدٍ بِيُؤْيُؤٍ سَمَّاهُ
مِسْعَرَ ٱلْحَرْبِ وَبِهِ كَنَّاهُ
عَلَى عِظَامِ ٱلطَّيْرِ قَدْ ضَرَّاهُ
فَهُوَ مُلَاقٍ كُلَّمَا يَلْقَاهُ
إِذَا بِشَــزْرِ لَحْظِـهِ رَمَاهُ
فَنَاتِلٌ مِنْ جَوْفِهِ مِعَاهُ
بِشَثْنَـةٍ تَغِيبُ فِي حَشَاهُ
حَتَّى يُوَارِي رُسْغَهَا كُلَاهُ
فَرُبَّ يَوْمٍ سَاقِطٍ نَدَاهُ
غِبَّ سَحَابٍ هَمَرَتْ عَزْلَاهُ
قَدْ أَحْرَزَتْنَا طَائِرًا كَفَّاهُ
يَشْبَعُ مِنْهُ كُلُّ مَنْ عَفَاهُ
أَكْرِمْ بِهِ أَكْرِمْ وَذَا ثَنَاهُ

~ 89 ~

Warmonger

He crossed the dark with Warmonger,
a merlin trained to charge big birds
head-on, after shooting a side glance at her prey,
ripping out intestines with her brute claws,
sinking her legs deep in kidneys, extracting guts.
On a rainy day, once the clouds emptied,
the birds proved no match for her. We ate
our fill of her gifts. Honor her with praise!

نعت العقاب وهو أرجوزة

~ ٩٠ ~

قال ينعته [الرجز]

قَدْ أَغْتَدِي بِلَقْوَةٍ صَيُودِ
أَحْمِلُهَا وَحْدِي عَلَى قُتُودِي
كَأَنَّهَا شَيْخٌ عَلَى قَعُودِ
بَعِيدَةِ ٱلْمَطْرَحِ فِي ٱلتَّحْدِيدِ
مِخْلَبُهَا مَخَالِبُ ٱلْأُسُودِ
وَهَامَةٌ كَٱلصَّخْرَةِ ٱلصَّيْخُودِ
فَمَرَّ سِرْبٌ كَٱلْحِقَابِ ٱلْقُودِ
مِثْلَ ٱلْحِسَانِ ٱلْخُرَّدِ ٱلنُّهُودِ
يَمْشِينَ فِي ٱلْبِيعَةِ يَوْمَ ٱلْعِيدِ
فَخِلْتَهَا كَٱلْبَاسِلِ ٱلْحَرِيدِ
فَٱتَّبَعَتْ أَوَائِلَ ٱلْجُنُودِ
فَدَقَّتِ ٱلصُّلْبَ مَعَ ٱلْعَمُودِ
فَٱلْقَوْمُ مِنْ مُقْتَدِرٍ مُجِيدِ
وَآخَرٍ غَادٍ عَلَى ٱلثَّرِيدِ

Eagle Description: One *Urjūzah*

~ 90 ~

A Snarling Lion

I crossed the dark alone with an eagle,
a trained hunter carried on my saddle
like an elder on a camel—a bird with keen, long-
range sight, talons like a lion's claws,
and a crown like an immovable rock.
A herd of deer like broad-necked, white-
bellied onagers passed like a procession
of lovely, pert-breasted maidens
in church on a saint's day.
Picture her—a lone, snarling lion
chasing the vanguard, crushing spines
at dawn's first pillar of light.[111]
Some of the troop were gracious;
others dined on bread and water broth!

نعت الجلاهق وقوسها وهو ثماني أرجوزات

~ ٩١ ~

قال ينعتها [الرجز]

قَدْ أَغْتَدِي وَٱلطَّيْرُ فِي أَوْكَارِهَا
بِشِقَّةٍ كَٱلْوَرْسِ فِي ٱصْفِرَارِهَا
يَخَالُ ٱلنَّاظِرُ فِي ٱسْتِدَارِهَا
قُلْبَ نُضَارٍ صِيغَ مِنْ قِنْطَارِهَا
كَأَنَّمَا ٱلْمَائِلُ مِنْ فَقَارِهَا
غُصْنٌ مِنَ ٱلْبَانِ عَلَى أَصْوَارِهَا
تُمِيدُهُ ٱلْأَرْوَاحُ فِي تَكْرَارِهَا
سِتَّةَ أَشْبَارٍ عَلَى ٱقْتِدَارِهَا
فَٱلظَّهْرُ يَحْكِي ٱلْقُلْبَ مِنْ نُضَارِهَا
وَٱلْقَرْنُ مِثْلَ ٱلْقَارِ فِي ٱنْتِشَارِهَا
وَلَيْلَةٍ طَالَتْ عَلَى سُمَّارِهَا
تَأَوَّهُ ٱلْأَنْفُسُ فِي أَسْحَارِهَا
شَوْقًا يُهَيِّجُهَا إِلَى أَطْيَارِهَا
غَابَتْ دَوَاعِي ٱلنَّجْمِ عَنْ طِيَارِهَا
أَرِقْتُ وَٱلْقَوْمُ عَلَى أَسْحَارِهَا
حَتَّى إِذَا نَحْنُ عَلَى مَدَارِهَا

Pellet Bow Descriptions: Eight *Urjūzah*s

~ 91 ~

Drops of Milk in the Sky

The birds were still in their nests.
I crossed the dark with a curved
wooden staff, safflower yellow—
a pure gold bracelet, it almost seemed.
From its back hangs a string, thin
as a *bān* twig, tossing in the breeze,
six spans long. The shaft
is like a gold bangle, the cord
loose, black as pitch.
The night was too long for talk,
and we heaved a sigh, our souls
pining for the birds. The last stars
set, like drops of milk in the sky:
we kept our dawn vigil as the night
revolved above us. Then they arrived,

طَلَعْنَ مِثْلَ ٱلْإِبْلِ فِي قِطَارِهَا
فَصَكَّنَا ٱلرَّاعِي عَلَى حُدَّارِهَا
صَكًّا فَلَمْ يَسْلَمْنَ مِنْ قَرَارِهَا
بِبُنْدُقٍ مِثْلَ شَرَارِ نَارِهَا
ثُمَّ تَنَازَعْنَا إِلَى كِبَارِهَا
تَنَازُعَ ٱلْكَمْأَةِ فِي مَغَارِهَا
وَضُوعَةٍ تَأْوِي إِلَى أَوْتَارِهَا
أَذَقْتُهَا ٱلْمَوْتَ عَلَى تَغْرَارِهَا
بِرَمْيَةٍ تَصْعَدُ فِي أَقْطَارِهَا
رَدَدْتُهَا مُرًّا عَلَى إِمْرَارِهَا
هٰذَا وَمَا أَرْدَيْتُ مِنْ شَوَارِهَا
كِبَارُهَا أَنْزَعُ مِنْ صِغَارِهَا
كَمْ قَائِلٍ وَٱلطَّيْرُ فِي تَمْرَارِهَا
أَنْتَ لَهَا أَسْوَرُ مِنْ سَوَّارِهَا
بَهْرَامُ جُورَانَ عَلَى ٱفْتِخَارِهَا
لَا مِثْلَ بُورَانَ عَلَى ٱخْتِيَارِهَا

like a line of large camels taken to water
by their drover, but their home wasn't safe
from the sparks of our pellet fire.
As if digging for truffles, our hands rushed
for the bigger missiles, readied in their pouch—
the pellets gave the innocent birds a taste
of Death as the shots peppered their flesh.
I stretched the string even tighter and killed
several plump birds, far pluckier
than the rest. The flock flew past.
Shouts resounded: "What a hunter,
fiercer than a lion!"

For all their boasts, 31
given the choice she made,
Būrān is no Bahrām Jūrān![112]

~ ٩٢ ~

وقال ينعتها [الرجز]

وَمَنْهَلٍ نَاءٍ عَنِ ٱلْفَلَاتِ
مُسْتَلَبِ ٱلْجِرْيَةِ فِي ٱنْصِلَاتِ
جَنَّ بِهِ تَهَاوُلُ ٱلنَّبَاتِ
عَلَى ٱلتَّنَاهِي وَعَلَى ٱلضِّفَّاتِ
تَرْعَى بِهِ غُرُّ ٱلشَّرُوقِيَّاتِ
مُشَنَّفَاتٍ وَمُقَرَّطَاتِ
وَطِيطَوِيَّاتٍ مُكَحَّلَاتِ
حُمْرَ ٱلْمَنَاقِيرِ مُخَضَّبَاتِ
مِثْلَ ٱلْأَبَارِيقِ مُصَفَّفَاتِ
وَٱلْبُغْثُ كَٱلْجُرْبِ ٱلْمُهَنَّآتِ
أَسْرَابُ شِيقٍ وَلَقَلَّقَاتِ
وَرَفْرَفَانَاتٍ مُرَتَّعَاتِ
بِنَاصِعِ ٱلْأَلْوَانِ مَوْشِيَّاتِ
وَبِٱلدَّبَابِيجِ مُوَشَّحَاتِ
وَتَدْرُجِيَّاتٍ مُرَاعِيَاتِ
صَبَّحْتُهُنَّ غَيْرَ مَذْعُورَاتِ
خَرَائِطًا حُمْرًا مُنَقَّشَاتِ
ذَوَاتِ آذَانٍ مُسَتَّرَاتِ
فِيهَا حُتُوفُ ٱلطَّيْرِ كَامِنَاتِ
مُدَحْرَجَاتٍ مُتَشَابِهَاتِ
قَطَعْتُهُ وَٱللَّيْلُ ذُو هَنَاةِ

~ 92 ~

A Shrill Chorus

A pool of stagnant water
far from the flats, its banks
covered in a riot of plants,
home to early risers
in their bright finery: dark *ṭīṭawī*s
with red beaks and kohled eyes,
like ibriks set in a row, ibis black
as tarred skins, flocks of teal,
storks, and *rafrāf*s in luxury's
lap, embroidered in vivid colors
and patterned silks, coursers
feeding peacefully with no cause
for alarm. In our early visit
we brought red pouches, decorated,
fitted with handles, kept covered
and safe. Their contents spelled
death for the birds: round pellets,
each alike. On a doom-laden night

بِكُلِّ هَفْهَافِ ٱلْحَشَا مِصْلَاتِ
أَغَرَّ ذِي أُكْرُومَةٍ مُوَاتِي
كَرِيمِ آبَاءٍ وَأُمَّهَاتِ
وَحِينَ نُودِي ٱلْقَوْمَ فِي ٱلْغَدَاةِ
وَفَثَأَ ٱلصُّبْحُ دُجَى ٱلظُّلْمَاتِ
وَٱلْقَوْمُ مِنْهُنَّ عَلَى صِمَاتِ
تَأَهَّبُوا تَأَهُّبَ ٱلرُّمَاةِ
مُجْتَمِعِينَ غَيْرَ مَا أَشْتَاتِ
وَجَرَّدُوا جُرْدًا مُخَطَّمَاتِ
بِشِقَقٍ خُضْرٍ بَرَوْصِيَّاتِ
صُفْرِ ٱللِّحَاءِ وَخَلُوقِيَّاتِ
جُدِلْنَ حَتَّى إِضْنَ كَٱلْحَيَّاتِ
أَنْفَهُنَّ غَيْرَ مُصْطَفَّاتِ
عَمْرُو بْنُ عُصْفُورٍ عَلَى ٱسْتِثْبَاتِ
رَشَائِقًا غَيْرَ مُؤَنَّبَاتِ
ذَوَاتَ أَعْجَازٍ مُؤَزَّرَاتِ
بِدَسْتَبَانَاتٍ مُخَمَّلَاتِ
عَلَى ٱلْمَذَابِحِ مُكَفَّرَاتِ
يُوسَدْنَ فِي ٱلْجَوِّ مُذَمَّرَاتِ
مُصَاعَدَاتٍ وَمُحَدَّرَاتِ
مُفَدَّيَاتٍ وَمُعَلَّمَاتِ
يُتْبِعْنَ مِنْهَا شُعَبَ ٱلْهَامَاتِ
وَحَيْثُ مُنْتَاطُ كُلَى ٱلْحَيَّاتِ
عَنِ ٱلتَّنَادِي غَيْرَ غَافِلَاتِ

I traveled there with a troop
of lean-bellied comrades, men
of action and fine deeds
and bright brows, all
from noble sires. We armed
the archers first, as dawn
threw cold water on night's
boiling cauldron. Silently
they geared up for combat
and, keeping in formation, removed
the bows fitted with strings[113]
from their covers, dark shafts
from Barwaṣ, with yellowish red
inner bark, bent to resemble
serpents, planed with skill
by ʿAmr ibn ʿUṣfūr and kept
in a heap, beyond reproach,
fast shooters, with gloves padded
with shaggy cloth above notches
kneeling in position,[114] roaring
when pointed and fired into the air,
shafts naturally straight, their strings
twisted tight, light in the hand,
carrying their owner's mark,
attached to prongs at the head
and to where the snakes' kidneys[115] are tied,
ever ready to answer the call

ثُمَّ صَبَحْنَ ٱلطَّيْرَ رَاتِعَاتِ
كَأْسَ ٱلْمَنَايَا مُتَبَارِيَاتِ
فَهُنَّ مِنْ بَيْنِ مُجَوَّرَاتِ
نَوَازِعُ حَشْرَجَةَ ٱلْأَمْوَاتِ
بِمُهَجِ ٱلْأَجْوَافِ شَاغِلَاتِ
وَفِي ٱلدِّمَاءِ مُتَضَرِّجَاتِ
وَفِي حَوَايَاهُنَّ وَاطِئَاتِ
كَأَنَّمَا زَمَاجِرُ ٱلْأَصْوَاتِ
مِنْهُنَّ تَرْجِيعُ مُغَنِّيَاتِ
حَتَّى إِذَا آنَسْنَ نَاظِرَاتِ
آنَسْنَنَا وَٱنْصَعْنَ جَافِلَاتِ
فَٱسْتَوْثَقَ ٱلنَّزْعُ بَوَاسِقَاتِ
فَلَا يَذَرْنَ صُقَلَ ٱللَّبَّاتِ
كَشِدَّةِ ٱلطُّغَاةِ لِلطُّعَاةِ
يُبْذَلُ لِلْقَانِعِ وَٱلْعُفَاةِ
عَفْوًا وَلِلْجِيرَانِ وَٱلْجَارَاتِ

to war. The contest began.
The bows attacked the feeding birds,
giving them a drink from Death's cup—
some lay prostrate, struggling to draw
their last breath, bellies bleeding
profusely; others, spattered with gore,
trod on their guts, voices raised
in a shrill chorus of song.
When they spotted us, they quickly took
to the air, but the string-shot bullets
caught their chests and flanks
as they flew, like the violence of a tyrant
visited on anyone seeking protection,
be they loyal subject, petitioner, or supplicant.

وقال ينعتها [الرجز]

لَمَّا تَوَلَّى عَجُزُ ٱلشِّتَاءِ
مُتَّبِعًا أُولَاهُ بِٱسْتِقْصَاءِ
كَأَنَّهُ حَادٍ عَلَى حُدَاءِ
قُلْتُ لِوَارِي ٱلزَّنْدِ ذِي سَنَاءِ
مَحْضِ ٱلْجُدُودِ مَاجِدِ ٱلْآبَاءِ
طَوْعَكَ لَا يَعْصِيكَ بِٱلْتِوَاءِ
بَاكِرْ بِنَا مَنَابِتَ ٱلْقَصْبَاءِ
مَا بَيْنَ أَعْلَى ٱلْغَابِ ذِي ٱلْأَشَاءِ
إِلَى أَدَانِي دَمِثِ ٱلْمَيْثَاءِ
فَهَبَّ مِثْلَ ٱلرِّيحِ ذَا ٱلْتِوَاءِ
يَحْمِلُ صَفْرَاوَيْنِ فِي ٱلرِّوَاءِ
كَشِقَّتَيْنِ مِنْ عَصَى سَرَّاءِ
كَأَنَّ بَيْنَ ٱللِّيْطِ وَٱللِّحَاءِ
لِمَا جَرَى فِيهِ مِنَ ٱلصَّفَاءِ
مِنَ ٱنْمِلَاسِ ٱلْأَكْعُبِ ٱلظِّمَاءِ
بَرِيقُ سَيْفٍ مُحْدَثِ ٱلْجِلَاءِ
وَمِقْبَضَانِ لَيِّنَا ٱلْوِطَاءِ
قَدْ كُسِيَا حَاشِيَتَيْ رِدَاءِ
ثُمَّتَ أَوْفَيْنَا عَلَى ٱلْجَرْعَاءِ
مَبْثُوثَةٍ فِي ٱلسَّهْلِ وَٱلْأَنْحَاءِ
وَٱلطَّيْرُ مِثْلَ غَنَمِ ٱلرِّعَاءِ

~ 93 ~

Imagine the Clamor

Winter had turned its back, like a camel drover
following the paths of earlier herds.
I said to my page, strong of arm,
bright of brow, pure of ancestry,
dutiful and compliant, not headstrong,
"Tomorrow, take us to the reed-
beds between the palm-tree groves
above and the soft flats below!"
Quick as the wind, he tended to his task,
carrying two yellow bows like staves
of *sarrāʾ*, with smooth knots, so polished
between wood and bark they flash
like a freshly burnished blade, their grips
light to the touch, wrapped in the fringes
of a cloak.
We were atop a knoll 19
on the plain. In pools shallow and deep,
the birds, like camels driven by herders

يَرْتَعْنَ فِي ٱلضَّحْلِ وَغَمْرِ ٱلْمَاءِ
بَوَاكِيًا مِنْ غَيْرِ مَا بُكَاءِ
يَزِدْنَ ذَا ٱلشَّجْوِ مِنَ ٱلشَّجَاءِ
كَأَنَّهُ تَجَاوُبُ ٱلظِّبَاءِ
ثُمَّ ٱعْتَمَدْنَاهُنَّ بِٱلرِّمَاءِ
فَثَمَّ مَا شِئْتَ مِنَ ٱلضَّوْضَاءِ
مَا بَيْنَ غَمَّاسٍ إِلَى عَدَّاءِ
وَلَقْلَقٍ مُوَاشِكِ ٱلنَّجَاءِ
ذِي هُدُبٍ يَهْوِي إِلَى ٱلْبَيْدَاءِ
وَآخَرٍ يَهْوِي مِنَ ٱلسَّمَاءِ
إِلَى مَسِيلٍ أَخْضَرِ ٱلْفِنَاءِ
مُرْتَطِمٍ فِي ٱلْمَاءِ وَٱلْغَضْرَاءِ
لَمْ يُنْجِهِ ذَاكَ مِنَ ٱلْقَضَاءِ
أَنْ خَضَبَ ٱلْمَاءَ مِنَ ٱلدِّمَاءِ
ظَلْنَا بِخَيْرٍ حَسَنَيْ ثَوَاءِ
نَرْتَعُ فِي ٱلْقَدِيدِ وَٱلشِّوَاءِ

to pasture, cried as they fed,
though they had no cause to cry,
calling like a herd of gazelles
that fill the lover with yearning.
We began to shoot—imagine the clamor!
Some birds dove; others took flight;
the storks, with fringe-like feathers,
tried to escape by making for the desert;
others plummeted from the sky
to the riverbed, plopping
into the dark water and mud dyed
black with their blood, unable to escape
Fate. We enjoyed a double reward:
grilled and sun-dried meat.

~ ٩٤ ~

وقال ينعتها [الرجز]

لَمَّا بَدَا ضَوْءُ ٱلصَّبَاحِ فَحَسَرْ
فِي حَالِكِ ٱلْأَطْرَافِ مُحْمِرِّ ٱلطُّرَرْ
قُمْتُ إِلَى صَفْرَاءَ سَوْدَاءِ ٱلْوَتَرْ
لَمْ تُؤْتَ مِنْ طُولٍ بِهَا وَلَا قِصَرْ
وَلَمْ تُعَبْ نَاتِئَةً وَلَا زَوَرْ
إِذَا تَمَطَّى نَازِعٌ فِيهَا ذَمَرْ
ذَاتِ شَذًا تَنْزِعُ أَنْفَاسَ ٱلثُّغَرِ
عَنْ سَمْهَرِيٍّ سَدِلِ ٱلْفُوقِ مُمَرّْ
مُعْتَمِدًا مِنِّي بِجِدٍّ وَأَشَرْ
لِنَهْرِ حَسَّانٍ وَنَهْرِ ٱبْنِ عُمَرْ
وَفِتْيَةٍ مِثْلِ مَصَابِيحِ ٱلزَّهَرْ
غَيْرِ مُبَالِي شَبَحٍ وَلَا حَضِرْ
مِنْ كُلِّ مَشْبُوحِ ٱلذِّرَاعَيْنِ أَغَرّْ
إِذَا تَمَطَّى طَائِرٌ فَوْقَ ٱلنَّهَرْ
خَاضَ إِلَيْهِ غَيْرَ وَانٍ فَعَبَرْ
مُكْتَشِحَيْنِ مِنْ عُكَاظِي ٱلْجُوَرْ
مُرَقَّشَاتٍ بِتَهَاوِيلِ ٱلصُّوَرْ
فِيهَا حُتُوفُ ٱلطَّيْرِ تَفْرِي وَتَذَرْ
حَتَّى صَبَحْنَا كُلَّ نُحَّامٍ نَغِرْ
مِنْ عُصَبِ ٱلشِّيقِ وَأَسْرَابِ ٱلشُّوَرْ
يَرْعَيْنَ شَتَّى وَمَعًا ضَاحِي ٱلزَّهَرْ

~ 94 ~

The Archery Grew Intense

Dawn's light glowed, bundled in a dark,
red-hemmed gown. I fetched a yellow bow
with a black string, of perfect length,
flawless, free of kinks, prized as a sapling,
roaring when fired, a sharpshooter
that makes the tightly twisted Samharī string
breathe deep, loose at the notch.
Exulting in my good fortune, I made
for Ḥassān's River or Ibn ʿAmr's Brook,
with comrades bright as lamplight,
men of strong arms and noble brows,
lithe of limb, hale and hearty. A bird
flew over the river. Hastily they waded
in over the thick vegetation of the banks,
with pouches patterned in a riot of figures,
containing death for the birds—pellets
designed to cut and maim.[116]
We paid an early visit to the flocks
of noisy, quacking teal and plump
shiwārs, feeding singly and in groups

فَلَوْ تَـرَاهُنَّ وَقَدْ جَـدَّ ٱلذُّعُـرْ
إِذْ جَدَّ جِدُّ ٱلرَّمْيِ فِيهَا وَٱنْتَشَـرْ
وَهُـنَّ مِنْ بَـيْنِ صَرِيعٍ مُنْعَفَـرْ
وَبَـيْنَ مَقْصُورِ ٱلنِّيَـاطِ مُنْبَهِـرْ
لَاعٍ وَقَـدْ عَـايَنَ صَمَّـاءَ ٱلْغَـبَرْ
صَادَفَـهُ ٱلْحَيْنُ فَلَمْ يُنْجِ ٱلْحَذَرْ
وَكُلُّ شَيْءٍ بِقَضَـاءٍ وَقَـدَرْ

amid the blooms brightened by the sun—
if only you could have seen them gripped
by fear as the archery grew intense,
pellets flying everywhere. Some birds
lay prostrate in the dust; others panted
for breath, hearts twitching, staring
at the hard ground in terror. Caution
was futile—they were meeting with Death.
The divine decree is all-powerful.

~ ٩٥ ~

وقال ينعتها [الرجز]

يَا رُبَّ طَيْرٍ وُقَّعٍ رِتَاعِ
غَادَيْتُهَا مَعْ لُمْعَةِ ٱلشُّعَاعِ
بِشِقَّةٍ مِنْ طُولِ أَوْفَى بَاعِ
مُحْكَمَةٍ لَيِّنَةِ ٱلنِّزَاعِ
تَأْمَنُ مِنْهَا رَوْعَةَ ٱلسُّطَّاعِ
ثُمَّتَ أَوْفَيْتُ عَلَى ٱلْيَفَاعِ
مُدَرَّبًا أَحْسِرُ عَنْ ذِرَاعِي
وَٱلطَّيْرُ فِي مَرَاتِعِ ٱلْبِقَاعِ
نَوَافِرُ يَهْمُمْنَ بِٱسْتِجْمَاعِ
تَكَاثُفَ ٱلْجُنْدِ عَلَى ٱلْأَطْمَاعِ
فَظَلْتُ أَهْوِيهِنَّ لِلْجَعْجَاعِ
بِنَافِذَاتٍ صُيَّبٍ سِرَاعِ
كَأَنَّهُنَّ أَعْيُنُ ٱلْأَفَاعِي
فَبَيْنَ مَيْتٍ بَائِنِ ٱلْكُرَاعِ
شُدِّخَ مِنْهُ مَوْضِعُ ٱلْقِنَاعِ
وَآخَرٍ مُرَضَّضِ ٱلذِّرَاعِ
قَطَّعَهُ ٱلطَّاهِي عَلَى أَرْبَاعِ
لِفِتْيَةٍ مَسَاغِبٍ جِيَاعِ
وَلِعِتَاقِ ٱلطَّيْرِ وَٱلتِّبَاعِ

~ 95 ~

Gentle in the Draw

A glint of sun, and I was ready
for the birds as they fed
at ease, with a bow the length
of my outstretched arms,
well made, gentle in the draw,
too quiet to scare the long-
necks by creaking. Expertly,
I took my position on top
of a hill, baring my forearm
as the birds fed in the pools.
They scattered, then tried
to muster, crowding like soldiers
on payday. I dropped them
with viper-eyed bullets
shot with a sure aim.
Some birds lay dead, limbs
torn from their bodies, their chests
crushed, others with shattered
legs. The cook quartered them
to feed to our hungry, weary comrades,
our retinue, and our noble hunting birds.[117]

~ ٩٦ ~

وقال ينعتها [الرجز]

يَا رُبَّ نَهْرٍ جَائِلِ ٱلْأَطْيَارِ
جَمِّ ٱلرِّعَا مُتَّسِعِ ٱلْأَهْوَارِ
مُغَطْمِطِ ٱللُّجَّةِ غَيْرِ جَارِي
غَادَيْتُهُ وَٱللَّيْلُ ذُو ٱنْدِحَارِ
فِي مَعْشَرٍ صِيدٍ ذَوِي أَخْطَارِ
عِيدَانُهُمْ لَيْسَتْ بِذِي ٱخْوِرَارِ
حَتَّى إِذَا لَاحَ كَقَرْنِ ٱلنَّارِ
صُبْحٌ أَرَاحَ ٱللَّيْلَ بِٱلْأَسْفَارِ
وَبَشَّرَ ٱلنَّاعِبُ بِٱلنَّهَارِ
وَقَهْقَهَتْ فِي ذِرْوَةِ ٱلْأَشْجَارِ
بِٱلصُّبْحِ مُسْتَبْشِرَةُ ٱلْقَمَارِي
وَٱشْتَعَلَ ٱلشَّمْسُ بِنُورٍ وَارِي
سَابِحَةً فِي ٱلْفَلَكِ ٱلدَّوَّارِ
وَٱنْبَثَّتِ ٱلْأَطْيَارُ فِي ٱلصَّحَارِي
يَرْعَيْنَ كُلَّ مُؤْنِقِ ٱلثِّمَارِ
وَكُلَّ زَهْرٍ حَسَنِ ٱلنُّوَّارِ
كَأَنَّهُنَّ رُفَقُ ٱلسُّفَّارِ
فَقُلْتُ لِلْبَطَارِقِ ٱلْأَحْرَارِ
أَفْدِيكُمُ يَا مَعْشَرَ ٱلْأَخْيَارِ
ٱلْآنَ فَٱشْفُوا غُلَلَ ٱلْأَطْوَارِ
بِذِي ٱشْتِعَالٍ كَضِرَامِ ٱلنَّارِ

~ 96 ~

Bows That Never Creak

The river's banks teemed with birds,
its pools wide and full of food,
their waves plashing in the ponds.
As night was violently evicted,
I arrived with a troop of proud-
necked comrades, tried and tested,
armed with bows that never creak.
Like the crown of a flame, dawn
sent night off on its travels,
the pigeons cooed in the trees,
the crow welcomed in the day,
and the sun in its sphere
was ignited into a blaze of light.
The birds, fed on fine fruits
and bright-colored flowers, were spread
across the plain like groups of travelers.
To my freeborn lords I said,
"Good fellows, I wish you luck today—
go, slake your thirsty strings
with bows like raging fires,

عَارِضِ رَمْيٍ قَاهِرٍ مِدْرَارِ
فَٱنْتَدَبُوا فِي صُدُرٍ قِصَارِ
مَضْمُومَةِ ٱلْأَقْطَارِ بِٱلْأَزْرَارِ
وَكُلِّ قَوْسٍ ذَاتِ زَنْدٍ وَارِي
يَرُوقُ مِنْكَ ٱلْعَيْنُ بِٱصْفِرَارِ
مِثْلَ عَرُوسِ ٱلْخُرَّدِ ٱلْأَبْكَارِ
وَبُنْدُقٍ يَصْدَعُ مِثْلَ ٱلنَّارِ
ذِي لَهَبٍ أُحْكِمَ بِٱدْوِرَارِ
فَمَا دَنَا ٱلنِّصْفُ مِنَ ٱلنَّهَارِ
حَتَّى مَلَأْنَا ٱلطَّفَّ ذَا ٱلْأَشْجَارِ
مِنْ كُلِّ طَيْرٍ مُعْلِنِ ٱلْخُوَارِ
أَمْسَى عَنِ ٱلْإِلْفِ بَعِيدَ ٱلدَّارِ
أَوْدَتْ بِهِ مَشْحُوذَةُ ٱلشِّفَارِ

wide-shooters, triumphant,
abundant as milk from the udder."
In short tunics, tied with buttons
at the side, they answered my call
to war, with yellow bows that burst
into flame, a delight for the eyes
like brides amid their bridesmaids,
the pellets flying like sparks,
round, well-made balls of fire.
By midday, we'd covered the tree-lined
bank with loudly moaning birds
gutted by a whetted knife,
lying in their strange new land.

~ ٩٧ ~

وقال ينعتها [الرجز]

وَدُلْجَةٍ غَافَصْتُ بِٱنْبِتَاتِهَا
جَوَاثِمَ ٱلطَّيْرِ عَلَى ضَفَّاتِهَا
وَهُنَّ قَدْ كَنَسْنَ فِي نَبَاتِهَا
تَوَقِّيًا مِنْ مُدْلِجِي رُمَاتِهَا
فَخَافِتَاتٍ لِلْكَرَى سِنَاتِهَا
نَبَّهَهَا تَلْحِينُ صَافِرَاتِهَا
تَبَكِّيَ ٱلثَّكْلَى عَلَى أَمْوَاتِهَا
أَثَارَهَا ٱلْحَائِشُ فِي غَدَاتِهَا
وَٱلشَّمْسُ لَمْ يَبْدُ سَنَا مِرْآتِهَا
فَٱنْتَشَرَتْ تَهِيمُ فِي شِيَاتِهَا
مُوَائِلَاتٍ مِنْ شَذَا عِدَاتِهَا
لَوْ زَارَهَا ذٰلِكَ فِي حَيَاتِهَا
فَحَاشَهَا ٱلْحَيْنُ عَلَى غِرَّاتِهَا
فَسَكَّنَ ٱلْبُنْدُقُ مِنْ شِرَّاتِهَا
صَكًّا يُفَرِّي ٱللَّحْمَ فِي كِفَّاتِهَا
وَيُصْمِتُ ٱلْأَجْرَاسَ مِنْ أَصْوَاتِهَا
حَتَّى يَبِينَ ٱلْمَوْتُ فِي شَكَاتِهَا
مِنْهُنَّ صَرْعَى صَادَفَتْ آفَاتِهَا
وَمُقْصَعَاتٍ فِي ذَرَى حُمَاتِهَا
فَقَدَّرُوا ٱلسُّمَّانَ مِنْ جِلَّاتِهَا
وَلِلشِّوَاءِ ٱلْكُومَ مِنْ بَنَاتِهَا
هٰذَا تَمَامُ ٱلْوَصْفِ مِنْ صِفَاتِهَا

~ 97 ~

A Mad Panic

My night journey was almost finished.
I ambushed the birds asleep on their breasts,
hiding in the plants to guard against
marauding archers. Their silent slumber
was broken by screeches—like a mother
lamenting her dead child.
The beater flushed them early: the sun's
mirror had not yet glinted. A riot of birds
scattered in a mad panic, trying to escape
the terror. Little did they know they'd been flushed
by Death, as our bullets sapped their energy
in thwacks that sliced their flesh trapped
in the nets, silencing their pealing voices.
Then Death appeared in full armor.
Some found shelter; others lay there
fatally maimed. For the fire, we separated
fat birds from scrawny; plump females,
large as camel humps, from their daughters.
Here my description ends.

~ ٩٨ ~

وقال ينعتها [الرجز]

وَلَيْـلَةٍ ذَاتِ سُهَـــادٍ وَأَرَقْ
لَابِثَـةٍ لَا تَنْجَـلِي عَنِ ٱلْأُفُقْ
حَـائِـرَةٍ نُجُومُهَـا لَا تَنْصَفِقْ
كَأَنَّهَـا بَيْنَ ٱرْتِفَـاقٍ وَقَـلَقْ
حَتَّى إِذَا ٱلصُّبْحُ تَجَلَّى وَٱنْبَلَقْ
وَصَـاحَ بِٱللَّيْـلِ فَوَلَّى وَٱنْفَتَقْ
فَقَـامَ لَا فِي فَـتْرَةٍ وَلَا خُـرُقْ
كُلُّ طَوِيـلِ ٱلْبَاعِ سَامٍ مُخْتَلَقْ
أَرْوَاحُهُـمْ رُوحٌ لَدَى ٱلْأَمْرِ وُفُقْ
فَشَمَّرُوا مِنْ كُلِّ فَضْفَـاضٍ يَفَقْ
وَٱسْتَصْبَحُوا مَوْشِيَّةً ذَاتَ عُلُقْ
وَشَنَقُوا بَـرَاوِصًـا مِنَ ٱلْفَـلَقْ
بِكُلِّ مَـرْبُوعِ ٱلسَّـرَاةِ مُتَّسِقْ
ذَاتِ عُيُونٍ لَيْسَ فِيهِـنَّ حَـدَقْ
لَا كَحَـلٌ أَزْرَى بِهَـا وَلَا زَرَقْ
تَقْذِفُ مَا فِيهِنَّ مِنْ غَيْرِ غَسَقْ
مُذَمَّرَاتِ ٱلرَّكْضِ كَفِتَاتِ ٱلْحَلَقْ
مُوَكَّلَاتٍ بِٱلتَّنَادِي وَٱلْأَفَقْ
مُؤَزَّرَاتٍ بِمَخَامِيلِ ٱلْأَبَقْ
مِنْ تَحْتِهَا مَـذَابِحٌ ذَاتِ ذَلَقْ
مَسْنُونَةٌ فِيهِـنَّ رَدْعٌ مِنْ عَـلَقْ

~ 98 ~

Paralyzed by Fear

The sleepless night clung to the horizon;
the stars were lost, unable to dip and set,
as if caught between repose and alarm.
Dawn's gate opened, and night, its cloak
torn, heeded its call and turned away.
A troop of noble, skilled, and muscular
hunters rose briskly and with a single purpose—
in time of action, their souls were in complete
accord. They tied back their loose white
robes and visited a flower-patterned field,
tying to the notches of Barwaṣī shafts
strings of a fourfold twist, tightly wound,
bows with eyes that cannot see, unsullied
by kohl or disease, clearing their motes away
without tears or pus, bows that roar
when fired, fitted with swift rings,[118]
sure to react to expert touch, finely honed,
padded with cotton lumps above sharp-pointed
notches,[119] wood polished and stained

حَتَّى إِذَا كُنَّا بِفَيَّاحٍ أَنِقْ
مُجَاوِرٍ ضَفَّةَ طَامٍ مُنْفَهِقْ
ذِي زَهَرٍ عَالٍ عَلَى ٱلرَّوْضِ سَبِقْ
كَأَنَّ مَرْجَانًا بِأَطْرَافِ ٱلْوَرَقْ
حِينَ جَلَاهُ ٱلصُّبْحُ مِنْ مَاءٍ غَدِقْ
يَدْعُو ٱلْخَشَنْشَارُ بِهَا سِرْبَ ٱلشَّرَقْ
وَطَائِرَاتٍ نُسَّقٍ إِلَى نَسَقْ
وَٱلْعَاقِدَ ٱلْأَبْيَضَ إِنْ قَرْقَرَ نَقّْ
تَفَرَّقُوا فِيهِنَّ فَٱلْقَوْمُ فِرَقْ
فَهُنَّ بَيْنَ فَاغِرٍ فَاهُ خَرِقْ
وَبَيْنَ مَغْضُوضِ ٱلْجَنَاحِ مُنْخَرِقْ
وَجَائِلٍ فِي جَوْلِهِ إِذَا غَفَقْ
يَعْثُرُ فِي جَنَاحِهِ مِنَ ٱلزَّعَقْ

blood-clot red. We were in a wide wadi
of fine blossoms, by the bank of a broad,
swollen pond, fields of tall flowers, early bloomers,
their leaves, as if tipped with coral, glinting in the light
against the water. The *khashanshār* summoned
the flock of dawn birds, the fowls all arranged
in a neat row, together with the white,
clucking supple-necks. In groups, our troop
spread out among them—some birds squawked,
their beaks open wide, paralyzed by fear;
some had smashed feathers; others fled panicked,
trying to flap their wings, only to trip and fall.

~ ٩٩ ~

وقال ينعتها [الرجز]

وَإِخْوَةٍ قَدْ عَطَفُوا عَلَى ٱلْإِخَا
وَصُيِّرَتْ أَهْوَاؤُهُمْ فِيهِ هَوَى
إِنْ قَالَ بَعْضٌ لَا أَجَابُوهُ بِلَا
عَطْفًا وَإِنْ قَالَ بَلَى قَالُوا بَلَى
شُخُوصُهُمْ شَتَّى وَهُمْ نَفْسُ فَتَى
لَمْ يَضْرَعُوا بُؤْسًا وَلَمْ يَطْغَوْا غِنَى
رَاحُوا بِسُمْرٍ ضُمَّرٍ فِيهَا ٱنْحِنَا
مِنْ بَرْوَصِيَّاتٍ خُلِقْنَ لِلرِّمَا
صُفْرٍ أَعَالِيهِنَّ زُرْقَاتِ ٱللِّحَا
قَدْ طُوِيَتْ أَعْنَاقُهَا عَلَى ٱلْبُرَى
مِنْ عَقَبٍ شُدَّ بِأَثْنَاءِ ٱلْقُوَى
وَسَدَلُوا خَرَائِطًا حُمْرًا طِرَا
مُزَرَّرَاتٍ قَدْ شُدِدْنَ بِٱلْعُرَى
فِيهَا حُتُوفٌ مُرْصَدَاتٌ لِلْفَنَا
مُدَحْرَجَاتٍ قَدْ عُمِلْنَ بِٱسْتِوَا
سَيَّانَ مِنْهَا مَا دَنَا وَمَا نَأَى
رَاحُوا فَبَاتُوا بِـزُرُوعٍ وَبِمَا
بِحَيْثُ بَاتَ ٱلطَّيْرُ فِيهِ وَرَعَى
لَمْ يَطْعَمُوا لَيْلَهُمْ طَعْمَ ٱلْكَرَى
حَتَّى إِذَا ٱلنَّجْمُ مِنَ ٱلْأُفْقِ دَنَا
وَشَقَّ ضَوْءُ ٱلصُّبْحِ سِرْبَالَ ٱلدُّجَى

~ 99 ~

Time's Lessons

A band of brothers, bonded as friends,
united in desire, men who'd reply, "No!"
if one of them said, "No!," their "Yes!"
echoing his "Yes!," sharing one soul
despite their different appearances,
accepting no insult, never going beyond
what is meet. At evening, they brought curved
brown shafts, thin *barwaṣīs* made
for firing, with yellow bark above a gray-blue
inner bark, their necks wrapped in bracelets
of sinews twisted into the folds of the strands.
From the shafts, there hung new red pouches,
Buttoned and tied at the handles, with death inside—
bullets made for ambush and destruction, pellets
perfectly balanced and round, identical
on every side.
The troop bivouacked in sown fields
by water where the birds slept at night
and fed by day. The men tasted no sleep.
As the Pleiades neared the horizon,
as night's gloomy gown was rent by dawn's

وَصَوَّتَ ٱلطَّيْرُ بِأَلْوَانِ ٱلنِّدَا
تَفَرَّقُوا فِي عُشُبٍ وَفِي كَلَا
وَسَتَرُوا قِسِيَّهُمْ فَمَا تُرَى
ثُمَّ مَشَوْا كَأَنَّ بِٱلْقَوْمِ حَفَا
خَتْلًا كَمَا يُمْشَى عَلَى جَمْرِ ٱلْغَضَى
حَتَّى إِذَا مَا قَرُبَ ٱلْقَوْمُ دَعَا
بَعْضُهُمْ بَعْضًا وَلَجُّوا فِي ٱلنِّدَا
وَتَرَكُوا ٱلْأَسْمَاءَ نَادَوْا بِٱلْكُنَى
أَبَا فُلَانٍ ٱرْمِ ذَاكَ وَٱرْمِ ذَا
وَصَعِدَ ٱلطَّيْرُ إِلَى جَوِّ ٱلسَّمَا
فَأَتْبَعُوا رِشْقًا كَرِجْلِ مَنْ دَبَى
مُشَيَّعَاتٍ بِٱلْقِرَاءِ وَٱلْفِدَا
وَبِٱكْتِنَاءٍ مَرَّةً وَبِٱعْتِزَا
مِنَ ٱلْمَجَانِيقِ أُمِرَّتْ لِلْعِدَا
وَأَدْرَكَتْهُنَّ وَهُنَّ بِٱلْهَوَا
فَٱنْصَعْنَ شَتَّى بَعْدَ أَنْ كُنَّ مَعَا
يَهْوِينَ فِي ٱلْجَوِّ كَمَا تَهْوِي ٱلدِّلَا
عَلَى ٱلْجَنَاحِ مَرَّةً وَلِلْقَفَا
وَأَقْبَلَ ٱلْقَوْمُ عَلَيْهَا بِٱلْمُدَى
حَزًّا وَنَهْسًا بِطَبِيخٍ وَشِوَا
ثُمَّ دَعَوْا غُلَامَهُمْ فَمَا وَنَى
مُذَفْذِفَ ٱلْخِلْقَةِ مَخْرُوطَ ٱلْقَبَا
فَصَفَّ فِي ٱلْبَيْتِ أَبَارِيقَ مِلَا
لَهَا رُؤُوسٌ مُشْرِفَاتٌ وَعُرَى

light, as the birds sang in a medley of calls,
they split up in the grass and undergrowth,
concealing their bows from sight, moving with stealth,
as if tiptoeing barefoot on burning coals.
When close, they shouted to one another,
using family rather than given names.
"Hey so-and-so, fire here, shoot there!"
The birds shot into the sky. With a step forward,
as if dawdling, accompanied with promises
of hospitality, prayers for success, family names,
and declarations of lineage,[120] the men fired salvos
from trebuchets tightly wound for warfare,
striking the birds in midair as the flock flew
in all directions, then plummeted from the sky
like buckets down a well, landing on their necks
or wings.
The men advanced with their knives,
cutting and tearing at the meat, boiled or grilled,
with their teeth. Then they called for their page,
who responded in haste, twig-thin in an ample gown,
swaying coquettishly as he arrived. Inside the tent,
he laid out the ibriks, full to the brim, pulsing

تَضْحَكُ عَنْ أَمْثَالِ أَوْدَاجِ ٱلظِّبَا
تَرْعُفُ إِنْ خَرَّتْ وَإِنْ قَامَتْ رَقَا
تَغُرُّ أَفْرَاخًا فَيَنْهَضْنَ رِوَا
تَدُورُ فِيمَا بَيْنَهُمْ دَوْرَ ٱلرَّحَى
تَمْضِي رِوَاءً ثُمَّ تَأْتِيهِمْ ظِمَا
فَبَيْنَمَا نَحْنُ عَلَى حَالِ ٱللِّقَا
تَقْصُرُ عَنْ غَايَتِنَا فِيهِ ٱلْمُنَى
إِذْ قَعَدَ ٱلدَّهْرُ عَلَيْنَا فَٱتَّكَا
وَفَرَّقَ ٱلْأُلَّافَ مِنْ بَعْدِ ٱللِّقَا
فَمِنْهُمُ مَنْ شَطَحَتْ بِهِ ٱلنَّوَى
وَمِنْهُمُ مَنْ صَارَ فِي دَارِ ٱلْبِلَى
فَٱلْعَيْنُ تَبْكِيهِمْ وَمَا يُغْنِي ٱلْبُكَا
فَمَنْ رَأَى بَعْدَهُمْ فَقَدْ رَأَى
مِنْ وَاعِظَاتِ ٱلدَّهْرِ مَا فِيهِ ٱكْتَفَى
ثُمَّ تَبَدَّلْتُ بِإِخْوَانِ ٱلصَّفَا
قَوْمًا يَرَوْنَ ٱلْمَجْدَ تَطْوِيلَ ٱللُّحَى
لَا عِلْمَ دُنْيَا عِنْدَهُمْ وَلَا تُقَى
غُذُّوا صِغَارًا ثُمَّ سُيِّبُوا سُدَى
بِغِرَّةِ ٱلْجَهْلِ وَتَأْدِيبِ ٱلنِّسَا
فَلَوْ تَرَى شَيْخَهُمْ إِذَا ٱحْتَبَى
ثُمَّ ٱبْتَدَا بِوَصْفِ شَيْءٍ إِذْ بَدَا
مِنْ رُخْصِ سِعْرٍ أَوْ مِنْ إِفْرَاطِ غَلَا
وَرَفَعُوا أَصْوَاتَهُمْ بَلَى بَلَى
حَسِبْتَهُمْ ضَأْنًا تَدَاعَوْا بِثُغَا

with bright wine like a gazelle's aorta,
spilling if tipped, staunched when upright,
deceiving youths into standing up to take their fill,[121]
doing the rounds like a millstone on a shaft,
leaving the thirsty drinkers slaked. In such a company,
they couldn't want for more, while Time
reclined before again scattering the friends.
Some live far away; others reside in the land
of the dead. I weep for them, but what good
does that do? Since those days, I've learned many
of Time's lessons.
I exchanged this brotherhood
of affection for people who think glory means
boasting a big beard—they don't know the world,
they have no true faith, they are fed like children,
then left to roam like camels without a drover,
educated like women, emboldened by ignorance.
Should you see their shaykh take his place
to teach and begin to describe a thing
by undervaluing its cost or inflating its price
and hear them shout, "Aye! Aye!," you'd think
they were a herd of bleating sheep or a flock

أَوْ سِرْبَ بَطٍّ جَاوَبَتْ سِرْبَ قَطَا
فَذٰلِكَ ٱلدَّأْبُ إِلَى وَقْتِ ٱلْعِشَا
فِي كُلِّ يَوْمٍ مَا بَقُوا وَمَا بَقَى
فَٱلْعَقْلُ يَزْدَادُ صَدًى إِلَى صَدَى
بِقُرْبِهِمْ وَٱلْعِلْمُ يَزْدَادُ فَنَا
وَكُلُّهُمْ فِي ٱلْعِلْمِ يَمْشِي ٱلْقَهْقَرَى
يُرِيدُ قُدَّامًا فَيَجْرِي مِنْ وَرَا

of ducks answering a troop of sandgrouse.
They do this each and every day until night falls,
and for as long as they breathe, they won't cease.
In their midst, my brain is starved of sustenance,
my learning shrinks: their knowledge is backward—
they try to advance yet only move in reverse.

نعت الديك والحمام والفرس وهو ستّ أرجوزات

~ ١٠٠ ~

قال ينعت ديكًا [الرجز]

أَنْعُتُ دِيكًا مِنْ دُيُوكِ ٱلْهِنْدِ
كَرِيمَ عَمٍّ وَكَرِيمَ جَدِّ
نِسْبَتُهُ لَيْسَتْ إِلَى مَعَدِّ
وَلَا قُضَاعِيٍّ وَلَا فِي ٱلْأَزْدِ
مُفَتَّحَ ٱلرِّيشِ شَدِيدَ ٱلزَّنْدِ
ضَخْمَ ٱلْمَخَالِيبِ عَظِيمَ ٱلْعُضْدِ
حَتَّى إِذَا ٱلدِّيكُ ٱرْتَأَى مِنْ بُعْدِ
وَنَجْمُهُ فِي ٱلنَّحْسِ لَا فِي ٱلسَّعْدِ
رَأَيْتَهُ كَٱلْفَارِسِ ٱلْمُعَدِّ
يَخْطِرُ تِيهًا مِثْلَ خَطْرِ ٱلْأُسْدِ
يُعِيُّهُ بِٱلْكَدِّ بَعْدَ ٱلْكَدِّ
وَتَعَبٍ مُوَصَّلٍ بِجَهْدِ
حَتَّى تَرَى ٱلدِّيكَ لَهُ كَٱلْعَبْدِ
مُكَفَّرًا يُعْظِمُهُ بِٱلسَّجْدِ
يَا لَكَ مِنْ دِيكٍ رَبَا فِي ٱلْمَهْدِ

Gamecock, Pigeon, and Horse Descriptions: Six *Urjūzah*s

~ 100 ~

His Foe's Star Is Bad

A gamecock description:

I sing of an Indian gamecock
of noble pedigree, grandfather
and uncle both, though not descended
from Maʿadd, Quḍāʿah, or Azd,
with wings open wide, strong
legs, thick claws, mighty thighs.
He spots his opponent from afar—
his foe's star is bad, he's out of luck.
Look, our cock's a cavalryman geared
up for battle, swaggering and exulting
like a lion: he wearies his foe, kicks
him again and again, tires him out
with his stamina and brute force.
Look, now the other bird is his slave,
an infidel lying prostrate in homage.
What a gamecock, bred in the yard!

~ ١٠١ ~

وقال ينعته [الرجز]

أَنْعَتُ دِيكًا مِنْ دُيُوكِ ٱلْهِنْدِ
أَحْسَنَ مِنْ طَاؤُوسِ قَصْرِ ٱلْمَهْدِي
أَشْجَعَ مِنْ غَادِي عَرِينِ ٱلْأُسْدِ
تَرَى ٱلدَّجَاجَ حَوْلَهُ كَٱلْجُنْدِ
يُقْعِينَ مِنْ خِيفَتِهِ لِلسَّفْدِ
لَهُ سُقَاعٌ كَدَوِيِّ ٱلرَّعْدِ
مِنْقَارُهُ كَٱلْمِعْوَلِ ٱلْمُحَدِّ
يَقْهَرُ مَنْ نَاقَرَهُ بِٱلنَّقْدِ
عَيْنَاهُ مِنْهُ فِي ٱلْقَفَا وَٱلْخَدِّ
وَهَامَةٌ وَعُنُقٌ كَٱلْوَرْدِ
لَهُ ٱعْتِدَالٌ وَٱنْتِصَابُ قَدِّ
كَأَنَّهُ ٱلْهُدَّابُ فِي ٱلْفِرِنْدِ
مُحْدَوْدِبُ ٱلظَّهْرِ كَرِيمُ ٱلْجَدِّ
كَأَنَّهُ قُلَّةُ طَوْدٍ صَلْدِ
طَاوٍ شَبَاهُ عِنْدَ كَدِّ ٱلرَّدِّ
يَعْتَقِبَانِ رَأْسَهُ بِٱلْقَفْدِ
مُفَحِّجُ ٱلرِّجْلَيْنِ عِنْدَ ٱلنَّجْدِ
ثُمَّ وَظِيفَانِ لَهُ مِنْ بَعْدِ
وَشَوْكَتَانِ خُصَّتَا بِحَدِّ
كَأَنَّمَا كَفَّاهُ عِنْدَ ٱلْوَخْدِ
فِي خَطْرِهِ كَٱلْمَسَدِ ٱلْمُرْبَدِّ

~ 101 ~

A Cheetah Lunge

I sing of an Indian gamecock
more gorgeous than the peacock
in al-Mahdī's palace, braver
than the hunter in a lion's den.
Look at him, surrounded by his hens
as if by his troops, fearful, ready for mating.
His crow is a thunderclap, his keen
pickaxe beak conquers with a brutal peck.
His opponent runs away, looking back
and to the side, his head and neck
rose-red, while he stands there poised
and erect, like cords hanging from a sword-
belt. He's a pedigree, his back curved
like a tall peak. His claws, tucked in,
kick back an attack, slapping his foe's
head time and again in a pigeon-toed
victory walk. He boasts long leg bones
and special sharp spurs,[122] an ostrich
stride with feet like dark palm rope,

فَٱلْقِرْنُ مِنْهُ أَبَدًا يُعَدِّي
كَمْ طَائِرٍ أَرْدَى وَكَمْ سَيُرْدِي
بِٱلْجَمْزِ وَٱلْقَفْزِ وَصَلْبِ ٱلْجِلْدِ
كَدًّا لَهُ بِٱلْخَطْرِ أَيَّ كَدِّ
كَمَا يُسَدِّي ٱلْحَائِكُ ٱلْمُسَدِّي
إِنْ وَقَفَ ٱلدِّيكُ ثَنَى بِٱلشَّدِّ
وَٱلْوَثْبُ مِنْهُ مِثْلَ وَثْبِ ٱلْفَهْدِ
لَيْسَ لَهُ مِنْ غُلْبِهِ مِنْ بُدِّ
فَٱلْحَمْدُ لِلّٰهِ وَلِيِّ ٱلْحَمْدِ

pounding the ground. His challengers
scamper away—he's killed so many birds
and will kill many more. With his tough skin,
he struts, jumps, and thumps the ground
like a weaver stitching the warp on the frame.
If a rival confronts him, he sprints back
in a cheetah lunge—and victory is assured.
Praise God, worthy of our praise!

~ ١٠٢ ~

وقال ينعت طيور يعفور [الرجز]

يَا أَيُّهَا ٱلْمُطْنِبُ ذُو ٱلْغُرُورِ
فِي صِفَةِ ٱلسُّودِ مِنَ ٱلطُّيُورِ
فِي ٱلْحُسْنِ وَٱلْهِدَاءِ وَٱلتَّخْيِيرِ
رَيْبُ شَهَادَاتٍ لِدَعْوَى زُورِ
اِسْمَعْ فَمَا نَبَّاكَ كَٱلْخَبِيرِ
مِنْ ذِي صِفَاتٍ حَاذِقٍ نِحْرِيرِ
صِفَاتُهُ مُحْكَمَةُ ٱلتَّحْبِيرِ
مَا جُعِلَ ٱلْأَسْوَدُ كَٱلْيَعْفُورِي
أَطْيَارُ يَعْفُورَ ذَوَاتُ ٱلْخَيْرِ
أَوْلَى بِفَضْلِ ذِكْرِهَا ٱلْمَذْكُورِ
هٰذَا ثَنَاءُ حُسْنِهَا ٱلْمَشْهُورِ
يَا حُسْنَهَا فَوْقَ أَعَالِي ٱلدُّورِ
فِي حُجَرٍ شَامِخَةِ ٱلتَّحْجِيرِ
إِذَا تَهَادَيْنَ مِنَ ٱلْوُكُورِ
بِعَرْصَةِ ٱلْإِنَاثِ وَٱلذُّكُورِ
وَطَرْدِ ٱلْغَيُورِ لِلْغَيُورِ
تَكْرِيرَ تَهْدِيلٍ عَلَى تَكْرِيرِ
كَأَنَّ فِي هَدِيلِهَا ٱلْجَهِيرِ
تَرَنُّمَ ٱلْعِيدَانِ وَٱلزَّمِيرِ
أَوْ كَدَوِيِّ ٱلنَّحْلِ لِلنَّفِيرِ

~ 102 ~

The Jinni's Night Song

A description of Ya'fūr's birds:

Chitter-chatter away with your long-
winded, deluded descriptions of black birds—
their beauty, their homing skills, their virtues.
A false claim puts testimony into doubt.
Listen to me, to my expert account,
a wordsmith's carefully worked claim:
black pigeons are inferior to Ya'fūr's birds,[123]
which are wondrous and fine,
fully worthy of their reputation!
I hereby sing the praises
of their well-known beauty!
How charming they are in their lofts
built high and proud on the rooftops,
males and females leaving their nests
to bob-walk on the patio, dominant birds
chasing their rivals away in a loud chorus
of coo-roo, coo-roo like the sound
of a fife-and-lute concert or the battle-
buzz of a swarm of bees attacking

مِنْ مُجْتَنِي ٱلذَّوْبِ أَخِي ٱلتَّغْرِيرِ
ذَوَاتِ هَامٍ جَهْمَةِ ٱلتَّدْوِيرِ
وَأَعْيُنٍ أَصْفَى مِنَ ٱلبِلَّورِ
فِي لَامِعٍ مِنْ حُمْرَةٍ مُنِيرِ
لَمْعَ ٱلْيَوَاقِيتِ مَعَ ٱلشُّذُورِ
إِلَى قَرَاطِمٍ نِبَالٍ خُورِ
كَتَوْأَمَاتِ ٱللُّؤْلُؤِ ٱلْمَنْثُورِ
فَوْقَ مَنَاقِرَ قِصَارٍ صُورِ
كَرَنَّةِ ٱلْبَمِّ وَرَجْعِ ٱلزِّيرِ
ذَوَاتِ رِيشٍ كَمَدَارِي ٱلْحُورِ
وَأَرْجُلٍ فِي حُمْرَةِ ٱلْحَبِيرِ
جُرْدٍ كَظَهْرِ ٱلْأَدَمِ ٱلْمَبْشُورِ
بِيضِ ٱلْبُطُونِ مُلْسِ ٱلظُّهُورِ
مَا بَيْنَ ذِي سَبْطٍ وَذِي تَنْمِيرِ
كَمْ طَائِرٍ مِنْهُنَّ ذِي تَشْمِيرِ
حَزَوَّرٍ ذِي ذَنَبٍ قَصِيرِ
مِنْ مِزْجَلٍ أُرْسِلَ فِي ٱلنُّحُورِ
فَشَقَّ هَوْلَ ٱلْجَوِّ وَٱلْغُمُورِ
كَفِعْلِهِ بِٱلْحَزْنِ وَٱلْوُعُورِ
كَٱلْخَالِقِ ٱلْكَاسِرِ لِلتَّغْوِيرِ
أَوْ سَهْمِ رَامٍ قَاصِدٍ طَرِيرِ
أَوْ لَفْتِ بَازٍ بِيَدِ ٱلْمُشِيرِ
حَتَّى هَوَى لِلْوَكْرِ كَٱلْمَنْظُورِ
فَضَعْضَعَ ٱلْحُجْرَةَ بِٱلنَّعِيرِ

a gutsy honey gatherer with his sack.
Their crowns are blunt and round, their eyes
clearer than crystal with shiny, bright-
red pupils set like rubies amid gold beads.
Their ceres are soft and fine, like safflower
seeds or Taw'am pearls scattered from a necklace,[124]
set in short, curved beaks; their plaints
are like the lute twang of the *bamm* or the *zīr*,
feathers like an iron comb in a maid's lustrous
hair, silky red feet, as bald and smooth
as a tanned hide, white bellies, and sleek
backs. Some are long and tall; others sport
a leopard's spots. So many birds primed
for action—short tails, breasts that sing
the jinni's night song.[125] Across seas
and rugged flats, they speed through the terrors
of the air,[126] as swift as a saber's sharp battle
slash or a skilled archer's lethal arrow;
or, at the signal, they wheel like the gos
attacking a nest and razing it with a shrill war cry.

وَكَبَّرُوا وَأَيَّمَا تَكْبِيرِ
فَرُبَّ سَاعٍ عِنْدَهَا بَشِيرِ
أُبِرَّ مِنْهُ قَسَمُ ٱلنُّذُورِ

When the pigeons return, the gamblers shout,
"Allahu akbar!" in joy, their bets cashed in.

~ ١٠٣ ~

وقال أيضاً بنعت الحمام [الرجز]

وَصَاحِبَاتٍ نُفَّرٍ مِنْ زَاعِقِ
يَطِرْنَ فِي ٱلْجَوِّ بِأَعْلَى حَالِقِ
بَوَاسِطٍ بِرِيشِهَا خَوَافِقِ
يَتْبَعْنَ لِلْعَادَةِ صَوْتَ نَاعِقِ
كَأَنَّمَا ٱسْتُقْنَ لَهُ بِسَائِقِ
مُغَلِّسَاتٍ لِذُرُورِ ٱلشَّارِقِ
لَا بِٱلْمَقَالِيعِ وَلَا ٱلْجَلَاهِقِ
يَبْعُدْنَ أَنْ يُبْلَغْنَ بِٱلْبَنَادِقِ
بِحَيْثُ يَأْمَنَّ لُحُوقَ ٱللَّاحِقِ
مِنْ كُلِّ بَازٍ مُطْعِمٍ وَبَاشِقِ
تَحْسَبُهُنَّ لُصَّقًا بِٱلْخَافِقِ
فَلَوْ حَمَلْنَ حَاجَةً لِعَاشِقِ
مُتَيَّمِ ٱلْقَلْبِ رَعُوبٍ خَافِقِ
رَسَائِلًا مِنْهُ إِلَى صَدَائِقِ
سَلَّيْنَ مِنْ شِدَّةِ شَوْقٍ شَائِقِ
يَقْطَعْنَ فِي مُدَّةِ نُطْقِ ٱلنَّاطِقِ
مَغَارِبَ ٱلْأَرْضِ إِلَى ٱلْمَشَارِقِ
إِلَى لُؤَيٍّ عُصَمِ ٱلْوَثَائِقِ
لَدَى ٱلْمُلِمَّاتِ وَفِي ٱلْحَقَائِقِ
بِشَرِّهِمْ قَبْلَ ٱلنَّوَالِ ٱللَّاحِقِ

~ 103 ~

From a Lover's Captive Heart[127]

Another pigeon description:

Comrades high in the sky, frightened
into flight toward a mountain peak,
fluttering wings outspread, heeding
the call of a leader driving them like camels
to a water hole at dawn's first break
at night's end. Too far to be shot
with pellets from sling or bow, safe
from attack by a sparrow hawk or a gos
with a nest to feed, you'd think they're stuck
to the horizon. Were they to carry petitions
to his beloved, those missives from a lover's
captive heart so prey to alarm and fear,
they'd bring solace to a yearning that sears,
crossing from west to east in the time
it takes a man to say, "To Lu'ayy,
true to his pledge and duty when disaster
strikes, first fierce, then generous—

كَٱلْبَرْقِ يَبْدُو قَبْلَ جَوْدٍ دَافِقِ
وَٱلْغَيْثُ يَخْفَى وَقْعُهُ لِلرَّامِقِ
إِنْ لَمْ يَجِدْهُ بِدَلِيلِ ٱلْبَارِقِ

when lightning flashes before a storm,
the watcher, unable to locate the lightning's
signs, knows not where the rain will fall."

~ ١٠٤ ~

وقال ينعت فرسًا [الرجز]

قَدْ أَغْتَدِي وَٱللَّيْلُ فِي إِهَابِهِ
أَدْعَجُ مَا غُسِّلَ مِنْ خِضَابِهِ
مُدَثَّرٌ لَمْ يَبْدُ مِنْ حِجَابِهِ
كَٱلْحَبَشِيِّ ٱنْسَلَّ مِنْ ثِيَابِهِ
بِهَيْكَلٍ قُوبِلَ مِنْ أَنْسَابِهِ
مُرَدَّدِ ٱلْأَعْوَجِ فِي أَصْلَابِهِ
يَهْدِيهِ مِثْلُ ٱلْقَعْوِ فِي ٱنْصِبَابِهِ
وَكَاهِلٍ وَعُنُقٍ نَأَى بِهِ
يُصَافِحُ ٱلْكَذَّانَ مَعْ أَطْرَابِهِ
بِوَقْحٍ يَقِيهِ فِي ٱنْسِيَابِهِ
شَبَا ٱلْمَطَارِيرِ وَحَدُّ نَابِهِ
حَتَّى إِذَا ٱلصُّبْحُ بَدَا مِنْ بَابِهِ
وَكَشَرَتْ أَشْدَاقُهُ عَنْ نَابِهِ
عَنَّ لَنَا كَٱلرَّأْلِ لَمْ يُورَأْ بِهِ
ذُو حُوَّةٍ أُفْرِدَ عَنْ أَصْحَابِهِ
يَقْرُو مِتَانَ ٱلْأَرْضِ مَعْ سِهَابِهِ
أَطَاعَهُ ٱلْحَوْذَانُ فِي إِسْرَابِهِ
فَقَدْ رَمَاه ٱلنَّحْضُ فِي أَقْرَابِهِ
وَٱلطِّرْفُ قَدْ زُمِّلَ فِي ثِيَابِهِ
قَائِدُهُ مِنْ أَرَنٍ يَشْقَى بِهِ

~ 104 ~

A Forest Fire

A horse description:

I crossed the dark-skinned, black-eyed night,
her unwashed hair still dyed with henna,
wrapped in a cloak and hidden in a hijab,
like a naked Ethiopian. I rode a horse
as huge as a temple, a true pedigree, whose spine
indicates his descent from Aʿwaj;[128] his head, in the reins,
moving like a pulley's iron wheel, his withers
and neck built for long-distance forays.
In the gallop, his hard hooves flatten the grasses
and pebbles, walled in by his toes and brute force.[129]
The sun left his lair, baring his fangs in a growl.
We spotted a brown ostrich in the flats, separated
from his comrades, oblivious, feeding on ripe *ḥawdhān*,
his muscular flanks hard and strong. Our horse
was covered with a blanket, his rider anxious

قُلْنَا لَهُ جَرِّدْهُ مِنْ أَسْلَابِهِ
فَلَاحَ كَٱلْحَاجِبِ مِنْ سَحَابِهِ
أَوْ كَٱلصَّفِيحِ ٱسْتُلَّ مِنْ قِرَابِهِ
فَسَدَّدَ ٱلطِّرْفَ وَمَا هَاهَا بِهِ
فَٱنْصَاعَ كَٱلْأَجْدَلِ فِي ٱنْصِبَابِهِ
أَوْ كَٱلْحَرِيقِ فِي هَشِيمِ غَابِهِ
مُلْتَهِبًا يَسْتَنُّ فِي إِلْهَابِهِ
كَأَنَّمَا ٱلْبَيْدَاءُ مِنْ نِهَابِهِ
فَحَازَهُ بِٱلرُّمْحِ فِي أَعْجَابِهِ
شَكَّ ٱلْفَتَاةِ ٱلدُّرَّ فِي أَخْرَابِهِ

to preserve his vigor. "Strip him!" we ordered.
He blazed bright, like the edge of a cloud
or a blade slipped from its sheath. The rider urged him on,
but there was no need to dig in a spur—
he exploded into a saker's stoop, a forest
fire at summer's height, his fierce leaps
and blazing pace stripping the desert bare.
He felled the ostrich, his lance spearing its rump
like a pearl threaded by a young girl.

~ ١٠٥ ~

وقال ينعته [الرجز]

لَمَّا بَدَا مِنْ سَاطِعٍ إِشْرَاقُهُ
وَٱنْجَابَ مِنْ ذِي ظُلَمٍ رِوَاقُهُ
وَحَانَ مِنْ نَهَارِنَا مِصْدَاقُهُ
قَرَّبْتُ سَهْمًا كَرُمَتْ أَعْرَاقُهُ
وَمَارَ فِي أَوْصَالِهِ إِحْرَاقُهُ
كَمَرَسٍ مُمِرَّةٍ أَطْلَاقُهُ
أَرْمَى بِهِ ٱلْغَيْثُ سَرَى بُعَاقُهُ
مِنْ نَوْءِ نَجْمٍ جَادَهُ ٱنْدِفَاقُهُ
أَسْعَدَهُ بِوَابِلٍ غَيْدَاقُهُ
وَٱلْغَيْثُ مُدَمَّمُ ٱلذُّرَى وَدَّاقُهُ
حَتَّى رَبَا مِنْ نِعْمَةٍ شِقَاقُهُ
لَمَّا دَنَوْنَا ذُعِرَتْ نُهَاقُهُ
وَٱلْمُهْرُ قَدْ هَيَّجَهُ ٱشْتِيَاقُهُ
فَلَاحَ مِنْ غَابِ ٱلطُّوَى فِرَاقُهُ
قُلْتُ لِعَبْدٍ رَعْبَلَتْ أَخْلَاقُهُ
ٱِرْكَبْ فَقَدْ أَقْلَقَنَا إِقْلَاقُهُ
لَمَّا ٱسْتَوَى فِي مَتْنِهِ خَفَّاقُهُ
أَرْسَلَهُ وَٱغْرَوْرَقَتْ أَحْدَاقُهُ
فَصَادَ عَيْرًا لَاحِقًا صِفَاقُهُ
بِطَعْنَةٍ مَجَّتْ لَهَا أَشْدَاقُهُ
نَجِيعَ جَوْفٍ شَابَهُ بُصَاقُهُ

~ 105 ~

Dropped to Earth

Rays lit up the sky and black night struck
camp, proof that it was day. I brought
out Colt, a pedigree stallion like an arrow,
fire coursing through his joints,
like a tightly twisted, knotted well rope,
dropped to earth by night clouds guided
by a rising star, showered with their gifts,
blessed by an endless deluge, the cloud
polls kohl-black with rain. He drank
from their bounty, and his limbs grew strong.

As we approached, the onagers neighed 12
in alarm. Colt stirred with lust.
One of the herd popped up, running from Ṭuwā's
holy trees.[130] To my rag-clad slave I said,
"Mount up! His energy is making me nervous."
He settled his light frame on Colt's back
and he gave the horse free rein, his eyes streaming
with water. He chased down a hard-loined jack—
a spear thrust caused its jaws to spew thick

عَنْ طَعْمِ مَوْتٍ مُمْقِرٍ مَذَاقُـهُ
مِنَ ٱلَّذِي أَبْـرَزَهُ إِبْـرَاقُـهُ
مِنَ ٱلرَّدَى إِذْ لَمَعَتْ أَعْنَاقُـهُ

belly blood mixed with spit, the bitter food
of death delivered by Colt, doom's lightning
burst, his neck a blaze of thunderbolts.

أرجوزة سقطت من نسخة الأصل

~ ١٠٦ ~

وقال ينعته [الرجز]

قَدْ أَغْتَدِي وَٱللَّيْلُ فِي ٱعْتِكَارِهِ
بِأَغْضَفَ يَمُوجُ فِي شَوَارِهِ
مُؤَدَّبٍ مَا يُصْطَلَى بِنَارِهِ
كَٱلْوَتَرِ ٱلْمُحْصَدِ فِي إِمْرَارِهِ
أَشْرَفَ مَتْنَاهُ عَلَى فَقَارِهِ
يَسْبِقُ مَرَّ ٱلرِّيحِ فِي إِحْضَارِهِ
لَا يُمْهِلُ ٱلظَّبْيَ عَلَى ٱقْتِدَارِهِ
قَلَّ رُجُوعُ ٱلطَّرْفِ عَنْ مِرَارِهِ
فَلَيْسَ كَلْبٌ يَنْتَمِي لِدَارِهِ
مَحَلُّهُ سَلُوقُ مَعْ وَبَارِهِ

A Poem Missing from MS Fateh 3773

~ 106 ~

The Wind Dawdles

Night was a confusion of black. I crossed the dark
with Drop Ear, bones jutting out under his flesh,
a trained killer, compactly fashioned
like a taut bowstring, his strong back arced
over vertebrae—when he sprints, the wind
dawdles behind. He gave the gazelles no respite,
his gaze focused on the chase. He's no home-
grown dog; he hails from Salūq and Wabār.

أرجوزة من رواية الصوليّ

A Poem Not Contained in al-Iṣfahānī's Recension and Found Only in al-Ṣūlī's Recension

~ ١٠٧ ~

وقال في البازي [الرجز]

قَدْ أَغْتَدِي قَبْلَ طُلُوعِ ٱلشَّمْسِ
بِأَحْجَنِ ٱلْخَطْمِ كَمِيِّ ٱلنَّفْسِ
غَرْثَانَ إِلَّا أَكْلَةً بِٱلْأَمْسِ
آنَسَ بِٱلطَّمْسِ وَمَاءِ ٱلطَّمْسِ
كَنَظْرَةِ ٱلْمَجْنُونِ أَوْ ذِي ٱلْمَسِّ
حَتَّى إِذَا أَقْصَدَ بَعْدَ ٱلْخَمْسِ
عِشْرِينَ مِنْ حُبَارَيَاتٍ قُعْسِ
مِثْلَ ٱلنَّصَارَى فِي ثِيَابٍ طُلْسِ
فَهُنَّ بَيْنَ أَرْبَعٍ وَخَمْسِ
صَرْعَى وَمُسْتَدْمٍ أَمِيمِ ٱلرَّأْسِ
وَخَرِبٍ يَشْفِنُ بَعْدَ ٱلتَّعْسِ
كَأَنَّمَا صَبْغَتُهُ بِوَرْسِ
مِنْ عَلَقِ ٱلْأَنْسَاءِ بَعْدَ ٱلْعَفْسِ

~ 107 ~

A Crazed Stare

A goshawk description:

Just before sunrise, I crossed the dark
with a hungry, curve-beaked, armor-
plated saker, last fed yesterday,
scanning the pond at Ṭams
with a crazed stare or the eyes
of a man in fever's grip. She felled
five then twenty plump-breasted
houbaras resembling dark-robed Christians,
lying dead in groups of four or five,
brains oozing from their skulls,
and a big male flat on his face
in the dust, a wild stare in his eyes,
as if, battle over, he were steeped
in spice from his bleeding thigh.

أراجيز من رواية توزون

Poems Found Only in Tüzün's Recension

~ ١٠٨ ~

وقال ينعت الكلب [الرجز]

عَلَّمَهُنَّ ٱلْحِرْصَ بِٱلتِّجْوَاعِ
وَٱلْأَدَبِ ٱلْمُحْكَمِ بِٱلْإِيزَاعِ
حَتَّى إِذَا إِضْنَ كَٱلْأَفَاعِي
وَقَلَّدَ ٱلْأَجْيَادَ بِٱلرِّصَاعِ
أَمَّ مَسَامَ ٱلْبَقَرِ ٱلرِّتَاعِ
وَصِدْنَ أَحْوَى أَحْسَمَ ٱلنِّزَاعِ
مُنَمْنَمَ ٱلْعُرْقُوبِ وَٱلْكُرَاعِ
يَأْخُذُ بِٱلسَّاقِ وَبِٱلذِّرَاعِ
مِثْلَ ٱلنَّصَارَى قُدَّسٍ رَعَاعِ
حَوْلَ عَظِيمٍ كَامِلِ ٱلْمَسَاعِي
يَا لَكَ مِنْ رَأْيٍ وَمِنْ سَمَاعِ

~ 108 ~

A Fighter to the End

A dog description:

> Skittish dogs, collars on necks, moving like vipers,
> starved, trained to behave. The huntsman made
> for the pasturelands where the oryx live at ease.
> Swarming around him like a throng of Christians
> worshipping a saint revered for his powers,
> the dogs killed a dark, hard-running bull
> with striped legs and hocks, a fighter to the end.
> What skill, what control the huntsman displayed!

وقال ينعت البازي [الرجز]

قَدْ أَغْتَدِي وَٱلشَّمْسُ فِي حِجَابِهِ
بِكُرَّزِيٍّ صَادَ فِي شَبَابِهِ
يَنْفُضُ عَنْهُ خُصَلاً يَأْذَى بِهِ
بِأَحْجَنِ ٱلْأَنْفِ إِذَا ٱفْتَلَى بِهِ
طَالَتْ خَوَافِيهِ عَلَى ٱزْلِغْبَابِهِ
كَأَنَّ صَوْتَ ٱلْحَلْقِ إِذْ صَأَى بِهِ
تَأَوُّهَ ٱلشَّاكِي لِمَا أَمْسَى بِهِ
وَحَلَّ مَا أَبْصَرَ إِذْ رَأَى بِهِ
مِنْ بَطْنِ مَلْحُوبٍ إِلَى أَعْجَابِهِ
فَٱنْقَضَّ كَٱلْجُلْمُودِ إِذْ غَلَا بِهِ
غَضْبَانَ قَوْمٍ فِئَةٍ رَمَى بِهِ
يَنْفُضُ عِطْفَيْهِ مِنَ ٱنْصِبَابِهِ
تَقَلُّبَ ٱلنَّيْزَكِ فِي ٱنْقِلَابِهِ
وَلَا يَزَالُ خَرَبٌ يَشْقَى بِهِ
مُنْتَزَعَ ٱلْفُؤَادِ مِنْ حِجَابِهِ
يَنْزُو وَقَدْ أَثْبَتَ فِي إِهَابِهِ
مَخَالِبًا يَنْشَبْنَ مِنْ إِنْشَابِهِ
مِثْلَ مُدَى ٱلْجَزَّارِ أَوْ قَصَّابِهِ
مِنْ كُلِّ شَحَّاجِ ٱلضُّحَى غَلَا بِهِ
يَخِرُّ لِلْأَنْفِ إِذَا كَرَا بِهِ

~ 109 ~

A Lover's Nightly Sighs

A goshawk description:

The sun was still veiled. I crossed the dark
with a molted goshawk on the glove,
a hunter since her youth, warding off harm
with the curved beak she wields like a blade.
Her downy feathers had long been replaced
by secondaries; her throat rasps with a lover's
nightly sighs. She fells all the plump-bellies
she spots, swooping in a rage, amid the troop
that hunts with her, like a rock from a trebuchet.
Out of the stoop, with a flick of her wings,
this scourge of houbaras with her assegai beak
mounts her prey, ripping hearts
from breasts with pounces like a butcher's
razor-sharp knives thrust fast in their hides,
tossing like a ball the clucking males
who lie flat on their beaks, brutalized.

~ ١١٠ ~

وقال ينعت الصقر ويذمّه وتروى لغيره [الرجز]

يَا لَكَ مِنْ صَقْرٍ لَقِيتَ حَتْفَكَا
أَلَا تَرَى إِذًا ٱلْحُبَارَى خَلْفَكَا
لَائِذَةً لَمْ تَلْقَ صَقْرًا قَبْلَكَا
وَأَرْنَبًا أُخْرَى ٱثْرَنَا هَالِكًا
تُقْبِلُ نَحْوِي وَتُوَلِّيهَا ٱسْتَكَا
لَقَدْ عَرَفْتُ إِذْ رَأَيْتُ نَوْمَكَا
تُدْخِلُ فِي ثِنْيِ ٱلْجَنَاحِ رَأْسَكَا
إِنَّكَ لَمَّا تَغْنَ عَنْكَ نَفْسُكَا

~ 110 ~

Your Bold Soul

A poem describing a saker the poet finds fault with; it is attributed to another poet.

My poor saker, you're dead!
Didn't you see the houbara
behind you? It had never seen
a saker before and was trying
to escape. A hare lay dead
in our tracks, and you were coming
to me, your back turned.
When I saw you sleep, head
folded in your wings, I knew
your bold soul hadn't achieved
its ambitions for you.

~ ١١١ ~

وقال ينعت الشاهين [الرجز]

لَمَّا بَدَا ذُو بُلَجٍ يُسْرَى بِهِ
يُنَفِّرُ ٱللَّيْلَ إِذَا حَدَا بِهِ
وَيُرَفِّعُ ٱلطُّرَّةَ مِنْ جِلْبَابِهِ
وَٱسْتَيْقَظَ ٱلْهَاجِدَ مِنْ أَسْرَابِهِ
كَبَلَقِ ٱلْحِصَانِ فِي أَقْرَابِهِ
أَوْ كَضِرَامِ قَابِسٍ يَسْعَى بِهِ
تُطِيرُهُ ٱلرِّيحُ عَلَى ثِيَابِهِ
طَوْرًا وَيَعْلُو سَنَنُ ٱلْتِهَابِهِ
تَذَكَّرَ ٱلْقَانِصُ فَٱغْتَدَى بِهِ
بِعَازِبٍ وَسْمِيُّهُ يُنْدَى بِهِ
قَفْرٍ كَأَنَّ ٱلصَّوْتَ مِنْ ذُبَابِهِ
تَغْرِيدُ نَشْوَانَ عَلَى شَرَابِهِ
وَفِتْيَةٍ صِيدٍ دَعَوْنَاهَا بِهِ
وَلَا يَكُونُ بَيْنَهُمْ يُجْوَى بِهِ
دَعَوْتُهُمْ لِمَنْزِلٍ بِتْنَا بِهِ
تُقْتَدَرُ ٱلْخِزْبَانُ أَوْ تُشْوَى بِهِ
فَقَامَ لِلطَّبْخِ وَلِٱحْتِطَابِهِ
أَبْلَجُ يَهْتَاجُ إِذَا هِجْنَا بِهِ
يُحَافِظُ ٱلطَّرْفَ إِذَا ٱجْتَلَى بِهِ
لِطُعْمَةِ ٱلْقُلُوبِ وَٱقْتَفَى بِهِ

~ 111 ~

A Lateral Attack

A peregrine description:

The dark was chased away by a glint of dawn
lifting the hem of its jilbab and rousing the flocks
of sandgrouse from their sleep. It shone like
the barrel of a piebald steed or a torch's
flickering flames lit by a man who tends them
till they're whipped up by a burst of wind
that sets fire to his clothes.
The hunter recalled 9
a field of wildflowers woven by the dew,
where insects screech like a drunk in his cups.
We summoned a group of braves, proud, young,
and true, to bivouac in a spot where houbaras
would soon be boiled or grilled.
A noble peregrine 17
was brought to provide us with food,
alert to our wishes when her hood's off,
directing her keen gaze to snatch souls.

يَمُجُّ مِنْهُ مِثْلَ مَا أَعْطَى بِهِ
مِنْ ثَمَنٍ أَقْسَمَ لَا يُشْرَى بِهِ
إِذَا هَبَطْنَا غَائِطًا غَادَى بِهِ
وَإِنْ عَلَوْنَا شَرَفًا رَأَى بِهِ
فَٱنْقَضَّ مِثْلَ لَمْحَةِ ٱضْطِرَابِهِ
يَلْمَعُ سَيْرَاهُ مِنَ ٱنْصِبَابِهِ
مِثْلَ مِدَقٍّ صُلَّبٍ رَمَى بِهِ
أَعْسَرَ أَهْوَاهُ فَمَا تَلَا بِهِ
يَخْضِبُهُ ٱلصَّيْدُ عَلَى خِضَابِهِ
وَإِنْ يُلَاقِ خُزَزًا طَحَا بِهِ
حَاصِرَهُ بِٱلرَّكْضِ مِنْ إِهْذَابِهِ
وَجَدَّدَ ٱلْمَنْكِبَ فَٱنْتَحَى بِهِ
حَتَّى تَرَاهُ بَعْدَمَا رُحْنَا بِهِ
يُعْدَلُ فِي ٱلسَّفْرَةِ أَوْ يُعْلَى بِهِ
لَا يَبْعُدِ ٱللَّهْوُ عَهِدْنَاهَا بِهِ
إِنْ كَانَ قَدْ وَدَّعَ لِٱنْقِلَابِهِ

Her owner vowed she'd never be sold,
her profits a match for her cost. Over hill
and wadi, in an early hunt, jesses glinting
in the dive like a darting glance, she stooped
like a mortar falling to the ground, sparing no effort
in her lust for the chase. Her plumage is dyed
in the blood of her prey. An encounter with a hare
took her far, as she harried it with repeated
bursts of her wings before launching
a lateral attack. At day's end, you could see
the peregrine carried high or held to the side.
Long ago, we knew such pleasure. May it
never depart even if, forever changed,
it has now said its farewells.

~ ١١٢ ~

وقال ينعت اليؤيؤ [الرجز]

قَدْ أَغْتَدِي بِيُؤْيُؤٍ زَيْرَكِّ
عَالٍ عَلَى أَتْرَابِهِ بِٱلْفَتْكِ
مُنَقَّطٍ سِرْبَالُهُ بِٱلْمِسْكِ
زَيْنِ يَدِ ٱلْحَامِلِ فَوْقَ ٱلمَشْكِ
كَأَنَّهُ حُلَاحِلٌ فِي مُلْكِ
فَلَوْ تَرَاهُ سَابِحًا فِي ٱلسَّلْكِ
عَلَى ٱثْرِ يَعْقُوبٍ وَإِثْرَ مُكِّ
قُلْتَ عُقَابٌ رَامَ صَيْدَ كُرْكِي
يَصُكُّهُ صَكًّا أَشَدَّ ٱلصَّكِّ
بِحَجِنٍ وَمِنْسَرٍ أَسَكِّ
حَتَّى تَلَاهُ شَائِلًا بِٱلْوَرْكِ
تَلْقَاهُ إِذْ تَلْقَاهُ غَيْرَ شَكِّ
حَزَوَّرًا نَهْمَتُهُ فِي ٱلسَّفْكِ
فَصَادَ قَبْلَ ٱلطَّعْمِ مَا لَمْ يَنْكِ
خَمْسِينَ مُسْتَحْيًى إِلَى مُنْفَكِّ

~ 112 ~

Dappled with Musk

A merlin description:

I crossed the dark with a merlin, a *zayrakk*
more brutal than her comrades, her coat
dappled with musk, as glorious on the glove
as a king on his throne. Should you see her
skim the air in the chase for chukar or lark, you'd say,
"An eagle hunting a crane!" She has curved
talons, a small-nared beak, and hoists
her prey by the thigh in a ferocious thwack.
Let there be no doubt—when you meet her,
her thirst for blood is unabated. Before she tasted
any prey as yet unharmed, she felled fifty,
some at death's door, others already departed.

~ ١١٣ ~

وقال ينعت الفرس [الرجز]

قَدْ أَغْتَدِي وَٱلصُّبْحُ مُحْمَرُّ ٱلطُّرَرْ
وَٱللَّيْلُ تَحْدُوهُ تَبَاشِيرُ ٱلسَّحَرْ
وَفِي تَوَالِيهِ نُجُومٌ كَٱلشَّرَرْ
بِسُحُقِ ٱلْمَيْعَةِ مَيَّالِ ٱلْعُذَرْ
كَأَنَّهُ يَوْمَ ٱلرِّهَانِ ٱلْمُحْتَضَرْ
طَاوٍ غَدَا يَنْفُضُ صِيبَانَ ٱلْمَطَرْ
عَنْ زِفِّ مِلْحَاحٍ بَعِيدِ ٱلْمُنْكَدَرْ
أَقْنَى يَظَلُّ طَيْرُهُ عَلَى حَذَرْ
يَلُذْنَ مِنْهُ تَحْتَ أَفْنَانِ ٱلشَّجَرِ
مِنْ صَادِقِ ٱلْوَقْعِ طَرُوحٍ بِٱلنَّظَرْ
كَأَنَّمَا عَيْنَاهُ فِي وَقْبَيْ حَجَرْ
بَيْنَ مَآقٍ لَمْ تُخَرَّقْ بِٱلْإِبَرْ

~ 113 ~

On Full Alert

A horse description:

Morning a broidered fringe of red,
but night welcomed this herald of dawn
as the late stars blazed like sparks.
I crossed the dark, mounted on a courser
pliant in the reins, long of stride.
In a packed race, she's like a saker in yarak
shaking off the hard morning showers
from her soft feathers, a persistent hunter
with a curved beak, flying on full alert,
swooping down from heights. Her prey hides
under trees and shrubs, but her keen eyes
are unerring in attack, her eyes
sunk in water-filled rock pools,
their lids never seeled by needle.

~ ١١٤ ~

وقال [الرجز]

قَدْ أَغْتَدِي بِأَعْوَجِيٍّ قَارِصِ
كَانَ رَبِيبَ حَلَبٍ وَقَارِصِ
ذِي مَحْزِمٍ نَهْدٍ وَهَادٍ شَاخِصِ
وَخُصَلٍ عَنْ أَيْبَسَيْهِ قَالِصِ
وَمُشُطٍ مِنَ ٱلْحَدِيدِ نَامِصِ

~ 114 ~

Raised on Milk

I move through the dark on an Aʿwajī steed,
full grown, raised on milk, fresh and sour,
with a taut girth, a barrel chest, a long neck,
a thick tail down to its shanks, its legs slender
and tall, its mane curried with an iron comb.

~ ١١٥ ~

وقال [الرجز]

قَدْ أَغْتَدِي قَبْلَ وَغَا ٱلْغَطَاطِ
وَٱللَّيْلُ مِثْلَ حَلَكِ ٱلْخِيَاطِ
رَحْبَ ٱلذِّرَاعِ وَاسِعَ ٱلْبِسَاطِ
بِذِي سَبِيبٍ نَاصِعِ ٱللِّيَاطِ
يَزِفُّ تَزْفَافَ سَرِيِّ ٱلرِّبَاطِ
كَأَنَّمَا جِيبَتْ لَهُ ٱلْقَبَاطِي

~ 115 ~

A Prize Stallion

Night was far-reaching, like a black thread
or a rug unfurled. Before the pin-tails' morning racket,
I crossed the dark on a thick-maned steed,
galloping gypsum bright as if clad in white
linen, a horse of the stables, a prize stallion.

~ ١١٦ ~

وقال ينعت الحيّة والحوّاء [الرجز]

أَنْعَتُ حَاوٍ جَاءَ مِنْ زَرَنْجِ
مُعَلَّقٌ صَاغِرَتَيْ خَلَنْجِ
وَسُفْرَةً نَوَّطَهَا بِطَنْجِ
لَمَّا رَأَى ٱلْحَاوِينَ فِي نِيرَنْجِ
شَدَّ حِزَامَيْنِ عَلَى بَرَطَنْجِ
عَلَى بُرَيْذِينٍ لَهُ خَوَنْجِ
غَالَى بِهِ فِي ٱلْجَانِّ وَٱلْإِسْفَنْجِ
كُلِّ رِوَنْدِيٍّ وَكُلِّ بَنْجِ
اِبْنَ أَرَّانَ وَٱبْنَ إِشْتَاخَنْجِ
وَالِي كَرِشِّيشَا وَكَارِدَنْجِ
فَسَارَ فِي ٱلزَّابَجِ أَوْ فِي ٱلزَنْجِ
فَأَرْضِ لُوقِينَ إِلَى هَرَنْجِ
إِلَى مُدِرٍّ فِلْفِلٍ فَمُنْجِ
فَمُنْبِتِ ٱلزَّرْنَبِ فَٱلْفَلَنْجِ
حَيْثُ تَقُولُ ٱلْهِنْدُ يَكِّي بَنْجِ
حَتَّى أَتَى بِحَيَّةٍ لَا يُنْجِي
مِنْهَا نَجَاءُ ٱلْهَارِبِ ٱلْمُسْتَنْجِي
أَشْجَعَ مِنْ حَيَّاتِ بَارَطَنْجِ
ذِي حُمَّةٍ أَفْلَتَ مِنْ بَرْزَنْجِ
مِنْ بَعْدِمَا أَحْرَزَهُ فِي خُرْجِ

~ 116 ~

Where Tigers Roam

A snake charmer and his snake:

I describe a snake charmer from Zaranj
who set up two small bowls of *khalanj*
and a cloth in Ṭanj. He had seen the snake
charmers at their tricks, and tied
two thongs to the saddle strap of a small,
rented packhorse. Amid the harmless snakes
and healing roots, the rhubarb and henbane
vendors, he offered the snake at a great price
to Ibn Arrān and Ibn Ishtākhanj, lord
of Karishshīshā and Kāridanj.
Through Zābaj 11
or Zanj he had traveled, through Lūqīn
as far as Haranj, to where pepper and *munj*
abound, where aromatic *zarnab* grows
and tigers roam, where the Indians say,
"*yakkī banji*," and brought back a ferocious snake,
lethal if it attacks you in the toilet,
more vicious than plantain-grove serpents,
a slithering, venomous creature from Barzanj,

وَشَدَّهُ مِنْ خَلْفِهِ بِٱلسَّرْجِ
أَبْتَرَ مِنْ بَيْدَقِ أَلشِّطْرَنْجِ
يَسْلَحُ مِنْهُ صَاحِبُ ٱلْقَوْلَنْجِ
لَا يَرْتَجِي ٱلْبُرْءَ مِنْهُ مُنَجِّي
ذَرْقَ حُبَارَى ٱلْخُضَّرِ ٱلْخُرْفَنْجِ

secured in a pouch tied to his saddle,
a snake with a tail smaller than a pawn—
at the sight of it, a patient suffering
from incurable colic defecates stools
like houbara mutes amid fresh plants.

أراجيز من كتاب الأنوار ومحاسن الأشعار من تأليف الشمشاطيّ

Poems Attributed to Abū Nuwās, Preserved Only in al-Shimshāṭī's *Kitāb al-Anwār wa-maḥāsin al-ash'ār*

~ ١١٧ ~

وله أيضاً فيه [الرجز]

وَلَيْسَ لِلطِّـرَادِ إِلَّا فَهْـدُ ١
كَأَنَّمَا أَلْقَتْ عَلَيْـهِ ٱلْكُـرْدُ
مِنْ خُلْقِهَا أَوْ وَلَدَتْهُ ٱلْأُسْدُ ٣

~ 117 ~

A Gift from the Kurds

A cheetah's the only way to hunt!
Like the offspring of mighty lions,
his courage a gift from the Kurds.

~ ١١٨ ~

وله أيضًا [الرجز]

جَاءَ مُطِيعًا بِمُطَاوِعَاتِ
عُلِّمْنَ أَوْ قَدْ كُنَّ عَالِمَاتِ
تُرِيكَ آمَاقًا لَهَا مُخَطَّطَاتِ
سُودًا عَلَى ٱلْأَشْدَاقِ سَائِلَاتِ
تَلْوِي بِأَذْنَابٍ مُعَقَّفَاتِ
عَلَى ظُهُورِ ٱلْخَيْلِ مُرْدَفَاتِ
حَتَّى إِذَا كُنَّا عَلَى ٱلْمَجْرَاتِ
حَيْثُ تَظُنُّ ٱلْوَحْشَ آخِذَاتِ
وَهُنَّ فِي ٱلْأَدْغَالِ كَالْحَاتِ
طَوَامِحَ ٱلْأَبْصَارِ شَاخِصَاتِ
عَلَى ٱلْبُطُونِ مُتَبَطِّحَاتِ
ثُمَّ حَدَوْنَ ٱلْوَحْشَ مُقْبِلَاتِ
فَوَاثَبَتْهُنَّ مُشَمِّرَاتِ
وَثْبَ ٱلشَّيَاطِينِ ٱلْمُسَلَّطَاتِ
فَلَوْ تَرَى ٱلْوُحُوشَ مُضْجَعَاتِ
مِنْ بَعْدِ مَا كُنَّ رَاتِعَاتِ
مَا أَقْرَبَ ٱلْمَوْتَ مِنَ ٱلْحَيَاةِ

~ 118 ~

Dead in the Dust

He brought along obedient hunters,
mounted on horses' rumps, well-trained
students but wild as innate predators
with bright, flecked eyes, black lines
stretching down their cheeks, and coiled
twitchy tails. We reached the flats,
where, their eyes raised, lying low
on their stomachs, ready to attack,
they thought they'd surprise the jumpy game
scowling in their coverts. On the return run,
they drove the oryx hard and, like despotic
ravening demons, pounced at top speed.
How I wish you'd seen those bulls, once free,
lying dead in the dust. Death is never far away!

~ ١١٩ ~

ولأبي نواس في طير الماء والشاهين [الرجز]

يَا رُبَّ وَادٍ زَاهِرِ ٱلنَّبَاتِ
تَهْوِي إِلَيْهِ ٱلطَّيْرُ كَاسِرَاتِ
أَغْنِجَةً خُضْرًا مُطَوَّسَاتِ
بِبَلَقِ ٱلرِّيشِ مُوَلَّعَاتِ
صُفْرَ ٱلْحَمَالِيقِ مُقَرَّطَاتِ
أَقْرِطَةً تَضْحَكُ فِي ٱللَّبَّاتِ
بِفَاخِرِ ٱلْوَشْيِ مُرَدَّيَاتِ
وَبِٱلدَّبَابِيجِ مُوَشَّحَاتِ
صَوَامِتًا طَوْرًا وَصَارِخَاتِ
مُلَحِّنَاتٍ وَمُرَجِّعَاتِ
بَوَاكِيًا يُسْعِدْنَ بَاكِيَاتِ
لَمْ يَشْجِهِنَّ عَدَمُ ٱلْأَمْوَاتِ
بَاكَرْتُهَا بِصَادِقِ ٱلْكَرَّاتِ
عَلَى ٱلشِّمَالِ حَسَنِ ٱلثَّبَاتِ
فَمَرَّ نَحْوَ ٱلطَّيْرِ ذَا ٱلْتِفَاتِ
يَحْفِزُهُ قَلْبٌ لَهُ مُوَاتِي
يَمْنَحُهَا مَشْقًا عَلَى ٱلسَّرَاتِ
ضَرْبَ أَخِي ٱلطَّبْطَابِ لِلْكُرَاتِ
فَكُلُّهُنَّ لَافِظُ ٱلْحَيَاتِ
لَمَّا تَوَافَيْنَ مِنَ ٱلْمِيقَاتِ

~ 119 ~

A Chorus of Shrill Cries

A poem by Abū Nuwās on waterfowl and a peregrine:

A wadi full of plants in bloom.
The birds alight with folded wings.
They resemble coquettes,
comely and dark, stippled
with pied feathers, golden
eye sockets, dressed in their finery—
plumes like earrings glint
brightly on their breasts,
in cloaks of sumptuous weave
and patterned damask tunics,
now silent, now squawking
a chorus of shrill cries,
still strangers to the taste
of throat-throttling death.
I arrived early, a peregrine
on my left hand—she's true
in attack, perfectly still. With twists
and turns, she flew at the birds,
urged by an obedient heart,
and flogged their backs
pitilessly, the thuds as loud
as balls struck by a *ṭabṭāb* player.
Her victims, meeting their last hour
en masse, spat out their souls.

~ ١٢٠ ~

وللحكميّ في قصب الدبق [الرجز]

رُبَّ خَفِيِّ ٱلشَّخْصِ قَدْ أُرِقَّا
عَنْ أَنْ يَجُوبَ لِفَلَاةٍ خَرْقَا
فَصَارَ لِلْعِيشَةِ يَبْغِي ٱلطَّرْقَا
بِقَصَبَاتٍ قَدْ جُعِلْنَ لِفْقَا
يَجْعَلُ فِي أَطْرَافِهِنَّ دِبْقَا
تَهْبِطُ أَحْيَانًا وَحِينًا تَرْقَى
تَدْمَعُ عَيْنَاهُ إِذَا مَا نَقَّا
دَمْعًا مُلِحًّا مَا يَكَادُ يَرْقَى
تَظُنُّهُ قَدْ حَنَّ أَوْ قَدْ رَقَّا
وَهْوَ أَفَظُّ مَا يَكُونُ خَلْقَا
يَا بُؤْسَ لِلْعُصْفُورِ مَاذَا يَلْقَى
مِنْ بَأْسِهِ كَتْفًا لَهُ وَخَنْقَا

~ 120 ~

Tears of Pus

A poem by Abū Nuwās on lime sticks:

A wretched hunter, skilled at hiding,
unable to cross deserts after game.
For food, he's resorted to the night-
time ambush with tightly tied reeds,
their bobbing tips smeared with
birdlime. When he cleans his eyes,
they weep tears of pus he's unable
to wipe away. Do you imagine he could
be tender or kind? He's a callous brute.
Pity the sparrow he meets—he pins
back its wings and wrings its neck.

~ ١٢١ ~

وله أيضًا [الرجز]

رُبَّ بُنَيٍّ لِلرَّدَى مَنْصُوبِ
حَانِي ٱلظِّهَارِ مُحْكَمِ ٱلتَّعْصِيبِ
كَمَا تُشَدُّ ٱلْقَوْسُ لِلتَّعْقِيبِ
مُوَتَّرٍ بِوَتِدٍ قَطُوبِ
آخِذُهُ بِوَسَطِ ٱلْأُنْبُوبِ
ضَمَّ ٱلْعُرُوقِ عَصَبَ ٱلظُّنْبُوبِ
مُنْخَنِسٍ عَنْ نَاظِرِ ٱلْمَنْكُوبِ
أُودعَ حَيًّا فِي يَدَيْ شَعُوبِ
يَنْتَزِعُ ٱلْحَبَّ مِنْ ٱلْقُلُوبِ
لَمَّا أَتَى ٱلْعُصْفُورُ مِنَ قَرِيبِ
لَاحَظَهُ لَحْظَةَ مُسْتَرِيبِ
مُرَجِّمًا فِي ٱلظَّنِّ بِٱلْغُيُوبِ
ثُمَّ دَعَاهُ ٱلْحَيْنُ لِلتَّكْذِيبِ
بِمَا ٱرْتَأَى فِيهِ مِنَ ٱلْخُطُوبِ
فَرَامَ لَقْطَ ٱلْحَبِّ بِٱلتَّقْلِيبِ
حَتَّى إِذَا أَمْكَنَ لِلْوُثُوبِ
هَوَتْ أَكُفُّ ٱبْنِ ٱلرَّدَى ٱلْمَنْصُوبِ
مِنْهُ إِلَى جُؤْجُؤِهِ ٱلنَّكِيبِ

~ 121 ~

God's Unseen Realm

The snare, death's child, was set up,
its back ropy, its twine tightly twisted
like a bow secured for sinews to be fitted
to its limbs. It was gripped by an iron peg
fixed in the midst of the shaft's knots,
its base held in place by shinbone tendons.
Hidden from the wary gaze, it traps souls
and surrenders them to death's grip,
stopping hearts from beating. The sparrow
approached from nearby and looked
at the snare suspiciously, trying to fathom
the secrets of God's unseen realm.
But Fate led it to ignore the danger
that lay before its eyes—for it desired the seeds.
The hands of death's child swooped
and trapped the sparrow's ill-starred breast
just as it was about to leap into flight.

وله أيضًا قصيدتان فيهما وصف الطرد

Two Qasidas with Hunting Scenes

وقال يمدحه [الكامل]

خَلُقَ ٱلزَّمَانُ وَشِرَّتِي لَمْ تَخْلُقِ   وَرَمَيْتُ فِي غَرَضِ ٱلشَّبَابِ بِأَفْوُقِ
تَقَعُ ٱلسِّهَامُ أَمَامَهُ وَكَأَنَّهُ   إِثْرَ ٱلْخَوَالِفِ طَالِبٌ لَمْ يَلْحَقِ
وَأَرَى قُوَايَ تَكَاءَدَتْهَا رَيْثَةٌ   فَإِذَا بَطَشْتُ بَطَشْتُ رِخْوَ ٱلْمِرْفَقِ
وَلَقَدْ غَدَوْتُ بِدَسْتَبَانِ مُعَلَّمٍ   صَخِبِ ٱلْجَلَاجِلِ فِي ٱلْوَظِيفِ مُسَبَّقِ
حُرٍّ صَنَعْنَاهُ لِتُحْسِنَ كَفُّهُ   عَمَلَ ٱلرَّفِيقَةِ وَٱسْتِلَابَ ٱلْأَخْرَقِ
يَجْلُو ٱلْقَذَى بِعَقِيقَتَيْنِ ٱكْتَنَّتَا   بِذَرَى سَلِيمِ ٱلْجَفْنِ غَيْرِ مُخَرَّقِ
أَلْقَى زَآبِرَهُ وَأَخْلَفَ بِزَّةً   كَانَتْ حِيَاكَةَ صَانِعٍ مُتَنَوِّقِ
فَكَأَنَّهُ مُتَدَرِّعٌ دِيبَاجَةً   عَنْ قَالِصِ ٱلتُّبَّانِ غَيْرِ مُسَوَّقِ
وَإِذَا شَهِدْتَ بِهِ ٱلْوَقِيعَةَ أَقْعَلَتْ   عَنْهُ ٱلْغَيَايَةُ وَهْوَ حُرُّ ٱلْمَصْدَقِ
فَتَرَى ٱلْإِوَزَّ فُوَيْقَ خَطْمٍ مُشَيَّعٍ   شَهْوَانَ يَنْتَشِطُ ٱلشَّوَاكِلَ سُوذَقِ
يَعْتَامُ جُلَّتَهَا وَيَقْصُرُ شَأْوُهَا   بِمُؤَنَّفٍ سَلِبِ ٱلشَّبَاةِ مُذَلَّقِ
حَتَّى رَفَعْنَا قِدْرَنَا بِرِضَامِهَا   وَٱللَّحْمُ بَيْنَ مُوَذَّرٍ وَمُوَشَّقِ

~ 122 ~

Ambrosial to the Tongue

A panegyric for Hārūn al-Rashīd:

Time may be worn thin, but not so my lust for life.
I take aim at youth and fire my broken arrows,
but they fall short and are cast aside. Their target
shifts like a quest with no end in sight.
I watch as lethargy creeps into my virility—
when I launch an assault, how feeble my limbs!

Yet not so long ago I would be out early 4
with a gos on the glove, bell tinkling on a leg
tied with a jess, freeborn, fully trained,
taught to have a deft clutch, to be both delicate
and brutal. Dust motes can be seen
in her carnelian eyes under their sheltering brows,
her lids intact, never sewn; after her molt,
she is clad in sumptuous garb, the handiwork
of an exquisite craftsman, as if she's wearing
silk chain mail above short breeches
that sit high on her arms. You watch her,
brave and true in combat when the murk
opens like a flower, and you see the geese
a fraction out in front, ahead of her keen beak,
as, ravening, she selects big birds
now flagging and weary, and fastens
nimbly to their flanks with her pounces—
javelins with tips well honed, razor-sharp spurs.
Then we set the cauldron on the stones
and serve the deboned meat in slices.

هٰذَا أَمِيرُ ٱلْمُؤْمِنِينَ ٱنْتَاشَنِي　　　وَٱلنَّفْسُ بَيْنَ مُحَنْجَرٍ وَمُخَنَّقِ
نَفْسِي فِدَاؤُكَ يَوْمَ دَابِقَ مُنْعِمًا　　　لَوْلَا عَوَاطِفُ حِلْمِهِ لَمْ أُطْلَقِ
حَرَّمْتَ مِنْ لَحْمِي عَلَيْكَ مُحَلَّلًا　　　وَجَمَعْتَ مِنْ شَتَّى إِلَى مُتَفَرِّقِ
فَٱقْذِفْ بِرَحْلِكَ فِي جَنَابِ خَلِيفَةٍ　　　سَبَّاقِ غَايَاتٍ بِهَا لَمْ يُسْبَقِ
إِنَّا إِلَيْكَ مِنِ ٱلصُّلَيْبِ فَجَاسِمٍ　　　طَلَعَ ٱلنِّجَادَ بِنَا وَجِيفُ ٱلْأَيْنُقِ
يَتْبَعْنَ مَائِرَةَ ٱلْمِلَاطِ كَأَنَّمَا　　　تَرْنُوا بِعَيْنِ مُضِلَّةٍ لَمْ تَفْرُقِ
خَنْسَاءَ تَنْشُدُهُ شَقَائِقَ عَالِجٍ　　　وَبِهَا إِلَيْهِ صَبَابَةٌ كَٱلْأَوْلَقِ
حَتَّى إِذَا وَجَدَتْهُ لَمْ تَرَ عِنْدَهُ　　　إِلَّا مَجَرَّ إِهَابِهِ ٱلْمُتَمَزِّقِ
يَأْبَى لِهَارُونَ ٱلْخَلِيفَةِ عُنْصُرٌ　　　زَاكٍ تَمَكَّنَ فِي ٱلْمُصَاصِ ٱلْمُعْرِقِ
مَلِكٌ يَطِيبُ طِبَاعُهُ وَمِزَاجُهُ　　　عَذْبُ ٱلْمَذَاقِ عَلَى فَمِ ٱلْمُتَذَوِّقِ
يَلْقَى جَمِيعَ ٱلْأَمْرِ وَهْوَ مُقَسَّمٌ　　　بَيْنَ ٱلْمَنَاسِكِ وَٱلْعَدُوِّ ٱلْمُوفِقِ
تَحْمِيكَ مِمَّا يَسْتَسِرُّ فُؤَادُهُ　　　ضَحِكَاتُ وَجْهٍ لَا يُرِيبُكَ مُشْرِقِ
حَتَّى إِذَا أَمْضَى عَزِيمَةَ رَأْيِهِ　　　أَخَذَتْ بِسَمْعِ عَدُوِّهِ وَٱلْمَنْطِقِ

You saved me, Commander of the Faithful, 13
when I was on the verge of death, and my soul
was moving up my throat and out of my mouth.[131]
I pledge you my soul in return for your gift
at Dābaq that day—because of your kindness
and clemency, I am a free man.
You could have destroyed me, rightfully,
but you declared my person inviolate
and repaired so many pieces that were broken.

Riders, untie your saddles, set them down 16
in the courtyard of a caliph who achieves goals
never before attained! From Ṣulayb and Jāsim
we sped to you across the uplands[132] on mounts
racing along behind a smooth-running,
strong-legged camel, staring with the eyes
of an oryx cow who, realizing her calf
is missing, now sets out in search of it,
a snub-nosed female singing out in the sand
valleys of the ʿĀlij desert, wild with grief.
When she finds it, all she can see are the marks
where its lacerated hide was dragged away.

Hārūn, our caliph, you are guided by a pure essence 21
bolstered by noble ancestry, a monarch
with a temperament ambrosial to the tongue
when tasted. Your rule is indivisible, though your energies
are divided between pilgrimage and war
against our enemies, their bows ever at the ready.
Your countenance, radiant and benevolent, sets us at rest,
protecting us from any designs devised and concealed
in your heart: when your resolve turns to action,
your foes no longer know how to speak and hear.

إِنِّي حَلَفْتُ عَلَيْكَ جُهْدَ أَلِيَّةٍ   قَسَمًا بِكُلِّ مُقَصِّرٍ وَمُحَلِّقِ
لَقَدِ ٱتَّقَيْتَ ٱللهَ حَقَّ تُقَاتِهِ   وَجَهَدْتَ نَفْسَكَ فَوْقَ جَهْدِ ٱلْمُتَّقِي
وَأَخَفْتَ أَهْلَ ٱلشِّرْكِ حَتَّى أَنَّهُ   لَتَخَافُكَ ٱلنُّطَفُ ٱلَّتِي لَمْ تُخْلَقِ
وَبِضَاعَةُ ٱلشُّعَرَاءِ إِنْ نَفَّقْتَهَا   نَفَقَتْ وَإِنْ أَكْسَدْتَهَا لَمْ تَنْفُقِ

I swear you a most solemn oath, an oath sworn 26
both by those whose plans fail and those who succeed—
you show God all the fear and respect due to Him!
Your devotions even surpass the efforts of the God-fearing!
You have terrified the polytheists—even their unborn
children, seed yet to be created, are terrified of you!
You determine a poet's worth—if you declare
a market for his goods, then they'll sell briskly.
If not, without buyers, he'll soon be out of business!

قال يهجو هاشم بن حديج وكان مدحه فحرمه [المتقارب]

وَدَارٍ تُؤَدَّبُ فِيهَا ٱلْبُزَاةُ   وَتُمْتَحَنُ ٱلْفَهْدُ وَٱلْفَهْدَهْ
وَصَلْتُ عُرَاهَا إِلَى بَلْدَةٍ   بِهَا نَحَرَ ٱلذَّابِحُ ٱلْبَلْدَهْ
إِذَا ٱعْتَامَهَا قَرِمُ ٱلْمُعْتَفِينَ   طُرُوقًا غَدَا زَهِمَ ٱلْمِعْدَهْ
وَلِيٌّ قَفَا بَعْدَ وَسْمِيِّهِ   فَهَمُّكَ مِنْ كَمْأَةٍ مَعْدَهْ
وَصَيْدٍ بِأَسْفَعَ شَاكِي ٱلسِّلَاحِ   شَدِيدِ ٱلْإِغَارَةِ وَٱلشَّدَّهْ
رَزِينٍ إِذَا ٱمْتَحَنَتْهُ ٱلْأَكُفُّ مُنْتَصِبِ ٱلزَّوْرِ وَٱلقَعْدَهْ
فَتِيقِ ٱلنَّسَا أَنْمَرِ ٱلدَّفَّتَيْنِ   خَفِيفِ ٱلْخَمِيصَةِ وَٱللِّبْدَهْ
يُقَلِّبُ طَرْفًا طَحُورَ ٱلْقَذَى   يُضِيءُ بِمُقْلَتِهِ خَدَّهْ
بِذِي شِيَةٍ أَعْرَفِ ٱلْحَوْصَلَاءِ   كَأَنَّكَ رَدَّيْتَهُ بُرْدَهْ
فَلَمَّا ٱسْتَحَالَ رَأَى تِسْعَةً   رِتَاعًا وَوَاحِدَةً فَرْدَهْ
فَكَفْكَفَ مُنْتَصِبَ ٱلْمَنْكِبَيْنِ   لِفَرْطِ ٱلشَّهَامَةِ وَٱلنَّجْدَهْ
فَقُلْنَا لِسَائِسِهِ مَا تَرَى   فَأَطْلَقَهُ سَلِسَ ٱلْعُقْدَهْ
فَمَرَّ كَمَرِّ شِهَابِ ٱلظَّلَامِ   لِيَفْعَلَ دَاهِيَةً إِدَّهْ
فَأَنْحَى لَهَا فِي صَمِيمِ ٱلْقَذَالِ   فَشَكَّ ٱلْمُذَمَّرَ أَوْ قَدَّهْ
وَثَنَّى لِأُلَّافِهَا ٱلْغَائِرَاتِ   فَكَمَّلَ عَشْرًا بِهَا ٱلعِدَّهْ

~ 123 ~

Kindah's Mighty Hero

A lampoon of Hāshim ibn Ḥudayj, who refused to remunerate Abū Nuwās for a panegyric he had dedicated to him.[133]

I came to a region where hawks are trained,
where cheetahs are put through their paces,
where animals are slaughtered as holy law dictates,
yet where meat-hungry travelers can arrive
in the dead of night and next morning suffer bellyaches.
It was desert truffle season, during the late
spring rains. I was hunting with a rufous falcon,
armed cap-a-pie, a brutal raider, savage
in the attack, calm when handled, keel held high,
sitting still, with sharp pounces, striped mail,
a light feather coat and mantle. Her eyes
in their roving gaze wash away the dust and light up
her cheeks; her breast is clad in embroidery,
her gorge and throat in a ruff collar. She spotted
distant shapes—nine gazelles out and about,
foraging in a group, and one doe, isolated, alone—
a raise of her wrists, a flap of her wings,
a surge of energy and battle lust.
I asked her handler, "What do you think?"
He untied the jess and let her go, as fast
as a star across the night sky,
unleashing death and destruction.
Sidling in, she cut and tore the nape,
binding onto the back of the head,
then doubled back to the gazelle's comrades
running to ground—making it a round ten.

قِفُوا مَعْشَرَ ٱلرَّاحِلِينَ ٱسْمَعُوا　　أُنَبِّئُكُمْ عَنْ فَتَى كِنْدَهْ
وَرَدْنَا عَلَى هَاشِمٍ مِصْرَهُ　　فَبَارَتْ تِجَارَتُنَا عِنْدَهْ
وَأَلْهَاهُ ذُو كَفَلٍ نَاشِئٌ　　شَدِيدُ ٱلْفَقَارَةِ وَٱلْبَلْدَهْ
سِبَطْرٌ يَمِيدُ إِذَا مَا مَشَى　　تَرَى بَيْنَ رِجْلَيْهِ كَٱلصَّعْدَهْ
يَجُوبُ بِهَا ٱللَّيْلَ ذَا بِطْنَةٍ　　كَحَشْوِ ٱلْمَدِينِيَّةِ ٱلْقِلْدَهْ
رَأَيْتُكَ عِنْدَ حُضُورِ ٱلْخِوَانِ　　سَفِيهًا عَلَى ٱلْعَبْدِ وَٱلْعَبْدَهْ
لَذَا وَكْزَةٌ مِنْكَ مَعْلُومَةٌ　　وَذَا نَقْفَةٌ وَلَذَا قَفْدَهْ
وَتَحْتَدُّ حَتَّى يَخَافُ ٱلْجَلِيسُ　　شَذَاكَ عَلَيْهِ مِنَ ٱلْحِدَّهْ
وَتَخْتِمُ ذَاكَ بِفَخْرٍ عَلَيْهِ　　بِكِنْدَةَ فَٱسْلَحْ عَلَى كِنْدَهْ
وَإِنَّ حُدَيْجًا لَهُ هِجْرَةٌ　　وَلٰكِنَّهَا زَمَنَ ٱلرِّدَّهْ
وَمَا كَانَ إِيمَانُكُمْ بِٱلرَّسُولِ　　سِوَى قَتْلِكُمْ صِهْرَهُ بَعْدَهْ
تَعُدُّونَهَا مِنْ مَسَاعِيكُمُ　　كَعَدِّ ٱلْأَهِلَّةِ مُعْتَدَّهْ
وَمَا كَانَ قَاتِلُهُ فِي ٱلرِّجَالِ　　لِحَمْلٍ لِطُهْرٍ وَلَا رِشْدَهْ
فَلَوْ شَهِدَتْهُ قُرَيْشُ ٱلْبِطَاحِ　　لَمَا مَحَشَتْ نَارُكُمْ جِلْدَهْ

Travelers, stop and pay heed! Let me tell you 16
about Kindah's mighty hero. We stayed with Hāshim
in Cairo, when all our goods were consumed.
He was served by a fat-assed lad with a broad back
and a deep chest, tall and haughty—
as he sauntered by, you could see the lance
between his legs, wielded all night long
to pierce a glutton, like a woman stuffing dates
with barley. When the food was brought
on the tray, I saw him badly mistreat his slaves,
shoving one (he's famous for this), hitting another
on the head, slapping a third on the nape of the neck,
so irate his guest would think he's next.
At the end of the meal, he boasted about Kindah—
who gives a shit about Kindah?
His father may have taken part in the hegira,
but this was during the Wars of Apostasy,
and his people declared their faith in the Prophet
by murdering his kinsman—a murder he counts
as one of their great deeds, like a divorcée
counting the days of her monthly bleeds.[134]
But the perpetrator was not trueborn:
he was the child of an unclean pregnancy.
If Quraysh had been present, Kindah
wouldn't have dared burn him in the fire!

Notes

1 Wagner's edition contains an extra verse: "starved into being a tyrant in the early morning": Abū Nuwās, *Dīwān al-Ḥasan ibn Hāni'*, ed. Wagner, 2.185.5.

2 The spotted pin-tailed sandgrouse (*qaṭā*) makes a "queeto-queeto" (*qaṭṭ*) sound. The sandgrouse is proverbial for its speed, though the exact point of the image is obscure.

3 The point of this fantastic image is that the dog leaves no tracks behind because his feet do not touch the ground long enough: as he walks, the carouser drags the hem of his garments behind him, removing his footprints in the process.

4 Al-Iṣfahānī offers the following: "if he wanted to bring his head and his legs together, he could do so because he was so lean": Abū Nuwās, *Dīwān al-Ḥasan ibn Hāni'*, ed. Wagner, 2.191.18.

5 Coals of *ghaḍā* (*Haloxyletum persici*) are specified.

6 Three verses included in Wagner's edition (Abū Nuwās, *Dīwān al-Ḥasan ibn Hāni'*, ed. Wagner, 2.195.7–8) are not in our MS: "Look—their thighs are branded, each goes by a pet name, with long snouts in snug muzzles."

7 The MS reads *khabātihā*; Wagner (Abū Nuwās, *Dīwān al-Ḥasan ibn Hāni'*, ed. Wagner, 2.196.7) reads *ḥayātihā*. I take *khabāt* to be a poetic plural, unattested in the lexica, of *khabt*, "flat land."

8 Wagner (Abū Nuwās, *Dīwān al-Ḥasan ibn Hāni'*, ed. Wagner, 2.196.2) reads an extra two lines: "The swoosh of an eagle's wings spurred on by hunger's bite, with the hoarse mumble of jinn at play." In this complex and many-layered image, the sound of the dogs chasing their quarry is described first (metaphorically) as the flapping of an eagle's wings and then as the noises made by jinn when, as a commentator says, "they sit down to enjoy themselves and drink" (Abū Nuwās, *Dīwān al-Ḥasan ibn Hāni'*, ed. Wagner, 2.196.6).

9 The poem (which is probably extant in a defective version) combines economically (at least in the version translated here) an oryx and a hare hunt.

10 There is an echo of Q Furqān 25:13–14 in the word *thubūrā* ("destruction").

11 Fully, "He understood the messages he received: the whistles and the hand motions, whether you were nodding instructions or pointing."

12 Wagner's edition contains two extra verses after this one: "truly blessed and honored, gracing minbar and throne." See Abū Nuwās, *Dīwān al-Ḥasan ibn Hāni'*, ed. Wagner,

2.198.16; *Dīwān Abī Nuwās*, ed. al-Ḥadīthī, 284.6. According to al-Iṣfahānī's commentary, the emir is Dāwūd ibn Sulaymān ibn Abī Ja'far.

13 The commentator notes that the skins are turned inside out when they are stripped from the fox. Presumably the point of the description is that some foxes had been skinned, while others were as yet unskinned.

14 In Arabic: *dhī nakafin muswaddī*. The term *nakaf* is glossed in the lexica as either the roof of the mouth or a ganglion at the base of the jaw. Cheetahs have black teardrop patterns on their cheeks. I have interpreted *nakaf* as a reference to prominent masseter muscles, used in mastication.

15 This verse is not included by Wagner in his edition of the poem: Abū Nuwās, *Dīwān al-Ḥasan ibn Hāni'*, ed. Wagner, 2.201.12. My translation is conjectural: *zard*, or *zarad*, means a "coat of mail, made of interlocking links." It seems here to designate some aspect of the mount, on the back of which the cheetah would have been transported to the hunting grounds, to preserve its strength and keep it fresh.

16 *Idd* is an echo of Q Maryam 19:89.

17 There is some disagreement about *'irbadd* in the lexica. Two common meanings are given: of a snake that puffs but does not harm; and of a vicious, venomous viper. The puff adder (*Bitis arietans*) is found in southern Arabia.

18 Compare Q Zumar 39:60, the "blackened faces" (*wujūhuhum muswaddah*) of those who lie to God on the Day of Resurrection.

19 Presumably the name of one of the poet's comrades or patrons, or even the owner of the gos.

20 The fingers were folded, bent, or straightened to indicate numerical units. Here the forefinger and thumb form a circle, to indicate the number ten.

21 Both al-Ṣūlī and al-Iṣfahānī justify their inclusion of this poem in the section of the diwan devoted to poems of the hunt. Al-Ṣūlī, *Dīwān Abī Nuwās*, ed. al-Ḥadīthī, 229.4–5: "A panegyric in honor of al-Ṣaqr ibn al-Ṣaffāq ibn Hujr, one of the Banū l-Julandā, whose folk had taken up residence in Sīf al-Baḥr beyond Shiraz. Some say the poet is describing Ṣaqr, and the majority think so too, apart from those who have studied and edited poetry."

22 I have construed *ḥurūf* as plural for the dual, *ḥarfā l-ra's*, "the lateral halves of the head."

23 There is a Qur'anic allusion in the epithet "captive," *al-'akūf*: see Q Fatḥ 48:25.

24 Wagner's edition (Abū Nuwās, *Dīwān al-Ḥasan ibn Hāni'*, ed. Wagner, 2.215.1–12) has eight extra verses not included in MS Fātiḥ 3773: "In the lists—there's a swift thwack, and like a tent peg her beak is hammered into their brains. Please have her carried by a fleet courier like a nimble camel, who senses the snowstorm powdering the mountaintops like teased cotton, his stout boots eating up the highlands."

25 Wagner (Abū Nuwās, *Dīwān al-Ḥasan ibn Hāniʾ*, ed. Wagner, 2.217.1) reads *bi-l-aḥwāz*, with the waders as the antecedent: "long-term residents of the breakwaters." His extra two verses come next: "Bound to on the vast empty plain, caught with a swift jab."

26 The Arabic reads *janān al-rūḥ* ("the very core of his soul"), which I suspect is a scribal error for *junūn al-rūḥ* ("the demonic possession of his spirit"). I have retained the text in the Arabic edition but have translated the latter.

27 The epithet *quṭāmī* ("savage for flesh") is often applied to the saker. Clark, "The Noble Art of the Chase in the Arab World," 52, suggests that the *shāhīn quṭāmī* is the lanner falcon (*Falco biarmicus*). Viré, "Essai de détermination des oiseaux-de-vol mentionnés dans les principaux manuscrits arabes médiévaux sur la fauconnerie," 146, notes it is the designation of the hobby (*Falco subbuteo*).

28 The reading of Wagner (Abū Nuwās, *Dīwān al-Ḥasan ibn Hāniʾ*, ed. Wagner, 2.222.9) (*wa-hya*) has the hares run in a line, one behind the other.

29 Wagner's edition (Abū Nuwās, *Dīwān al-Ḥasan ibn Hāniʾ*, ed. Wagner, 2.229.9) contains an extra verse: "He trained and brought her up."

30 Wagner's edition (Abū Nuwās, *Dīwān al-Ḥasan ibn Hāniʾ*, ed. Wagner, 2.230.5) contains an extra verse: "all have drunk deep of her poison."

31 The epithet *azraq* probably indicates that the pallid or steppe merlin is meant and that this is a male.

32 The detail of the yellow eye ring identifies these "white-fronts" as lesser white-fronted geese (*Anser erythropus*); by *iwazz*, perhaps the greylag goose (*Anser anser*) is intended. I am unable to identify the fowl described as wearing a *yamlaq*, a "fur coat."

33 Wagner's edition (Abū Nuwās, *Dīwān al-Ḥasan ibn Hāniʾ*, ed. Wagner, 2.235.10) contains two extra verses: "well-built men, in tip-top condition, comely, neither cowards nor poltroons."

34 The term *shazr* denotes twisting a rope from left to right, upward against the body, as opposed to *yasr*, which is rolling a rope downward, with a twist from right to left. On bowstrings and the quadruple twist, see Latham and Paterson, *Saracen Archery: An English Version and Exposition of a Mameluke Work on Archery (ca. AD 1368)*, 21, and 197n9. *Fūq*, pl. *afwāq*, is the standard term for the nock piece, and sometimes also the nock, of an arrow: Latham and Paterson, *Saracen Archery*, 181. The wood of the pellet bow in this and the previous poem is manufactured by a *barrāʾ*, a fletcher, and not a *qawwās*, a bowyer.

35 Or "their backs underneath four wing feathers."

36 Or, construing *al-simām* as poetic plural for singular, "like deadly venom."

37 The sandgrouse is a proverbially early riser, which is the point the poet intends: see Viré, "Ḳaṭā."

38 A commentator (Abū Nuwās, *Dīwān al-Ḥasan ibn Hāniʾ*, ed. Wagner, 2.242.6) explains the point by stating that "the Armenians are knowledgeable about goshawks."

39 Lit., "a letter *nūn*." Wagner's edition (Abū Nuwās, *Dīwān al-Ḥasan ibn Hāniʾ*, ed. Wagner, 2.232.18) reads an extra verse here: "Assegais grip the glove with whetted, sharpened tips."

40 Another refence to dactylology.

41 Fully: "cloth spun with the finesse of <the weavers> of Sābir." I construe *ḥiyāl* as plural of *ḥāʾilah*, with the meaning of "finesse, skill."

42 This is a reference to the *talbiyah*, the shouting of a pious formula in which the expression *labbayka* ("Here I am, Lord") features.

43 Of this poem, al-Ṣūlī remarks: "What I have to say about this poem is the same as what I said about the preceding poem: some people do not include it in their transmission, whereas others do, so we have included it" (*Dīwān Abī Nuwās*, ed. al-Ḥadīthī, 203.4). The preceding poem is a *rāʾiyyah* in *rajaz*: see Abū Nuwās, *Dīwān Abī Nuwās*, ed. al-Ḥadīthī, 199–203; *Dīwān al-Ḥasan ibn Hāniʾ*, ed. Wagner, 2.264–69, which al-Ṣūlī introduces with the following remarks: "A description of a dog—a bad poem that some intelligent critics do not ascribe to him, included here because so many people say it is by him."

44 Or equally: "They drew out the pace in him and he responded, kicking up the stones against his loins."

45 One commentator (Abū Nuwās, *Dīwān al-Ḥasan ibn Hāniʾ*, ed. Wagner, 2.252.17) notes that the phrase *fī* (or *dhī*) *jildah* has been construed as a reference to the *dastabān*, the hunting glove (*jildah* can refer to an animal pelt), but I take it here to mean "a hard and compact" date, i.e., the glans of the member.

46 See Q Taḥrīm 66:4, where the word *ẓahīr*, "help," is used of angels.

47 The extra verse in Wagner's edition (Abū Nuwās, *Dīwān al-Ḥasan ibn Hāniʾ*, ed. Wagner, 2.255.5) is: "She catches hare and dust-dark deer."

48 The extra verse in Wagner's edition (Abū Nuwās, *Dīwān al-Ḥasan ibn Hāniʾ*, ed. Wagner, 2.255.9) reads: "never complaining of exhaustion and fatigue."

49 The lexica explain the feature denoted by *zawar*, here translated as "protruding," as a distortion of the *zawr*, the uppermost part of a camel's or horse's chest, when one side protrudes more than the other; *maḥniyyah*, here rendered as "curved," denotes a stick or piece of wood that has been bent or curved.

50 My translation of *al-bazz*, lit., "the weapons," as denoting the "sticks" is conjectural. Presumably this individual fulfills the function of the official later known as the *jūkandār*, "responsible for the care of the *čawgān*s" (i.e., the polo mallets) "and for the conduct of the game" (Massé, "Čawgān"). He appears from this poem also to be in charge of looking after the wagers.

51 I presume this implies that, in this instance, the *jūkandār* was himself a renowned player of the game.

52 Reading *dhī ḥabāb*; or, reading *dhī ḥibāb*, "like beet juice in jars."

53 I have presumed that by the "birds" (*al-ṭayr*) in verse 16 the clubs are intended.

54 Wagner's edition (Abū Nuwās, *Dīwān al-Ḥasan ibn Hāni'*, ed. Wagner, 2.258.13–14) contains two verses not included in MS Fātiḥ 3773: "the clubs screech in fear of the strike, like shrill scolds who know they've got to leave."

55 Wagner's edition (Abū Nuwās, *Dīwān al-Ḥasan ibn Hāni'*, ed. Wagner, 2.258.15–16) contains three verses missing from MS Fātiḥ 3773: "some of the clubs dove like eagles into the water, others raced on the bank."

56 Lit., "it occupies less space than the support of a *mīm* or the dot under the wing of a *jīm*."

57 The point of this is unclear to me. Wagner, *Abū Nuwās*, 289, renders it: "Er wird in Abessinien und in Byzanz geboren" ("born in Abyssinia and Byzantium").

58 The epithet *mufarzaj* (which the lexica do not record) can either be from *fayrūzaj*, a pigment or type of dye, or *farzajah*, a suppository, which could also be the intended meaning in view of the adjective *aḥbaj* in the next verse, which means the salukis are not constipated, presumably because they have not been fed.

59 The dictionaries explain the verb *qarnaṣa* as meaning to keep a hawk or falcon tied up in the mews until it is reclaimed and has molted. This seems to be borne out by the phrase *fī burdi ḥibālin*, lit., "in a striped cloak of ropes."

60 The Arabic text has *kawmaj*, for which I can find no meaning. One possible reading could be *kawnaj*, Persian for the hobby (*Falco subbuteo*); however, Viré, "Essai de détermination," 145, notes that in Iraq the male saker is called *kūbaj*. I have used "tarsell," a variant spelling of "tiercel," to avoid confusion with the male goshawk, uniformly referred to in this book as a "tiercel."

61 *Minsam* usually denotes the weaver's loom, though I have in mind a weaver's knife similar to the Pakistani churi, which resembles a raptor's beak.

62 The male houbara has an impressive mating display of feathers. That may be the reference here.

63 "Dyed dark as blood" is presumably used proleptically, to signal their ultimate fate.

64 Dog collars were apparently made from or decorated with shells or gems.

65 Or, reading *siffan*: "like a flying snake in hellfire winds." There is an echo of Q Nisā' 4:56 in *al-nuḍḍaj* ("scorching").

66 Two of the nouns in this list (*al-ḥazn* and *al-ṣammān*) are located in northeastern Arabia, but here they seem not to designate toponyms as such but rather to function as descriptors of terrain: see ʿAntarah ibn Shaddād, *War Songs*, Map 2.

67 The verse describes the way in which the dog's hindquarters are drawn up to its chest when it runs.

68 The lexica explain *al-nuwāsī* as choice grapes that make good raisins.

69 There is a pun in the use of the adjectives *ghālin* ("rare," lit., "costly") and *rakhīṣ*, ("common," lit., "cheap,"), which can also mean "fat flesh meat" and "soft, tender," respectively.

70 The image derives from camel husbandry. In times of drought, camels could be slaughtered and the water in their stomachs drunk.

71 The syntax of my reading (*fa-ʿtāba-hu ʿalaqayni fī ghtiṣābi-hi*) is just possible at a stretch. Professor Wagner is also perplexed.

72 Wagner (Abū Nuwās, *Dīwān al-Ḥasan ibn Hāniʾ*, ed. Wagner, 2.275.8) reads an extra verse: "wondrously crafted by our Maker."

73 Properly: "two arrows shot by alternating archers aiming at one target."

74 The spears in this hunting scene apparently refer to the dog's claws, not his teeth, judging by the elaboration of the familiar image from saluki descriptions in which the dogs are said to tear their ears with their nails as they sprint after game.

75 The saliva of the poet's beloved is often compared to musk or fragrant wine. Here the image is inverted.

76 Or possibly, reading *karīmin* and *al-muntahib(u)* for *karīmi l-muntahab(i)*: "Blessed is he who receives the spoils of a noble dog."

77 For the image, cf. Ibn al-Muʿtazz, *In Deadly Embrace*, Poem 10, line 11. The line alludes to Q Fajr 89:13. Wagner's edition (Abū Nuwās, *Dīwān al-Ḥasan ibn Hāniʾ*, ed. Wagner, 2.277.9) reads an extra verse here: "A blessed beast, kind and giving."

78 As the commentator explains, the point is that the hunter is so sure of a successful chase that he shouts out the *basmalah*, as is done at the start of an activity, and in the same breath, the *takbīr* ("Allāhu Akbar") and the *ḥamdalah*, as is done upon the completion of an activity.

79 I am unsure what is intended by *kilāb*, "dogs," as quarry.

80 It was thought that the queen bee was male.

81 Properly, *zamaʿ* denotes the hair that grows on the cartilage at the back of the leg, between the pastern and hoof of the sheep, goat, or oryx.

82 Wagner's edition (Abū Nuwās, *Dīwān al-Ḥasan ibn Hāniʾ*, ed. Wagner, 2.283.2) reads two verses after this verse: "He hunted him down on the steepest slope. When he was in front of me, he said."

83 *Dibq*, the dog's name, means "birdlime."

84 An echo of Q Raḥmān 55:37.

85 Animal physiognomy was an important part of animal breeding.

86 Al-Iṣfahānī (Abū Nuwās, *Dīwān al-Ḥasan ibn Hāni'*, ed. Wagner, 2.285.2) rather cryptically explains this unusual image as follows: "the mountains are obscured in the mirage."

87 Wagner's edition (Abū Nuwās, *Dīwān al-Ḥasan ibn Hāni'*, ed. Wagner, 2.287.13) reads an extra verse here: "makes his plans properly."

88 Lit., "a stone pestle that has fallen from its supports."

89 These two verses seem to literally mean: "just as the man who counts <with his fingers> folds that with which he counts fifty, counting with both hands like one who is doing the counting."

90 The word *ʿayr* normally means the "wild ass" but is used here in its sense of "lord," "chief," or "leader."

91 I construe the subject of lines 30–33 to be the owner of the goshawk.

92 Or: "in a group of fine young men from the people of Najd."

93 The verb *inḥajara* (here rendered as "hide out at home") is unattested, though not impossible as a reflexive of the first form. Perhaps we should read *inḥajaza*, which fits the sense perfectly.

94 Lit., "maternal aunts and grandparents an equal match."

95 See Q Baqarah 2:187 for the phrase *al-khayṭ al-abyaḍ* ("the white thread") and *al-khayṭ al-aswad* ("the black thread").

96 This feature is more in keeping with the peregrine than the gos, as is the technique of towering described in the next line.

97 I have construed *marād* as poetic license for *marādah*, *maṣdar* of *marida*, "to be rebellious." It could conceivably be *marād* (from *r-w-d*), "a grazing land for camels."

98 An echo of Q Aʿrāf 7:182 and Q Qalam 68:44.

99 The translation of these last two verses is highly conjectural. Perhaps the point of the second verse is that the party feasts on the game killed by the gos and so by extension consumes the unborn offspring of the game too. In the previous verse, "pleasure" (*lahw*) is said to be "magnanimous" and to "be active through the night" (*mudlij*), just like the raptor in the third line of the poem.

100 The translation of *abī l-mufarrajī* ("the father of him whose sorrows God has cleared away," i.e., "the one whose sorrows God has cleared away") is conjectural.

101 Abū Nuwās's poetry sometimes refers to the practice of sodomizing unconscious drinkers at such gatherings. A play on the words *faraj* ("relief, happiness") and *farj* ("genitalia") runs through the last four verses.

102 I expect that by *ḥamām* here, the *qaṭā*, the pin-tailed sandgrouse, is meant, proverbial for its early visits to the water hole.

103 This style of hunting is typical of peregrine falcons, not goshawks.

104 He means that the hawks provide him with enough food so he does not have to rely on the milk of milch camels for nourishment.

105 Lit., "all the benefits, old and new." The phrase refers to property that has long been in one's possession and property that is newly acquired.

106 I have been unable to identify the event referred to here.

107 Wagner (Abū Nuwās, *Dīwān al-Ḥasan ibn Hāniʾ*, ed. Wagner, 2.297.18) reads *wa-l-farraqah* (with a question mark). In the absence of a better suggestion, I have construed it as a poeticism for *farīqah*, a wooden box designed to trap raptors.

108 I have retained the repeated rhyme word *mufarraqah* in the last two verses, though Wagner's reading (Abū Nuwās, *Dīwān al-Ḥasan ibn Hāniʾ*, ed. Wagner, 2.298.6) *mugharraqah* ("drowned") is definitely better.

109 Wagner's edition (Abū Nuwās, *Dīwān al-Ḥasan ibn Hāniʾ*, ed. Wagner, 2.299.12) reads an extra verse here: "scorching the draped earth."

110 I translate *ṭāwin* here in the sense explained by Viré, "Falconaria arabica (III)," 157. Viré describes this form of attack as typical of the goshawk, though, not the saker. The term may mean "hungry, starved."

111 The *ʿamūd al-ṣubḥ* is the first rays of sunlight, commonly designated in Arabic as a pillar of light.

112 The point of this assertion is unclear to me.

113 The bows are carried unstrung: they have strings attached that need to be tightened before use.

114 The meaning of *madhābiḥ* is uncertain; see also Poem 98, line 20.

115 In Arabic, *kulā l-ḥayyāt*. The *kulyah* ("kidney") is the part of the bow on either side of the grip (*kabid*); the reference to snakes is obscure.

116 Line 16 contains the rare word *muktashaḥayni* and the otherwise unattested term *ʿukāẓ*, also the name of a township outside of Mecca where poetic competitions were said to have been held in the pre-Islamic era and where leather goods were manufactured. Lines 16 and 17 contain a conventional description of the pellet pouches, but there is no referent for the passive participle *muraqqashshātin*.

117 The poet notes that the game he has hunted with the pellet bow is fed to the birds of prey he has brought along with him on the expedition.

118 It is unclear which part of the bow the phrase "swift rings" (*kaftāti l-ḥalaqi*) indicates.

119 Or possibly "above their knives fitted with pivots," reading *dhātu dhalaqī*.

120 The *iʿtizāʾ* ("declarations of full lineages") involved saying, "I am X, the son of Y"; it also carried the meaning of a war cry by means of which combatants would know the identity of fellow combatants.

121 The wine deceives the young drinkers because it is much more potent than they expect (and can handle) and robs them of their sense such that they break with etiquette and stand up.

122 Gamecocks may have had blades fitted to their legs, either spurs (known as "gaffs") or knives.

123 The epithet *ya'fūrī* is not generally used of the pigeon but rather of the *ẓaby*, meaning "dirt-colored, dust-colored." Ya'fūr is also a proper noun and is, for example, the name of the hoopoe sent by Solomon to locate water when on his pilgrimage to Mecca (Wensinck, "Hudhud").

124 The detail of the next two lines in Wagner's edition (Abū Nuwās, *Dīwān al-Ḥasan ibn Hāni'*, ed. Wagner, 2.321.10) is obscure: pearls "intercalated (i.e., set on a string and alternating gold beads and pearls), tied together from the scattered <necklace>."

125 The sound made by heat escaping from the sands in the desert at night was traditionally identified as the grumbling and groaning of the jinn.

126 Wagner (Abū Nuwās, *Dīwān al-Ḥasan ibn Hāni'*, ed. Wagner, 2.321.17–322.1) reads four extra verses: "swift as a hunted beast in a panic, several days' journey in one day, quicker than the vulture's keen eye, than the snatch of eagle or saker."

127 Al-Iṣfahānī comments (Abū Nuwās, *Dīwān al-Ḥasan ibn Hāni'*, ed. Wagner, 2.322.6–7): "Another poem describing pigeons (*ḥamām*) I found in one of the manuscript copies (*nusakh*) with the phrase: 'He uttered the following poem in praise of a group of Quraysh.'"

128 I have emended the *al-a'raj* ("the lame <thing>") of the manuscript to *al-a'waj*, the name of a stallion.

129 A horse's toe is the front part of the wall (i.e., the visible part) of his hoof.

130 This line contains allusions to Q Ṭā Hā 20:12 and Q Nāzi'āt 79:1 (al-Ṭuwā, the hallowed valley in which God spoke to Moses), Q Kahf 18:78 (Moses and the mysterious companion), and Q Qiyāmah 75:28 (Judgment Day).

131 It was widely supposed that the soul left the body through the mouth.

132 The topography of this section of the poem is Syrian. According to one commentator (see Abū Nuwās, *Dīwān al-Ḥasan ibn Hāni'*, ed. Wagner, 1.117.4–5), the alternative toponyms, Dāsim and Ṣulayb, are located in Najd; Yāqūt has no entry for Dāsim and locates Ṣulayb (a mountain) on the eastern Arabian littoral in the premodern province of al-Baḥrayn. Ṣulayb is used here as a poetic diminutive of Ṣalb, a wadi tributary of the Tigris.

133 Some of the invective Abū Nuwās directs against Hāshim involves the actions of his grandfather: see Pellat, "Mu'āwiya b. Ḥudaydj"; Hawting, "Muḥammad ibn Abī Bakr."

134 *'Iddah* is the "term for the duration of widowhood or, rather, the period of abstention from sexual relations imposed on a widow or a divorced woman, or a woman whose marriage has been annulled, before she may re-marry" (Bellefonds, "'Iddah").

Glossary

Many of my identifications of fauna and flora are approximate at best and conjectural at worst. For flora, I rely principally on Mandaville, *Flora of Eastern Saudi Arabia.* I have not been able to identify many of the places where hunting occurred: they are not referred to in the poems with toponyms as such but with evocative names such as "Jaggy Rocks."

ʿAbbās al-ʿAbbās ibn ʿAbd al-Muṭṭalib ibn Hāshim, ancestor of the Abbasid caliphs (r. 132–656/750–1258) and uncle of Prophet Muḥammad.

Ahwaz a town on the Karun River in the Khuzistan plain, Iran.

ʿĀlij the great Nafud Desert in north Arabia.

ʿAmr ibn ʿUṣfūr see *Ibn ʿUṣfūr.*

ʿarfaj *Rhanterium epapposum,* a shrub grazed on by livestock that grows in soft soil and is highly combustible when dried.

arms the legs of a raptor, from the thigh to the foot.

arṭāh *Calligonum comosum,* also known as fire bush, a shrub with white older branches and flexible green shoots, found in the deeper sands.

atḥamī a striped outer garment.

Azd an ancient lineage group of southern Arabia.

al-Aʿwaj a famous Arabian stud descended from a Yemeni stallion said to have been given by King Solomon as a gift to an Arab delegation.

Awṭās a wadi in the tribal lands of the Hawāzin, who dwelled in western Najd and the Hijaz.

al-ʿAyyūq the star Alpha Aurigae, also known as Capella or the Goat Star, the brightest star in the Auriga constellation.

Bahrām Jūrān Sassanian King Vahram V (r. AD 420–38).

bamm the lowest string of the lute.

bān *Moringa oleifera,* the ben tree.

Barwaṣī a designation applied to the lath of the pellet bow, perhaps in origin a toponym or a proper noun.

Barzanj a town in the region of Arrān. See also *Ibn Arrān.*

beams a raptor's primary feathers.

bechins a term for beakfuls of food.

bind to a raptor "binds to" when she catches and holds her quarry in the air.

black-bellies either the black-bellied sandgrouse (*Pterocles orientalis*) or the small pin-tailed sandgrouse (*Pterocles exustus*).

block a perch for raptors.

boxthorn (Ar. ʿawsaj) *Lycium shawii,* a thorny shrub with edible leaves, popularly thought to be an abode of the jinn.

bulbul a passerine songbird member of the *Pycnonotidae* family, not to be confused with the nightingale.

Būrān the daughter of Khosro II (r. AD 590, 591–628), queen from 630 to 631. It was also the name of the wife of Caliph al-Maʾmūn (d. 218/833).

burd a mantle of striped woolen cloth manufactured in Yemen.

calmed with water when a raptor becomes agitated, a falconer may spray water from his mouth to calm her down, especially during training.

cheetah (Ar. fahd) *Acinonyx jubatus,* trained for the hunt and carried on horseback behind the rider to preserve its strength.

chukar (Ar. yaʿqūb) *Alectoris chukar,* a member of the pheasant family.

coverts a set of feathers that cover other feathers.

courser (Ar. tadruj) *Cursorius cursor,* the cream-colored courser that winters in the Middle East.

crane (Ar. kurkī) *Grus grus,* the Eurasian crane, a large wetland bird.

crines the hair like feathers that lie upward across the cere, the yellow waxy skin around the bird's nares, i.e., its nostrils.

crown a raptor's head.

Dābaq a place four *farsakh*s (approximately fifteen miles/twenty-four kilometers) from Aleppo.

dabbūq an unidentified child's toy.

dastaband a Zoroastrian dance in which the dancers hold one another by the arms.

Dāwūd ibn Sulaymān ibn Abī Jaʿfar the owner of a cheetah, or possibly a dog, that is praised by Abū Nuwās.

deer (Ar. ḍaʾn) The Arabic word usually designates "goat," but in these poems it refers to gazelle. See also *gazelle* and *ẓaby*.

Dayr Ṣalībā a monastery on the outskirts of Damascus.

Dhanūb a small group of mountains in the territory of Asad.

Dhū Simāṭ an unidentified place.

Dune's Edge either a toponym, or a geographical term that evokes a place.

eagle (Ar. liqwah, ʿuqāb) *Aquila chrysaetos daphanea*, the Asian golden eagle. The practice of hunting with Asian golden eagles is known from the Central Asian steppes.

enseamed a raptor is said to be enseamed when she has been brought out of her molt by managing her diet and weight and by exercise.

eyas a raptor taken from the nest while still a chick.

flags a raptor's secondary feathers.

fox (Ar. thaʿlab) the Arabian red fox (*Vulpes vulpes arabicus*), well adapted to desert life and found in Syria, Jordan, and Iraq.

francolin (Ar. durraj) *Francolinus francolinus arabistanicus*, the black francolin, found in southeastern Turkey, southern Iraq, and western Iran through to Turkmenistan and northeast India.

full-summed a raptor is full-summed when her new feathers are full length, with their quills hard.

gadwall (Ar. shīqah) *Mareca strepera*, a common wetland dabbling duck that feeds by submerging its head rather than by diving.

gamecock a rooster used in cockfighting.

gazelle (Ar. ẓaby) either an idmi, *Gazella gazella*, the mountain gazelle, a species that lives on mountain ridges and desert plateaus, or a rhim, *Gazella arabica*, an Arabian subspecies of the mountain gazelle. See also *ẓaby*.

ghaḍā *Haloxyletum persici*, a large saltbush prized as firewood.

gharb unidentified shrub or grass.

goose (Ar. iwazz) either *Anser albifrons*, the greater white-fronted goose; *Anser erythropus*, the lesser white-fronted goose; *Anser anser*, the greylag goose; or *Branta ruficollis*, the red-breasted goose.

ḥādh *Cornulaca arabica*, a prickly shrub with numerous branches.

halsband a soft cord fitted around the neck of a raptor, held in the falconer's left hand in order to move the bird to a crouching position and ensure a vigorous launch when the bird is cast off.

Haranj an unidentified place.

hard-penned a raptor is said to be hard-penned once her feathers have grown and hardened, with their bases white.

hare (Ar. arnab) *Lepus capensis arabicus*, a mammal in the genus *Lepus*.

Hārūn al-Rashīd fifth Abbasid caliph (r. 170–93/786–809).

Hāshim Hāshim ibn ʿAbd Manāf was the great-grandfather of Prophet Muḥammad.

Hāshim ibn Ḥudayj an individual first praised, then lampooned by Abū Nuwās when he refused to remunerate him for his panegyric. Some of the events the poet satirizes relate to the conduct of Hāshim's grandfather, Muʿāwiyah ibn Ḥudayj, who took part in the conquest of Egypt and was loyal to the fourth caliph, ʿUthmān. Muʿāwiyah exacted revenge on Muḥammad ibn Abī Bakr, referred to in the poem as "the Prophet's kinsman," for his involvement in the murder of ʿUthmān. Muʿāwiyah is said to have killed Muḥammad ibn Abī Bakr by placing his corpse inside the skin of a donkey and burning it in a fire.

Ḥassān's River an unidentified place.

ḥawdhān *Picris babylonica*, an abundant annual herb that grows in sand in numerous habitats.

Ḥazīz an unidentified place, perhaps characterized by jagged rocks.

High Homes an unidentified place, probably in the agricultural lands, the Sawād, of Iraq.

hobby (Ar. kawnaj) *Falco subbuteo*, the Eurasian hobby, a small falcon with long wings, superb in the air.

hocks well let down low hocks, short hocks, or hocks that are "well let down" suggest a breed of dog suitable for tasks that demand endurance.

hood used to prevent the raptor from becoming stressed. There are few unambiguous references to the use of the hood in the corpus. Some experts argue that the hood did not come into use until the thirteenth century.

hoopoe (Ar. hudhud) *Upupa epops*, the Eurasian hoopoe.

houbara (Ar. ḥubārā) *Chlamydotis macqueenii*, MacQueen's bustard, a large bustard that nests in areas of dense scrub vegetation; when hunted, it rises into the air and spirals, in order to confuse the pursuer.

hyena (Ar. ḍabuʿ) *Hyaena hyaena*, the striped hyena (not to be confused with the more famous spotted hyena), a shy nocturnal scavenger that sports a bushy mane and lives largely off carrion.

ibex (Ar. waʿil) *Capra nubiana*, the Nubian ibex, a species of goat that lives in mountainous areas. Ibex have long horns that grow up and then downward and backward. They are light brown with a white underbelly and white legs; the males have a dark dorsal stripe.

ibis (Ar. bughth) *Geronticus eremita*, the northern bald ibis.

Ibn ʿAmr's Brook unidentified place.

Ibn Arrān designation of the ruler of Arrān, a region next to Azerbaijan.

Ibn al-Dāyah Yūsuf ibn Ibrāhīm, known as Ibn al-Dāyah ("Son of the Wet Nurse"), a foster brother of Caliph al-Muʿtaṣim (r. 218–27/833–42) and an expert on the poetry of Abū Nuwās who composed an anthology of his poetry.

Ibn Ishtākhanj "the son of the Ishtākhanj," the title of a ruler of a region of Khurasan.

Ibn ʿUsfūr "the Son of Sparrow," explained as a friend of Abū Nuwās who made bows. ʿUṣfūr al-Azdī is also mentioned in some sources as a famous bowyer.

ibrik (Ar. ibrīq) a container with a spout used for pouring liquids.

intermewed a raptor that has molted in captivity.

isabelline a pale gray-yellow horse color.

jack a tiercel merlin.

Jaggy Rocks either a toponym, or a phrase that evokes a place.

Jahm either Jahm al-Sāmī, a native of Khurasan who occupied various administrative offices under the caliphs al-Maʾmūn (r. 198–218/813–33) and al-Wāthiq (r. 227–32/842–47), or Jahm ibn Khalaf, who composed hunting poems.

Jāsim a settlement eighty *farsakh*s (just under 300 miles/480 kilometers) west of Damascus.

jess a strap made of leather tied to a raptor's leg.

jilbab (Ar. jilbāb) a long and loose-fitting outer garment worn by women.

jīm the Arabic letter *j* (ج).

jinn, sg. jinni like humans, a class of intelligent beings in the created world.

al-Julandā ibn Masʿūd the chief of the Azd, elected by the Ibadis (members of the third sect of Islam, after Sunnis and Shiʿis) as their first imam, attacked in an expedition sent in 134/752 by the caliph al-Ṣaffāḥ (r. 132–36/749–54). See also *Azd*.

jumayl possibly a name for the lark; explained in the lexica as a small bird, like a bulbul. See also *bulbul*.

Kāridanj an unidentified place.

Karishshīshā an unidentified place.

keel a raptor's breast.

khalanj a tree with streaky wood from which bowls were made.

khashanshār an unidentified type of waterfowl.

Khusro (Ar. Kisrā) the name of two Sassanid rulers, used in Arabic as a general regnal title for Persian rulers.

Khufāfān either a water hole in the territory of ʿAmr ibn Kilāb, branch of the ʿĀmir ibn Ṣaʿṣaʿah federation in Arabia, or Khaffān, a place on the pilgrim route from Kufa.

Kindah a South Arabian tribal group who had, in the form of an insurrection in Ḥadramawt, taken part in the Wars of Apostasy after the death of Prophet Muḥammad. Members of Kindah settled in Egypt.

kite (Ar. zurraqah) either *Elanus caeruleus caeruleus* or *Elanus c. vociferus*, respectively the African or the Asian black-winged kite.

Kulthūm a woman's name, common in the *nasīb* (amatory) section of a qasida.

Laʿlaʿ a settlement between Basra and Kufa.

lark (Ar. mukkāʾ) a passerine, member of the *Alaudidae* family.

leveret (Ar. khirniq) a young hare. See also *hare*.

lime stick (Ar. dibq) a twig smeared with glue used for trapping birds.

lion (Ar. asad) the Asiatic lion (*Panthera leo persica*), now extinct in Syria, Iraq, and Arabia.

long-necks (Ar. suṭṭāʿ) unidentified waterfowl.

Lūqīn Chia-chou in the region of Hanoi, Vietnam.

lure an imitation quarry tied to the end of a rope and used to entice a raptor back to her trainer.

Luʾayy a branch of the Quraysh, Prophet Muḥammad's tribe.

Maʿadd the main tribal confederation of the northern Arabs of Najd.

al-Mahdī Abbasid caliph (r. 158–69/775–85).

mail the breast feathers of a raptor.

mallard (Ar. shirwāq) *Anas platyrhynchos*, the wild duck.

manned a tamed raptor.

marw a type of shrub or grass.

Mashrafī a type of sword manufactured in Mashārif in Syria.

merlin (Ar. yuʾyuʾ) *Falco columbarius pallidus*, the pallid or steppe merlin, a swift hunter used to catch small birds.

mīm the Arabic letter *m* (م).

Muḍar a powerful confederation of tribes in ancient North Arabia.

mulled grape juice a fermented grape liquor from which any alcohol has been burnt off.

munj a type of psychotropic seed.

mutes a bird's droppings.

Nabataean an Abbasid designation for the agriculturalists of the Sawād of Iraq, the cultivated regions of lower Mesopotamia and the marshes between Kufa and Basra.

Najd the plateau region of North Arabia.

Naʿmān a mountain between Mecca and al-Ṭāʾif.

nares a raptor's nostrils.

naʾūr soot, used, along with indigo and antimony, in tattooing.

notch (Ar. madhbaḥ) a knife used for the ritual slaughter of an animal; the part of an arrow shaft between the fletchings and the notch. Its exact function in terms of the pellet bow is unclear.

nūn the Arabic letter *n* (ن).

onager (Ar. ḥimār waḥshī) *Equus hemionus hemippus*, the Syrian or Mesopotamian wild ass, an extinct subspecies once native to Arabia. The onager, typically 660 pounds (300 kg) in weight and six and a half feet (two meters) in length, could reach speeds of thirty-seven miles (sixty km) per hour.

oryx (Ar. baqar waḥshī) *Oryx leucoryx*, the Arabian oryx, a subspecies of antelope distinctive for its straight horns and white hide, black facial and caudal stripes, and dark-brown legs. Oryx are perfectly adapted to desert conditions and can go for long periods without water.

ostrich (Ar. raʾl or naʿām) *Struthio camelus*: when ready to mate, the ostrich cock's beak and shins turn bright red, and occasionally his neck will also change to a red color.

partridge (Ar. ḥajal or dayzaj) either *Ammoperdix heyi*, the sand-partridge, a galliform resident of dry, open, often hilly areas, or the see-see partridge (*Ammoperdix griseogularis*).

Pebbles either a toponym or a geographical term that evokes a place.

pellet bow (Ar. qaws al-bunduq) a wooden bow used for firing a pellet made of hardened clay, known in Arabic as *bunduq*, "hazelnut." The pellets were carried in pouches. Hunting with the pellet bow was a team sport.

peregrine (Ar. shahīn) *Falco peregrinus brookei*, the peregrine falcon, a powerful raptor, agile in the air, with a distinctive stoop on prey at great speeds, often catching its prey in the air. Peregrines have dark mustache marks under each eye.

pigeon (Ar. ḥamām) *Columba livia gaddi*, the Iranian rock dove, used as homing and racing pigeons.

pin-tailed sandgrouse (Ar. qaṭā or ghaṭāṭ) *Pterocles alchata*, a medium-sized bird that flies in flocks to water holes at dawn. See also *black-bellies*.

poison (Ar. dhirrīḥ) *Lytta vesicatoria*, cantharidin, a highly potent, vesicant substance produced by blister beetles.

polo played on horseback by players wielding curved sticks (called in Arabic *ṣawlajān*), polo was popular with the elite members of Abbasid society. There were two teams of four, and the game would begin when one of the players threw the ball as high into the air as he could. The object of the game was to strike the ball, generally made of leather, between two posts. Spectators would sit on the walls of the hippodrome or training ground where the game was played (*maydān*).

pounces a raptor's talons.

Qaḥṭān the reputed ancestor of the South Arabian peoples.

qildah a dish of dates, dried barley, and clarified butter.

Qubaybāt an area of Baghdad.

Quḍāʿah an ancient tribal federation based on shared lineage.

Qūhī adjective denoting an origin from Qūhistān, a mountainous and only partially arable province of Iran, renowned in the third/ninth century for the manufacture of fine linen textiles.

Quraysh the Meccan tribe to which Prophet Muḥammad belonged.

Quṭaybiyyāt a mountain range or a water hole in the territory of Asad.

rā' the Arabic letter r (ر).

Ravines an unidentified place, probably in the agricultural lands, the Sawād, of Iraq.

rafrāf an unidentified small waterfowl.

reclaimed a raptor is said to be reclaimed when she has been manned after the molt. See also *manned*.

Romans (Ar. Rūm) the Arabs referred to the Byzantine Greeks as "Romans."

sabahraj an epithet usually applied to the sparrow hawk, sometimes to the goshawk, to describe the gray-white coloration of its plumage.

Sābir (more commonly Sābūr), a place in Persia renowned for its textiles.

sails a raptor's wings.

saker (Ar. ṣaqr) *Falco cherrug milvipes*, the eastern saker falcon, a large rufous-brown falcon that prefers to hunt from a vantage point or from a height and to surprise its prey. It has excellent stamina and will tail-chase until the prey is exhausted. Females are larger than males.

saluki (Ar. salūqī) a sight hound widely used to hunt game, distinguished by its stamina and speed over long distances.

Salūq either a toponym (referring to a place in the Yemen or one west of the Caspian Sea) or the Arabic name of the dynasty of the Seleucids, the Hellenistic rulers of west Asia from 312 to 363.

samand epithet for a horse (designating an isabelline, i.e., a pale gray-yellow, horse, specifically with a black mane and tail) applied to a goshawk.

Samharī epithet for a hard spear shaft, often explained as originally crafted by an individual named Samhar who imported the shafts from India; also explained, more plausibly perhaps, as crafted in a village in Ethiopia.

al-Ṣaqr ibn al-Ṣaffāq ibn Ḥujr al-Azdī the dedicatee of a panegyric composed by Abū Nuwās requesting the gift of a goshawk. See also *al-Julandā*.

Ṣarīfūn a place in the Sawād, the agricultural lands, of Iraq.

sarrāʾ a type of tree whose wood was used for making bows.

sawdhanīq epithet usually applied to the saker, describing its reddish-white coloration.

scissor bite the normal bite for dogs with a long muzzle, referring to the relative positioning of the upper and lower incisors.

seeled the eyelids of a newly trapped bird were often sewn shut with silk thread before it could be reclaimed. See also *reclaimed*.

shiwār unidentified waterfowl.

Sīf the hot coastland on the Iranian side of the Arabian Gulf.

simʿ a crossbreed mentioned frequently in the lexica, explained as the offspring of a wolf and a hyena.

Sīraf a commercial port on the Arabian Gulf.

snake *Macrovipera lebetina obtusa*, the Lebetine blunt-nosed viper found in Syria and Iraq; also the aggressive Indian saw-scaled viper (*Echis carinatus*).

sparrow (Ar. ʿusfūr) a small member of the *Passeridae* family.

sparrow hawk (Ar. bāshiq) *Accipiter nisus*, the Eurasian sparrow hawk, a small hawk known to hunt by employing an undulating flight to allow it to close in on its quarry before it can escape.

spider possibly Walckenaer's huntsman spider (*Eusparassus walckenaeri*), commonly encountered in domestic settings and noted for its speed, or the smaller pantropical jumping spider (*Plexippus paykulli*), a cosmopolitan spider that does not use a web but chases and jumps upon its prey.

spice (Ar. wars) *Memecylon umbellatum,* a plant from whose leaves a yellow dye can be produced.

squirrel (Ar. sinjāb) *Sciurus vulgaris,* the Eurasian red squirrel.

stoop a falcon "stoops" when she dives at quarry from a great height.

stork (Ar. laqlaqah) *Ciconia ciconia asiatica,* the white stork, known to winter in Iran.

Sulayb diminutive of Ṣalb, a wadi tributary of the Tigris between Amid and Mayyafariqin (modern-day Silvan in Diyarbakır, Turkey).

Sulaymān ibn Khalṣah an expert on the poetry of Abū Nuwās.

Sulaymān ibn Sakhṭah an expert on the poetry of Abū Nuwās.

suhradāz an epithet applied to the goshawk, and occasionally the peregrine, to describe the gray-white coloration of its breast feathers.

swift (Ar. khaṭṭāf) *Apus apus,* the common swift, a superb aerial performer.

ṭabṭāb a club with a curved end and possibly a concave scoop used in a game similar to that played with a *ṣawlajān* (see *polo*). The game seems to have been played on foot and in the open, possibly in water, and may have involved a race between the players and a hunt for the ball. See also *polo.*

Ṭā'if a town in Arabia to the south of Mecca.

Tamīm a large and important ancient Arabian lineage group.

Ṭams an unidentified place.

Ṭanj a region in Khurasan.

tarsell (Ar. kūbaj) an obsolete form of "tiercel," used in this book to refer to the male saker falcon.

Taw'am a place in Oman renowned for the quality of its pearls.

Tawwaj an area west of Shiraz in Iran (where goshawks are said to come from); a place in Hijaz where falcons are said to come from.

teal (Ar. shıqah, burkah) *Anas crecca,* the Eurasian teal, a gregarious wetland bird.

tiercel (Ar. zurraq) *Accipiter gentilis,* the male northern goshawk, noticeably smaller than the female, known in Arabic as *bāz.* See also *goshawk.*

ṭīṭawī the jacana, the lily walker, a wader with elongated toes that enable it to walk on aquatic vegetation.

train a raptor's tail.

trap net (Ar. fakhkh) a trap for catching birds, with a trip hazard placed under a suspended net.

Ṭufayfāt a place between Basra and Kufa.

Tuktam a woman's name, encountered in the *nasīb*, the amatory section of a qasida.

Ṭuwā the hallowed valley in which God spoke to Moses.

urjūzah (pl. arājīz) a poem composed in *rajaz* meter, the basic foot of which is a diamb, i.e., a double iamb (v— v—).

vulture (Ar. nasr) *Gyps fulvus*, the Eurasian griffon vulture.

Wabār the ancestral home in Yemen of the pre-Islamic ʿĀd people.

wader (Ar. ṭuwwal) a bird whose exact identity is unknown.

Wars of Apostasy (Ar. ḥurūb al-riddah) a series of battles waged by the early Muslim community against the Arabian tribes. Beginning just before the death of Prophet Muḥammad, they lasted throughout the caliphate of Abū Bakr (r. 11–13/632–34).

wrist the point at which a raptor's wings are attached to its body.

wolf (Ar. dhi'b) *Canis lupus arabs*, a subspecies of gray wolf. It is adapted to the desert and lives in small packs.

Wood Pond either a toponym, or a phrase that evokes a place.

Yaʿfūr the name of a famous pigeon breeder in Basra.

yakkī banjī a nonsense term, a combination of *yak*, Persian for "one," and *panj*, Sanskrit for "five."

yarak when a falcon or a hawk is described as "in yarak," it is in a fit and proper condition for flying—that is, hunting.

ẓaby the general term in Arabic for a gazelle, be it an idmi, *Gazella gazella*, the mountain gazelle, a species that lives on mountain ridges and desert plateaus, or a rhim, *Gazella arabica*, an Arabian subspecies of the mountain gazelle. See also *gazelle*.

Zābaj an island in the Indian ocean, possibly Java, Sumatra, or Borneo.

Zanj Zanzibar.

Zaranj a place in Sijistan.

zarnab unidentified herb.

zayrakk an epithet of uncertain meaning applied to the merlin.

zīr the highest string of the lute.

Bibliography

Abū Nuwās, al-Ḥasan ibn Hāni'. *Dīwan al-Ḥasan ibn Hāni'*. Vol. 1, edited by Ewald Wagner. 2nd ed. Berlin: Das Arabische Buch, 2001. First published 1958 by Franz Steiner (Wiesbaden, Germany).

———. *Dīwan al-Ḥasan ibn Hāni'*. Vol. 2, edited by Ewald Wagner. Wiesbaden, Germany: Franz Steiner, 1972.

———. *Dīwan al-Ḥasan ibn Hāni'*. Vol. 3, edited by Ewald Wagner. Wiesbaden, Germany: Franz Steiner, 1988.

———. *Dīwan al-Ḥasan ibn Hāni'*. Vol. 4, edited by Gregor Schoeler. Wiesbaden, Germany: Franz Steiner, 1982.

———. *Dīwan al-Ḥasan ibn Hāni'*. Vol. 5, edited by Ewald Wagner. Beirut: Klaus Schwarz, 2003.

———. *Dīwān Abī Nuwās bi-riwāyat al-Ṣūlī*. Edited by Bahjat ʻAbd al-Ghafūr al-Ḥadīthī. Abu Dhabi: Dār al-Kutub al-Waṭaniyyah, 2010.

Allen, Mark. *Falconry in Arabia*. London: Orbis Books, 1984.

Allsen, Thomas T. *The Royal Hunt in Eurasian History*. Philadelphia: University of Pennsylvania Press, 2006.

ʻAntarah ibn Shaddād. *War Songs*. Edited and translated by James E. Montgomery. New York: New York University Press, 2018.

Armitage, Simon. *A Vertical Art: On Poetry*. Princeton, NJ: Princeton University Press, 2022.

Al-Azdı, Abū l-Muṭahhar. *The Portrait of Abū l-Qāsim al-Baghdādī al-Tamīmī* (*Ḥikāyat Abī l-Qāsim al-Baghdādī al-Tamīmī*). Edited and translated by Emily Selove and Geert Jan van Gelder. Oxford: Gibb Memorial Trust, 2021.

Baker, John A. *The Peregrine*. London: HarperCollins, 2017.

Bate, Jonathan. *The Song of the Earth*. London: Picador, 2001.

Bellefonds, Yvon Linant de. "ʻIddah." In *Encyclopaedia of Islam*. 2nd ed. Brill Online.

Bürgel, Johann-Christoph. "The Lady Gazelle and Her Murderous Glances." *Journal of Arabic Literature* 20, no. 1 (1989): 1–11.

Burnside, John. *The Music of Time: Poetry in the Twentieth Century*. London: Profile Books, 2019.

Clark, Terence. "The Noble Art of the Chase in the Arab World." *Asian Affairs* 35, no. 1 (2004): 47–55.

Cohen, Jeffrey J. *Medieval Identity Machines*. Minneapolis: University of Minnesota Press, 2003.

Cooperson, Michael. *Classical Arabic Biography: The Heirs of the Prophets in the Age of al-Ma'mūn*. Cambridge: Cambridge University Press, 2000.

———. "Bandits." In *Violence in Islamic Thought from the Qur'ān to the Mongols*, edited by Robert Gleave and István T. Kristó-Nagy, 191–99. Edinburgh: Edinburgh University Press, 2015.

Deleuze, Gilles. *Essays Critical and Clinical*. Translated by Daniel W. Smith and Michael A. Greco. Minneapolis: University of Minnesota Press, 1997.

Deleuze, Gilles, and Félix Guatarri. *A Thousand Plateaus: Capitalism and Schizophrenia*. Translated by Brian Massumi. Minneapolis: University of Minnesota Press, 1987.

Derrida, Jacques. "The Animal That Therefore I Am (More to Follow)." Translated by David Wills. *Critical Inquiry* 28, no. 2 (2008): 369–418.

Diamond, Cora. "The Difficulty of Reality and the Difficulty of Philosophy." In Cary Wolfe, Cora Diamond, Stanley Cavell, John McDowell, and Ian Hacking, *Philosophy and Animal Life*, 43–91. New York: Columbia University Press, 2008.

Ess, Josef van. *Theology and Society in the Second and Third Centuries of the Hijra: A History of Religious Thought in Early Islam*. Vol. 3, translated by Gwendolin Goldbloom. Leiden, Netherlands: Brill, 2018.

Foster, Charles. *Being a Beast: An Intimate and Radical Look at Nature*. London: Profile Books, 2016.

Hawting, Gerald R. "Muḥammad ibn Abī Bakr." In *Encyclopaedia of Islam*. 2nd ed. Brill Online.

Ibn al-Muʿtazz, Abū ʿAbd Allāh. *In Deadly Embrace*. Edited and translated by James E. Montgomery. New York: New York University Press, 2023.

Kohn, Eduardo. *How Forests Think: Toward an Anthropology beyond the Human*. Berkeley: University of California Press, 2013.

Al-Jāḥiẓ, Abū ʿUthmān. *Kitāb al-Ḥayawān*. Edited by Muḥammad ʿAbd al-Salām Hārūn. Cairo: Maṭbaʿat Muṣṭafā l-Bābī l-Ḥalabī, 1937–47.

Kennedy, Philip F. "Perspectives of a Ḫamriyya: Abū Nuwās' *Yā Saḥir al-Ṭarf*." In *Festschrift Ewald Wagner zum 65. Geburtstag. Band 2: Studien zur arabischen Dichtung*, edited by Wolfhart Heinrichs and Gregor Schoeler, 258–76. Beirut: Franz Steiner, 1994.

———. "Abu Nuwas (circa 757–814 or 815)." In *Arabic Literary Culture, 500–925*, edited by Michael Cooperson and Shawkat M. Toorawa, 21–33. Detroit, MI: Thomson Gale, 2005.

———. *Abu Nuwas: A Genius of Poetry*. Oxford: Oneworld Publications, 2005.

Latham, J. Derek, and W. F. Paterson, trans. *Saracen Archery: An English Version and Exposition of a Mameluke Work on Archery (ca. AD 1368)*. London: The Holland Press, 1970.

Mandaville, James P. *The Flora of Eastern Saudi Arabia*. London: Routledge, 2016.

Marvin, William. "Medieval Blood Sport." In *Animals, Animality and Literature*, edited by Bruce Boehrer and Molly Hand, 57–72. Cambridge: Cambridge University Press, 2018.

Massé, Henri. "Čawgān." In *Encyclopaedia of Islam*. 2nd ed. Brill Online.

Meisami, Julie. "Abū Nuwās and the Rhetoric of Parody." In *Festschrift Ewald Wagner zum 65. Geburtstag. Band 2: Studien zur arabischen Dichtung*, edited by Wolfhart Heinrichs and Gregor Schoeler, 246–57. Beirut: Franz Steiner, 1994.

Montgomery, James E. *Dīwān ʿAntarah ibn Shaddād: A Literary-Historical Study*. New York: New York University Press, 2018.

Montgomery, James E., ed. and trans. *Fate the Hunter: Early Arabic Hunting Poems*. New York: New York University Press, 2023.

Pellat, Charles. "Muʿāwiya b. Ḥudaydj̲." In *Encyclopaedia of Islam*. 2nd ed. Brill Online.

Robinson, Chase. *Empire and Elites after the Muslim Conquest: The Transformation of Northern Mesopotamia*. Cambridge: Cambridge University Press, 2004.

Al-Shabushtī. *The Book of Monasteries*. Edited and translated by Hilary Kilpatrick. New York: New York University Press, 2023.

Al-Shimshāṭī, Abū l-Ḥasan ʿAlī ibn Muḥammad. *Kitāb al-Anwār wa-maḥāsin al-ashʿār*. Edited by al-Sayyid Muḥammad Yūsuf. 2 vols. Kuwait: Maṭbaʿat Ḥukūmat Kuwayt, 1977.

Steel, Karl. *How to Make a Human: Animals and Violence in the Middle Ages*. Columbus: The Ohio State University Press, 2011.

Stetkevych, Jaroslav. *The Hunt in Arabic Poetry: From Heroic to Lyric to Metapoetic*. Notre Dame, IN: University of Notre Dame Press, 2016.

Tor, Deborah. *Violent Disorder: Religious Warfare, Chivalry, and the ʿAyyār Phenomenon in the Medieval Islamic World*. Würzburg, Germany: Ergon Verlag, 2007.

Vidal-Naquet, Pierre. *The Black Hunter: Forms of Thought and Forms of Society in the Greek World*. Translated by Andrew Szegedy-Maszak. Baltimore, MD: The Johns Hopkins University Press, 1986.

Viré, François. "Falconaria arabica. Glanures philologiques (III)." *Arabica* 9, no. 2 (1962): 152–92.

———. "Essai de détermination des oiseaux-de-vol mentionnés dans les principaux manuscrits arabes médiévaux sur la fauconnerie." *Arabica* 24 (1977): 138–49.

———. "Ḳaṭā." In *Encyclopaedia of Islam*. 2nd ed. Brill Online.

Wagner, Ewald. "Die Überlieferung des Abū Nuwās-Dīwān und seine Handschriften." Akademie der Wissenschaften und der Literature. *Abhandlungen des Geistes- und Sozialwissenschaftlichen Klasse* 6 (1957): 303–73.

———. *Abū Nuwās: Eine Studie zur arabischen Literatur der frühen 'Abbāsidenzeit.* Wiesbaden, Germany: Franz Steiner, 1965.

———. "Abū Nuwās." *Encyclopaedia of Islam.* 3rd ed. Brill Online.

Wensinck, Arent Jan. "Hudhud." *Encyclopaedia of Islam.* 2nd ed. Brill Online.

Further Reading

Al-Bāshā, ʿAbd al-Raḥmān. *Shiʿr al-ṭarad ilā nihāyat al-qarn al-thālith al-hijrī*. Beirut: Muʾassasat al-Risālah, 1974.

Capezzone, Leonardo. "Amorous or Scientific Metaphors? Abū Nuwās, the Beginning of the End of the Aristotelian Cosmos, and an Incoherence by al-Naẓẓām." *Studia Islamica* 111 (2016): 1–19.

Farrell, Jeremy. "Toward an Integral Abū Nuwās: Evidence of His Transgressive Religiosity in His Khamriyyāt and Zuhdiyyāt." In *"Passed Around by a Crescent": Wine Poetry in the Literary Traditions of the Islamic World*, edited by Kirill Dimitriev and Christine van Ruymbeke, 239–73. Beirut: Ergon, 2022.

Folz, Richard C. *Animals in Islamic Tradition and Muslim Cultures*. London: Oneworld Publications, 2017.

Gelder, Geert Jan van. "Some Types of Ambiguity: A Poem by Abū Nuwās on al-Faḍl al-Raqāshī." *Quaderni di Studi Arabi* 10 (1992): 75–92.

———. "Waspish Verses: Abū Nuwās's Lampoons on Zunbūr ibn Abī Ḥammād." *Annali di Ca' Foscari* 35 (1996): 447–55.

———. "Dubious Genres: On Some Poems by Abū Nuwās." *Arabica* 44 (1997): 268–83.

Hämeen-Anttila, Jaako. "Abū Nuwās and Ghazal as Genre." In *Ghazal as World Literature I: Transformations of a Literary Genre*, edited by Thomas Bauer and Angelika Neuwirth, 87–105. Beirut: Ergon, 2005.

Hamori, Andras. *On the Art of Medieval Arabic Literature*. Princeton, NJ: Princeton University Press, 1973.

Harb, Lara. "Persian in Arabic Poetry: Identity Politics and Abbasid Macaronics." *Journal of the American Oriental Society* 139, no. 1 (2019): 1–21.

Ibn Khālawayh. *Al-Ḥusayn ibn Aḥmad ibn Khālawayh's Names of the Lion*. Translated by David Larsen. Seattle, WA: Wave Books, 2017.

Ibn Mangli. *De la chasse*. Translated by François Viré. Paris: Sindbad, 1984.

Kennedy, Philip F. "Abū Nuwās, Samuel and Levi." *Medieval and Modern Perspectives on Muslim-Jewish Relations* 2 (1995): 109–25.

———. *The Wine Song in Classical Arabic Poetry: Abū Nuwās and the Literary Tradition*. Oxford: Clarendon Press, 1997.

Lyons, Malcolm. *Identity and Identification in Classical Arabic Poetry*. Warminster, UK: Aris and Philips, 1999.

Mattock, John N. "Description and Genre in Abū Nuwās." *Quaderni di Studi Arabi* 5–6 (1987–88): 528–40.

Mikhail, Alan. *Animals in Ottoman Egypt*. New York: Oxford University Press, 2017.

Montgomery, James E. "Revelry and Remorse: A Poem of Abū Nuwās." *Journal of Arabic Literature* 25, no. 2 (1994): 116–32.

———. "For the Love of a Christian Boy: A Song by Abū Nuwās." *Journal of Arabic Literature* 27, no. 2 (1996): 114–24.

———. "Abū Nuwās the Alcoholic." In *Philosophy and Arts in the Islamic World*, edited by Urbain Veermeulen and Daniel de Smet, 16–26. Leuven, Belgium: Peeters, 1998.

———. "Abū Nuwās, the Justified Sinner." *Oriens* 39, no. 1 (2011): 75–164.

Motoyoshi Sumi, Akiko. *Description in Classical Arabic Poetry: Waṣf, Ekphrasis, and Interarts Theory*. Leiden, Netherlands: Brill, 2004.

Payne, Mark. *The Animal Part: Human and Other Animals in the Poetic Imagination*. Chicago: The University of Chicago Press, 2010.

Al-Ṣāliḥī, ʿAbbās Muṣṭafā. *Al-Ṣayd wa-l-ṭarad fī l-shiʿr al-ʿarabī ḥattā nihāyat al-qarn al-thānī l-hijrī*. Baghdad: Maṭbaʿat Dār al-Salām, 1974.

Schoeler, Gregor. "Bashshār b. Burd, Abū ʾl-ʿAtāhiyah and Abū Nuwās." In *ʿAbbasid Belles-Lettres* (The Cambridge History of Arabic Literature), edited by Julia Ashtiany, T. M. Johnstone, J. D. Latham, and R. B. Serjeant, 275–99. Cambridge: Cambridge University Press, 1990.

———. "Iblīs in the Poems of Abū Nuwās." In *Myths, Historical Archetypes and Symbolic Figures in Arabic Literature: Towards a New Hermeneutic Approach (Proceedings of the International Symposium in Beirut, June 25th–30th, 1995)*, edited by Angelika Neuwirth, Birgit Embaló, Sebastian Günther, and Maher Jarrar, 271–90. Beirut: Franz Steiner, 1999.

———. "Abū Nuwās' Ghazal Mu'annathāt no. 25." In *Ghazal as World Literature I: Transformations of a Literary Genre*, edited by Thomas Bauer and Angelika Neuwirth, 181–95. Beirut: Ergon, 2005.

Shakib, Mahmood. "The Influence of Persian Culture during the Early ʿAbbāsid Times: A Study of Abū Nuwās' Poetry." PhD diss., University of Washington, 1982.

Smith, G. Rex. "Hunting Poetry (*Ṭardiyyāt*)." In *ʿAbbasid Belles-Lettres* (The Cambridge History of Arabic Literature), edited by Julia Ashtiany, T. M. Johnstone, J. D. Latham, and R. B. Serjeant, 167–84. Cambridge: Cambridge University Press, 1990.

Stetkevych, Jaroslav. "Name and Epithet: The Philology and Semiotics of Animal Nomenclature in Early Arabic Poetry." *Journal of Near Eastern Studies* 45, no. 2 (1986): 89–124.

Viré, François. "Falconaria arabica. Glanures philologiques (II)." *Arabica* 9, no. 1 (1962): 37–60.

———. "Falconaria arabica. Glanures philologiques." *Arabica* 8, no. 3 (1961): 273–93.

Wagner, Ewald. "Warum haben Ḥamza al-Iṣbahānī und al-Ṣūlī mehrere Weingedichte aus ihren Rezensionen des Abū Nuwās-Dīwānen ausgeschieden?" *Asiatische Studien* 62, no. 4 (2008): 1085–96.

Zakharia, Katia. "Figures d'al-Ḥasan ibn Hāni', dit Abū Nuwās, dans *Kitāb Aḫbār Abī Nuwās* d'Ibn Manẓūr." *Bulletin d'Études Orientales* 58 (2009): 131–60.

Index

جامعة نيويورك أبوظبي

NYU ABU DHABI

About the NYUAD Research Institute

The Library of Arabic Literature is a research center affiliated with NYU Abu Dhabi and is supported by a grant from the NYU Abu Dhabi Research Institute.

The NYU Abu Dhabi Research Institute is a world-class center of cutting-edge and innovative research, scholarship, and cultural activity. It supports centers that address questions of global significance and local relevance and allows leading faculty members from across the disciplines to carry out creative scholarship and high-level research on a range of complex issues with depth, scale, and longevity that otherwise would not be possible.

From genomics and climate science to the humanities and Arabic literature, Research Institute centers make significant contributions to scholarship, scientific understanding, and artistic creativity. Centers strengthen cross-disciplinary engagement and innovation among the faculty, build critical mass in infrastructure and research talent at NYU Abu Dhabi, and have helped make the university a magnet for outstanding faculty, scholars, students, and international collaborations.

Titles Published by the Library of Arabic Literature

For more details on individual titles, visit www.libraryofarabicliterature.org

Classical Arabic Literature: A Library of Arabic Literature Anthology
Selected and translated by Geert Jan van Gelder (2012)

A Treasury of Virtues: Sayings, Sermons, and Teachings of ʿAlī, by al-Qāḍī al-Quḍāʿī, with the **One Hundred Proverbs** attributed to al-Jāḥiẓ
Edited and translated by Tahera Qutbuddin (2013)

The Epistle on Legal Theory, by al-Shāfiʿī
Edited and translated by Joseph E. Lowry (2013)

Leg over Leg, by Aḥmad Fāris al-Shidyāq
Edited and translated by Humphrey Davies (4 volumes; 2013–14)

Virtues of the Imām Aḥmad ibn Ḥanbal, by Ibn al-Jawzī
Edited and translated by Michael Cooperson (2 volumes; 2013–15)

The Epistle of Forgiveness, by Abū l-ʿAlāʾ al-Maʿarrī
Edited and translated by Geert Jan van Gelder and Gregor Schoeler (2 volumes; 2013–14)

The Principles of Sufism, by ʿĀʾishah al-Bāʿūniyyah
Edited and translated by Th. Emil Homerin (2014)

The Expeditions: An Early Biography of Muḥammad, by Maʿmar ibn Rāshid
Edited and translated by Sean W. Anthony (2014)

Two Arabic Travel Books
Accounts of China and India, by Abū Zayd al-Sīrāfī
Edited and translated by Tim Mackintosh-Smith (2014)
Mission to the Volga, by Aḥmad ibn Faḍlān
Edited and translated by James Montgomery (2014)

Disagreements of the Jurists: A Manual of Islamic Legal Theory, by al-Qāḍī al-Nuʿmān
Edited and translated by Devin J. Stewart (2015)

Consorts of the Caliphs: Women and the Court of Baghdad, by Ibn al-Sāʿī
Edited by Shawkat M. Toorawa and translated by the Editors of the Library of Arabic Literature (2015)

What ʿĪsā ibn Hishām Told Us, by Muḥammad al-Muwayliḥī
Edited and translated by Roger Allen (2 volumes; 2015)

The Life and Times of Abū Tammām, by Abū Bakr Muḥammad ibn Yaḥyā al-Ṣūlī
Edited and translated by Beatrice Gruendler (2015)

The Sword of Ambition: Bureaucratic Rivalry in Medieval Egypt, by ʿUthmān ibn Ibrāhīm al-Nābulusī
Edited and translated by Luke Yarbrough (2016)

Brains Confounded by the Ode of Abū Shādūf Expounded, by Yūsuf al-Shirbīnī
Edited and translated by Humphrey Davies (2 volumes; 2016)

Light in the Heavens: Sayings of the Prophet Muḥammad, by al-Qāḍī al-Quḍāʿī
Edited and translated by Tahera Qutbuddin (2016)

Risible Rhymes, by Muḥammad ibn Maḥfūẓ al-Sanhūrī
Edited and translated by Humphrey Davies (2016)

A Hundred and One Nights
Edited and translated by Bruce Fudge (2016)

The Excellence of the Arabs, by Ibn Qutaybah
Edited by James E. Montgomery and Peter Webb
Translated by Sarah Bowen Savant and Peter Webb (2017)

Scents and Flavors: A Syrian Cookbook
Edited and translated by Charles Perry (2017)

Arabian Satire: Poetry from 18th-Century Najd, by Ḥmēdān al-Shwēʿir
Edited and translated by Marcel Kurpershoek (2017)

In Darfur: An Account of the Sultanate and Its People, by Muḥammad ibn ʿUmar al-Tūnisī
Edited and translated by Humphrey Davies (2 volumes; 2018)

War Songs, by ʿAntarah ibn Shaddād
Edited by James E. Montgomery
Translated by James E. Montgomery with Richard Sieburth (2018)

Arabian Romantic: Poems on Bedouin Life and Love, by ʿAbdallāh ibn Sbayyil
Edited and translated by Marcel Kurpershoek (2018)

Dīwān ʿAntarah ibn Shaddād: A Literary-Historical Study
By James E. Montgomery (2018)

Stories of Piety and Prayer: Deliverance Follows Adversity, by al-Muḥassin ibn ʿAlī al-Tanūkhī
Edited and translated by Julia Bray (2019)

The Philosopher Responds: An Intellectual Correspondence from the Tenth Century, by Abū Ḥayyān al-Tawḥīdī and Abū ʿAlī Miskawayh
Edited by Bilal Orfali and Maurice A. Pomerantz
Translated by Sophia Vasalou and James E. Montgomery (2 volumes; 2019)

Tajrīd sayf al-himmah li-stikhrāj mā fī dhimmat al-dhimmah: A Scholarly Edition of ʿUthmān ibn Ibrāhīm al-Nābulusī's Text
By Luke Yarbrough (2020)

The Discourses: Reflections on History, Sufism, Theology, and Literature—Volume One, by al-Ḥasan al-Yūsī
Edited and translated by Justin Stearns (2020)

Impostures, by al-Ḥarīrī
Translated by Michael Cooperson (2020)

Maqāmāt Abī Zayd al-Sarūjī, by al-Ḥarīrī
Edited by Michael Cooperson (2020)

The Yoga Sutras of Patañjali, by Abū Rayḥān al-Bīrūnī
Edited and translated by Mario Kozah (2020)

The Book of Charlatans, by Jamāl al-Dīn ʿAbd al-Raḥīm al-Jawbarī
Edited by Manuela Dengler
Translated by Humphrey Davies (2020)

A Physician on the Nile: A Description of Egypt and Journal of the Famine Years, by ʿAbd al-Laṭīf al-Baghdādī
Edited and translated by Tim Mackintosh-Smith (2021)

The Book of Travels, by Ḥannā Diyāb
Edited by Johannes Stephan
Translated by Elias Muhanna (2 volumes; 2021)

Kalīlah and Dimnah: Fables of Virtue and Vice, by Ibn al-Muqaffaʿ
Edited by Michael Fishbein
Translated by Michael Fishbein and James E. Montgomery (2021)

Love, Death, Fame: Poetry and Lore from the Emirati Oral Tradition, by al-Māyidī ibn Ẓāhir
Edited and translated by Marcel Kurpershoek (2022)

The Essence of Reality: A Defense of Philosophical Sufism, by ʿAyn al-Quḍāt
Edited and translated by Mohammed Rustom (2022)

The Requirements of the Sufi Path: A Defense of the Mystical Tradition, by Ibn Khaldūn
Edited and translated by Carolyn Baugh (2022)

The Doctors' Dinner Party, by Ibn Buṭlān
Edited and translated by Philip F. Kennedy and Jeremy Farrell (2023)

Fate the Hunter: Early Arabic Hunting Poems
Edited and translated by James E. Montgomery (2023)

The Book of Monasteries, by al-Shābushtī
Edited and translated by Hilary Kilpatrick (2023)

In Deadly Embrace: Arabic Hunting Poems, by Ibn al-Muʿtazz
Edited and translated by James E. Montgomery (2023)

The Divine Names: A Mystical Theology of the Names of God in the Qur'an, by ʿAfīf al-Dīn al-Tilimsānī
Edited and translated by Yousef Casewit (2023)

Bedouin Poets of the Nafūd Desert, by Khalaf Abū Zwayyid, ʿAdwān al-Hirbīd, and ʿAjlān ibn Rmāl
Edited and translated by Marcel Kurpershoek (2024)

The Rules of Logic, by Najm al-Dīn al-Kātibī
Edited and translated by Tony Street (**2024**)

Najm al-Dīn al-Kātibī's al-Risālah al-Shamsiyyah: An Edition and Translation with Commentary
By Tony Street (**2024**)

Arabian Hero: Oral Poetry and Narrative Lore from Northern Arabia, by Shāyiʿ al-Amsaḥ
Edited and translated by Marcel Kurpershoek (**2024**)

A Demon Spirit: Arabic Hunting Poems, by Abū Nuwās
Edited and translated by James E. Montgomery (**2024**)

English-only Paperbacks

Leg over Leg, by Aḥmad Fāris al-Shidyāq (**2 volumes; 2015**)
The Expeditions: An Early Biography of Muḥammad, by Maʿmar ibn Rāshid (**2015**)
The Epistle on Legal Theory: A Translation of al-Shāfiʿī's *Risālah*, by al-Shāfiʿī (**2015**)
The Epistle of Forgiveness, by Abū l-ʿAlāʾ al-Maʿarrī (**2016**)
The Principles of Sufism, by ʿĀʾishah al-Bāʿūniyyah (**2016**)
A Treasury of Virtues: Sayings, Sermons, and Teachings of ʿAlī, by al-Qāḍī al-Quḍāʿī, with the **One Hundred Proverbs** attributed to al-Jāḥiẓ (**2016**)
The Life of Ibn Ḥanbal, by Ibn al-Jawzī (**2016**)
Mission to the Volga, by Ibn Faḍlān (**2017**)
Accounts of China and India, by Abū Zayd al-Sīrāfī (**2017**)
A Hundred and One Nights (**2017**)
Consorts of the Caliphs: Women and the Court of Baghdad, by Ibn al-Sāʿī (**2017**)
Disagreements of the Jurists: A Manual of Islamic Legal Theory, by al-Qāḍī al-Nuʿmān (**2017**)
What ʿĪsā ibn Hishām Told Us, by Muḥammad al-Muwayliḥī (**2018**)
War Songs, by ʿAntarah ibn Shaddād (**2018**)
The Life and Times of Abū Tammām, by Abū Bakr Muḥammad ibn Yaḥyā al-Ṣūlī (**2018**)
The Sword of Ambition, by ʿUthmān ibn Ibrāhīm al-Nābulusī (**2019**)

Brains Confounded by the Ode of Abū Shādūf Expounded: Volume One, by Yūsuf al-Shirbīnī (2019)

Brains Confounded by the Ode of Abū Shādūf Expounded: Volume Two, by Yūsuf al-Shirbīnī and **Risible Rhymes**, by Muḥammad ibn Maḥfūẓ al-Sanhūrī (2019)

The Excellence of the Arabs, by Ibn Qutaybah (2019)

Light in the Heavens: Sayings of the Prophet Muḥammad, by al-Qāḍī al-Quḍāʿī (2019)

Scents and Flavors: A Syrian Cookbook (2020)

Arabian Satire: Poetry from 18th-Century Najd, by Ḥmēdān al-Shwēʿir (2020)

In Darfur: An Account of the Sultanate and Its People, by Muḥammad al-Tūnisī (2020)

Arabian Romantic: Poems on Bedouin Life and Love, by ʿAbdallāh ibn Sbayyil (2020)

The Philosopher Responds, by Abū Ḥayyān al-Tawḥīdī and Abū ʿAlī Miskawayh (2021)

Impostures, by al-Ḥarīrī (2021)

The Discourses: Reflections on History, Sufism, Theology, and Literature—Volume One, by al-Ḥasan al-Yūsī (2021)

The Book of Charlatans, by Jamāl al-Dīn ʿAbd al-Raḥīm al-Jawbarī (2022)

The Yoga Sutras of Patañjali, by Abū Rayḥān al-Bīrūnī (2022)

The Book of Travels, by Ḥannā Diyāb (2022)

A Physician on the Nile: A Description of Egypt and Journal of the Famine Years, by ʿAbd al-Laṭīf al-Baghdādī (2022)

Kalīlah and Dimnah: Fables of Virtue and Vice, by Ibn al-Muqaffaʿ (2023)

Love, Death, Fame: Poetry and Lore from the Emirati Oral Tradition, by al-Māyidī ibn Ẓāhir (2023)

The Essence of Reality: A Defense of Philosophical Sufism, by ʿAyn al-Quḍāt (2023)

The Doctors' Dinner Party, by Ibn Buṭlān (2024)

The Requirements of the Sufi Path: A Defense of the Mystical Tradition, by Ibn Khaldūn (2024)

Fate the Hunter: Early Arabic Hunting Poems (2024)

About the Editor–Translator

James E. Montgomery is Sir Thomas Adams's Professor of Arabic, Fellow of Trinity Hall at the University of Cambridge, and an Executive Editor of the Library of Arabic Literature. In 2024 he was elected Fellow of the British Academy.

www.ingramcontent.com/pod-product-compliance
Lightning Source LLC
Chambersburg PA
CBHW021847090426
42811CB00033B/2174/J

* 9 7 8 1 4 7 9 8 3 4 1 2 9 *